THIRD EDITION

ON COURSE

Strategies for Creating Success in College and in Life

Skip Downing
Baltimore City Community College

HOUGHTON MIFFLIN COMPANY   Boston   New York

To Jocelyn, Jill, and Guy

Director of College Survival: Barbara A. Heinssen
Assistant Editor: Shani B. Fisher
Editorial Assistant: Jonathan Wolf
Associate Project Editor: Kate Hartke
Editorial Assistant: Shanya Dingle
Senior Production/Design Coordinator: Sarah Ambrose
Senior Manufacturing Coordinator: Priscilla Bailey

Cover Image: Photonica © S.P.C.

Material in the Appendix is based on Jack Pejsa *Success in College Using the Internet,* First Edition. Copyright © 1998 by Houghton Mifflin Company. Reproduced by permission.

Additional permissions acknowledgments may be found on page 231, which constitutes an extension of the copyright page.

Printed in the U.S.A.

Library of Congress Control Number: 00-111873

ISBN: 0-618-11636-2

56789-DOC-05 04 03 02

As part of Houghton Mifflin's ongoing
commitment to the environment, this text
has been printed on recycled paper.

Contents

Preface

On Course is intended for college students of any age who want to create success both in college and in life. College may be unfamiliar now, but grab your compass (this text, *On Course*), your book bag, and your dreams, and start discovering yourself. Step onto the road to success and begin moving in the right direction. The right direction is certainly a very personal choice, but working through *On Course* can help you determine the choices you must make to succeed. While goals are very personal, there are common strategies for reaching goals that can be used successfully by most people.

Intended Outcomes of *On Course*

Whether you are taking a student success or a freshman seminar course, a composition course, or an "inward-looking" course of psychology, self-exploration, or personal growth, *On Course* will present you with practical and proven strategies for improving study skills. The essential study skills—reading, taking notes, studying, memorizing, taking tests, writing, and researching—are covered in the **Wise Choices in College** sections. However, that's just the beginning. Through articles, guided journals, case studies in critical thinking, and inventories, *On Course* shows you how to make wise choices that will empower you to experience greater self-awareness, self-management, creative and critical thinking skills, emotional intelligence, and lifelong learning skills.

New and Proven Features of the Third Edition

- **Articles on Success Strategies.** Thirty-one brief articles explain proven strategies for creating success in college and in life. Each article presents a strategy based upon the ideas of respected figures in psychology, philosophy, business, sports, politics, and personal and professional growth.

- **Focus Questions.** Preceding each article, focus questions encourage you to read to find personally valuable answers. By formulating questions before reading and seeking answers while reading, you improve your reading skills.

- **Guided Journal Entries.** A guided journal entry immediately follows each article, giving you an opportunity to apply the success strategy to enhance your outcomes in college and in life. *Believing in Yourself* journal activities appear in each chapter, reinforcing the importance of personal self-worth for long-term success.

- **Wise Choices in College.** Use this feature to learn the essential study skills necessary to succeed in college—reading, note taking, studying, memorizing, test taking, writing, and researching. In each section, an easy-to-read smorgasbord of strategies is presented, and you are encouraged to experiment with those that match your preferred way(s) of learning.

- **Case Studies for Critical Thinking.** Apply the strategies you learn to a real-life problem. The case studies, on topics like procrastination and collaborative work, spark lively discussions that assist you in seeing the importance and challenges of making wise choices. Because case studies have no right answer, they also encourage you to think critically and creatively.

- **On Course Principles at Work.** These new sections show how important the *On Course* success strategies are for choosing the right career, getting hired, and succeeding in the work world.

- **Personal Assessment Questionnaires.** *On Course* begins and ends with a personal assessment questionnaire. By completing the initial questionnaire, you see areas of growth that need attention. By completing the concluding questionnaire, you see your semester's growth. You now have the option of completing the questionnaire either in the text or online on the Houghton Mifflin College Survival Programs web site at the *On Course* location. You may take the personal assessment questionnaire by visiting the *On Course* web site at the College Survival discipline student page located on our web site at *http:// college.hmco.com.*

- **Quotations.** Marginal quotations express the wisdom of famous and not-so-famous people regarding the success strategies under consideration in articles throughout the text.

- **Poems and Cartoons.** Poems and cartoons throughout the book are thematically linked with the success strategies being explored.

Support for the Student and Instructor

We help you build community in a number of ways:

1. College Survival Consulting Services: College Survival is the leading source of expertise, support services, and materials for student success courses. We are committed to promoting and supporting effective success courses within the higher education community.

For more than fifteen years, Houghton Mifflin's College Survival consultants have provided consultation and training for the design, implementation, and presentation of student success and first-year courses. Our team of consultants have a wide variety of experience in teaching and administering the first-year course. They can provide help in establishing or improving your student success program. We offer assistance in course design, instructor training, teaching strategies, and much more. Contact us today at 1-800-528-8323, or visit us on the web at *college.hmco.com.*

2. College Survival Programs Web Site *(http://college.hmco.com).* This web site offers you new ways to interact with your peers, with us, and with yourself! Try the online exercise in time management, the discussion groups, and the *On Course* personal assessment questionnaire. Enjoy information, activities, and links to helpful resources. The *On Course* web site is located within the student and instructor College Survival discipline pages at *http://college.hmco.com.*

3. Facilitator's Manual. The facilitator's manual offers educators specific suggestions for using *On Course* in various kinds of courses and endeavors to answer questions that educators might have about using the text. It also includes numerous in-class exercises that encourage active exploration of the success strategies presented in the text. These exercises include role playing, learning games, dialogues, demonstrations, metaphors, mind-mappings, brainstorms, questionnaires, drawings, skits, scavenger hunts, and many others.

4. "Roundtable Discussions" Videotapes. These two videotapes, "Study Strategies" and "Life Skills," feature five college students who discuss and seek solutions to the problems they face in college and in life. Call 1-800-733-1717, visit the Student Success Programs web site, or contact your Houghton Mifflin representative for more information. A teaching unit for the videotapes is also available on the Student Success Programs web site.

5. Myers-Briggs Type Indicator® (MBTI®) Instrument*. This is the most widely used personality inventory in history—shrink wrapped with *On Course* for a discounted price at qualified schools. The standard form M self-scorable instrument contains 93 items that determine preferences on four scales: Extraversion-Introversion, Sensing-Intuition, Thinking-Feeling, and Judging-Perceiving.

6. Retention Management System™ College Student Inventory. The Noel Levitz **C**ollege **S**tudent **I**nventory instrument is available in a specially priced package with this text. This early-alert, early-intervention program identifies students with tendencies that contribute to dropping out of school. Students can participate in an integrated, campus-wide program. Advisors are sent three interpretative reports: The Student's Report, the Advisor/Counselor Report, and The College Summary and Planning Report. For more information, contact your College Survival consultant at 1-800-528-8323 or your local Houghton Mifflin Sales Representative.

*MBTI and Myers-Briggs Type Indicator are registered trademarks of Consulting Psychologists Press, Inc.

7. Instructor Trainings: The author conducts faculty development workshops for all educators who want to learn strategies for assisting students to be successful in both college and in life. Graduate Credits and CEUS are available for the 4-day *On Course* workshops. For information, contact the author toll-free at 1-888-597-6451, or go to the author's web site at *http://www.oncourseworkshop.com*. Houghton Mifflin offers On-Campus Training and Workshops to assist classroom instructors develop new and innovative ways of improving the success rate of their students. Call 1-800-528-8323 for more information.

8. Listserv Discussion Group. All college educators are invited to join the free *On Course* Discussion Group, an international community of more than one thousand five hundred dedicated university and college educators from all academic disciplines and from student affairs. The group is united by a commitment to learning and sharing practical strategies for helping students achieve more of their potential. To subscribe, send an email request to *skipdown@starpower.net*.

Acknowledgments

This book would not exist without the assistance of an extraordinary group of people. I can only hope that I have returned (or will return) their wonderful support in kind.

At Houghton Mifflin I would like to thank Barbara Heinssen for her support and guidance, and Jonathan Wolf for his unflagging attention to details. And especially Daryl Peterson—mentor and friend—thanks for sharing the vision.

At Baltimore City Community College, my thanks go to president Jim Tschechtelin for his enthusiastic support of the College Success Seminar. Also, I acknowledge the extraordinary work of my colleagues, the teachers of the College Success Seminar: Tessie Black, Paul Blaisdell, Joan Cobb, James Coleman, Carolyn Dabirsiaghi, Freida Davis, Lori Harris, Mona Hartz, Doug Holt, Synethia Jones, Lynn Kerr, Angela Lawler, Audrey Lawson, Tamara Lewis, Jon Mangana, Stanley Mazer, Art Mueller, Elliot Oppenheim, Asnah Perlman, Karlton Pressley, Anita Read, Ann Ritter, Robert Selby, Almeta Sly, Edith Sorrell, Alfred Sutton, Eric Wakefield, Mardie Walker, and Jerry Wood, all of whom made my job a treat. Eric Hallengren's constant encouragement picked me up and got me back on course more times than he will ever know—thanks, bud.

To Anita Read and Eric Wakefield, what would I have done without your wisdom, love, and unflagging support? To Tom Maze, Rich Rosen, John McDaniel, and Roxanne MacDougal, thanks for your active listening, your guidance, and most of all, your friendship.

Additionally, I'd like to thank Dave Ellis for inspiring me to make different choices as a teacher, Ron and Mary Hulnick and Norm Frye of the University of Santa Monica for creating the learning environment in which I could discover how to make wiser choices, and Pauline Signor and her colleagues at Harrisburg Area Community College for believing in my dream even before I did, and supporting me to make it come true.

A number of wise and caring reviewers have made valuable contributions to this book, and I thank them for their guidance:

Alicia Andujo, Long Beach City College, CA

Pamela Fletcher, N. Hennepin Community College, MN

Kathryn Jones, University of California–Riverside, CA

Patsy Krech, University of Memphis, TN

Judith Pula, Frostburg State University, MD

Warren Schlesinger, Ithaca College, NY

Judith Smith, South Piedmont Community College, NC

Ester Winter, Northwest Missouri University, MO

Finally, my deep gratitude goes out to the students who over the years have had the courage to explore and change their thoughts, actions, feelings, and beliefs. I hope, as a result, you have all lived richer, more personally fulfilling lives. I know I have.

S. D.

Travel With Me

On Course is the result of my own quest to live a rich, personally fulfilling life and my strong desire to pass on what I've learned to my students. As such, *On Course* is a very personal book, for me and for you. I invite you to explore in depth what success means to you. I suggest that if you want to achieve your greatest potential in college and in life, you will want to transform many of your beliefs, behaviors, and attitudes. In short, you will want to learn to make wiser choices.

During my first two decades of teaching college courses, I consistently observed a sad and perplexing puzzle. Each semester I watched students sort themselves into two groups. One group achieved varying degrees of academic success, from excelling to just squeaking by. Another group struggled: withdrawing, disappearing, or failing. But, here's the puzzling part. The struggling students often displayed as much academic potential as their more successful classmates, and in some cases more. What, I wondered, caused the vastly different outcomes of these two groups? And what could I do to help my struggling students achieve greater success?

Somewhere around my twentieth year of teaching, I experienced a series of crises in both my personal and professional life. In a word, I was struggling. After a period of feeling sorry for myself, I embarked on a quest to improve the quality of my life. I read, I took seminars and workshops, I talked with wise friends and acquaintances, I kept an in-depth journal, I saw a counselor, I even returned to graduate school for a masters degree in applied psychology. I was seriously motivated to change my life for the better.

If I were to condense all that I learned into one sentence, it would be this: Successful, happy people consistently make wiser choices than do struggling, unhappy people. I came to see that the quality of my life was essentially the result of all of my previous choices. I saw how the wisdom (or lack of wisdom) of my choices influenced every aspect of my life. The same, of course, was true of my struggling students.

For the past decade, I have continued my quest to identify the choices that support success both in college and in life. As a result of what I learned (and continue to learn), I created and teach a course at Baltimore City Community College called the College Success Seminar. This course teaches students how to make the essential choices that empower us all to achieve more of what we want in life. I teach this course in part because it has the power to change my students' lives for the better. I teach it for another, more personal reason. I teach the College Success Seminar and I wrote *On Course* because both activities keep me conscious of the wise choices I must consistently make to live a richer, more personally fulfilling life.

Now that much of my life is back on course, I don't want to forget how I got here!

Skip Downing

1 Getting On Course to Your Success

SUCCESSFUL STUDENTS . . .	STRUGGLING STUDENTS . . .
accept personal responsibility, seeing themselves as the primary cause of their outcomes and experiences.	see themselves as Victims, believing that what happens to them is determined primarily by external forces such as fate, luck, and powerful others.
discover self-motivation, finding purpose in their lives by discovering personally meaningful goals and dreams.	have difficulty sustaining motivation, often feeling depressed, frustrated, and/or resentful about a lack of direction in their lives.
master self-management, consistently planning and taking purposeful actions in pursuit of their goals and dreams.	seldom identify specific actions needed to accomplish a desired outcome. And when they do, they tend to procrastinate.
employ interdependence, building mutually supportive relationships that help them achieve their goals and dreams (while helping others do the same).	are solitary, seldom requesting, even rejecting, offers of assistance from those who could help.

Taking the First Step

> **FOCUS QUESTIONS** What does "success" mean to you? When you achieve your greatest success, what will you **have,** what will you be **doing,** and what kind of person will you **be?**

Congratulations on choosing to attend college! With this choice, you've begun a journey that can lead to great personal and professional success.

What is success?

I've asked many college graduates, "What did success mean to you when you were an undergraduate?" Here are some typical answers:

When I was in college, success to me was . . .

- . . . getting all A's and B's while working a full-time job.
- . . . making two free-throws to win the conference basketball championships.
- . . . having a great social life.
- . . . parenting two great kids and still making the dean's list.
- . . . being the first person in my family to earn a college degree.

College is a place where a student ought to learn not so much how to make a living, but how to live.

Dr. William A. Nolen

Notice that each response emphasizes *outer success:* high grades, sports victories, social popularity, and college degrees. These successes are public, visible achievements that allow the world to judge one's abilities and worth.

I've also asked college graduates, "If you could repeat your college years, what would you do differently?" Here are some typical answers:

If I had a chance to do college over, I would . . .

- . . . focus on learning instead of just getting good grades.
- . . . major in engineering, the career I had a passion for.
- . . . constantly ask myself how I could use what I was learning to enhance my life and the lives of the people I love.
- . . . discover my personal values.
- . . . learn more about the world I live in and more about myself . . . especially more about myself!

Notice that the focus some years after graduation often centers on *inner success:* enjoying learning, following personal interests, focusing on personal values, and creating more fulfilling lives. These successes are private, invisible victories that offer a deep sense of personal contentment, happiness, and self-worth.

Only with hindsight do most college graduates realize that, to be completely satisfying, success must occur both in the visible world and in the invisible spaces of our minds and hearts. This book, then, is about how to achieve both outer and inner success in college and in life.

There is only one success—to be able to spend your life in your own way.

Christopher Morely

To that end, I suggest the following definition of success: **Success is staying on course to your greatest dreams, creating wisdom, happiness, and unconditional self-worth along the way.**

As a college instructor, I have seen thousands of students arrive on campus with dreams, then struggle, fail, and fade away. I've seen thousands more come to college with dreams, pass their courses, and graduate having done little more than cram thousands of new facts into their brains. They've earned degrees, but in more important ways they have remained unchanged.

Our primary responsibility in life, I believe, is to realize the incredible potential with which each of us is born. All of our experiences, especially those during college, can contribute to the creation of our best selves.

On Course will show you how to use your college experience as a laboratory experiment. In this laboratory you'll learn and apply proven strategies that will help you create outstanding success—academically, personally, and professionally. Get ready to change the outcome of your life!

The deepest personal defeat suffered by human beings is constituted by the difference between what one was capable of becoming and what one has in fact become.

Ashley Montagu

To begin, consider a curious puzzle: Two students enter a college class on the first day of the semester. Both appear to have similar intelligence, backgrounds, and abilities. The weeks slide by, and the semester ends. Surprisingly, one student passes and the other fails. One fulfills his potential; the other falls short. Why do students with similar aptitudes perform so differently? More importantly, which of these students is you?

Teachers observe this puzzle in every class. I know you've seen it, too, not only in school, but wherever people gather. Some people have a knack for achievement. Others wander about confused and disappointed, unable to create the success they claim they want. Clearly, having potential does not guarantee success.

What, then, are the essential ingredients of success?

The power of choice

The main ingredient in all success is wise choices. That's because the quality of our lives is determined by the quality of the choices we make on a daily basis. Successful people stay on course to their destinations by wisely choosing their beliefs and behaviors.

Do beliefs cause behaviors, or do behaviors lead to beliefs? Like the chicken and the egg, it's hard to say which came first. This much is clear: Once you choose a positive belief or an effective behavior, you usually find yourself in a cycle of success. Positive beliefs lead to effective behaviors. Effective behaviors lead to success. And success reinforces the positive beliefs.

Here's an example showing how the choice of beliefs and behaviors determines results. Until 1954, most track-and-field experts believed it was impossible for a person to run a mile in less than four minutes. On May 6, 1954, however, Roger Bannister ran a mile in the world-record time of 3:59.4. Once Bannister had proven that running a four-minute mile was possible, within months, many other runners also broke the four-minute barrier. In other words, once runners chose a new belief (a person can run a mile under four minutes), they pushed their physical abilities, and suddenly the impossible became possible.

Consider another example. After a disappointing test score, a struggling student thinks, "I knew I couldn't do college math!" This belief will likely lead the student to miss classes and neglect assignments. These self-defeating behaviors lead to even lower test scores, reinforcing the negative beliefs. This student, caught in a cycle of failure, is now in grave danger of failing math.

Life is a self-fulfilling prophesy . . . in the long run you usually get what you expect.

Denis Waitley

In that same class, however, someone with no better math ability is passing the course because this student believes she *can* pass college math. Consequently, she chooses positive behaviors such as attending every class, completing all of her assignments, getting a tutor, and asking the instructor for help. Her grades go up, confirming her empowering belief. The cycle of success has this student on course to passing math.

Someone once said, "If you keep doing what you've been doing, you'll keep getting what you've been getting." That's why if you want to improve your life (and why else would you attend college?), you'll need to change some of your beliefs and behaviors. Conscious experimentation will teach you which ones need revision. Once these new beliefs and behaviors become a habit, you'll find yourself in the cycle of success, on course to creating your dreams in college and in life.

Write a great life

College offers the perfect opportunity to design a life worth living. A time-tested tool for this purpose is a journal, a written record of your thoughts and feelings, hopes and dreams. Journal writing is a way to explore your life in depth and discover your best "self." This self-awareness will enable you to make wise choices about what to keep doing and what to change.

Journal work is an excellent approach to uncovering hidden truths about ourselves. . . .

Marsha Sinetar

Because you will be writing about your life and your success, I urge you to buy a book especially for journal writing. You can buy an inexpensive composition book or a fancy journal book. Either way, your journal will become a valuable record of your growing wisdom.

Many people who keep journals do what is called "free writing." They simply write whatever thoughts come to mind. This approach can be extremely valuable for exploring issues present in one's mind at any given moment.

In *On Course,* however, you will write a guided journal. This approach is like going on a journey with an experienced guide. Your guide takes you places and shows you sights you might never have discovered on your own.

Before writing each journal entry, you'll read an article about proven success strategies. Then you'll apply the strategies to your own life by completing the guided journal entry that follows the article. Here are five suggestions (which are also listed on the inside back cover of this book) for creating a meaningful journal:

- **Copy the directions for each step into your journal (just the bold print):** When you find your journal in a drawer twenty years from now, having the directions in your journal will enable you to make sense of what you've written. (You may want to use different-color inks for the directions and for your response.)
- **Be spontaneous:** Write whatever comes to mind in response to the directions. Imagine pouring liquid thoughts into your journal without pausing to edit or rewrite. Unlike public writings, such as an English composition or a history research paper, your journal is a private document written primarily for your own benefit.
- **Be honest:** As you write, tell yourself the absolute truth; honesty leads to your most significant discoveries about yourself and your success.
- **Be creative:** Add favorite quotations, sayings, and poems. Use color, drawings, and photographs. Express your best "self."
- **Dive Deep:** When you think you have exhausted a topic, write more. Your most valuable thoughts will often take the longest to surface. So, most of all—DIVE DEEP!!

Relax

Before writing each journal entry, take a few moments to RELAX. You might be tempted to rush into your writing. Resist the urge. A few moments of relaxation will pay you back many times over.

Experiments have shown that relaxing before a learning session greatly improves the results. During a normal day, your brain is continually firing electrical waves at fourteen or more cycles per second. These waves, known as *beta* waves, are great for getting daily tasks done, but they are less efficient for learning something new.

When you take a few minutes to relax deeply, your brain waves slow down. These slower *alpha* waves occur at between seven and fourteen cycles per second. Studies have compared the impact of various types of brain waves on learning. The evidence is clear: *Alpha* waves improve learning.

When we experience alpha waves, our mind is better able to focus because it's less distracted by muscle tension or irrelevant thoughts. Relaxation also appears to allow the two sides of our brain—the logical, linear left brain and the creative, holistic right brain—to work together. All in all, alpha waves seem to tune up our brains for increased mental performance.

No matter what you want to learn—from guitar playing to real-estate law—you'll do better if you know how to relax.

Sheila Ostrander and
Lynn Schroeder

As if the mental benefits weren't enough, relaxation also aids physical health. Medical studies of people who do daily relaxation sessions reveal physical benefits that include lowered blood pressure, increased energy, relief from muscle tension and stress, a strengthened immune system, and improved general health. Furthermore, those who relax regularly have better emotional health, an increased sense of well-being, and even greater self-esteem.

To achieve deep relaxation, only four elements are required: 1) a quiet place; 2) a comfortable physical position; 3) a passive attitude; and 4) something on which to focus your thoughts.

Any quiet place where you'll be undisturbed is appropriate. One position that many people prefer is sitting in a comfortable chair with feet flat on the floor, toes pointing slightly outward. Rest your arms and hands in your lap, and tilt your head slightly forward. When you close your eyes, imagine looking at the tip of your nose.

There are many ways to achieve deep relaxation. One effective approach is described below. The directions are easy to follow, and you will be able to remember them easily after a few sessions.

Progressive Relaxation: Find a comfortable position and close your eyes. Breathing deeply through your nose, feel your stomach expand with air. Tighten the muscles in your feet, and hold your breath for a count of five. Now expel the air through your mouth and let your feet relax fully.

Keep doing this progressive relaxation as you move up your body. Breathe deeply, then (one at a time) tighten and relax the muscles in your calves, thighs, buttocks, lower back and abdomen, upper back and chest, shoulders and neck, then your face and scalp.

For fast-acting relief, try slowing down.
Lily Tomlin

Finally, taking one more deep breath, tighten all of the muscles of your body. Hold your breath and keep all of your muscles tight for a count of five. Now expel the air and let your whole body relax fully.

Enjoy the feeling. There is no rush. When you are ready, open your eyes. You will feel completely relaxed and refreshed.

Assess yourself

Before we examine the choices of successful students, take a few minutes to complete the self-assessment questionnaire on the next two pages. Your scores will identify behaviors and beliefs you may wish to change to achieve more of your potential in college and in life. In the last chapter, you will have an opportunity to repeat this self-assessment and compare your two scores. I think you're going to be pleasantly surprised!

This self-assessment is not a test. There are no right or wrong answers. The questions simply give you an opportunity to create an accurate and current self-portrait. Be absolutely honest and have fun with this activity, for it is the first step on an exciting journey to a richer, more personally fulfilling life.

Self-Assessment

You can take this self-assessment on the Internet by visiting the *On Course* web site at the College Survival discipline student page located at *http://college.hmco.com/collegesurvival/students.* You'll receive your score immediately . . . and see how others scored as well.

Read the statements below and score each one according to how true or false you believe it is about you. To get an accurate picture of yourself, consider what **IS** true about you (not what you want to be true). Obviously there are no right or wrong answers. Assign each statement a number from zero to ten, as follows:

Totally false   0 1 2 3 4 5 6 7 8 9 10   Totally true

1. ___ I control how successful I will be.
2. ___ I'm not sure why I'm in college.
3. ___ I spend most of my time doing important things.
4. ___ When I encounter a challenging problem, I try to solve it by myself.
5. ___ When I get off course from my goals and dreams, I realize it right away.
6. ___ I'm not sure how I learn best.
7. ___ Whether I'm happy or not depends mostly on me.
8. ___ I'll truly accept myself only after I eliminate my faults and weaknesses.
9. ___ Forces out of my control (like poor teaching) are the cause of low grades I receive in school.
10. ___ If I lose my motivation in college, I know how to get it back.
11. ___ I don't need to write things down because I can remember what I need to do.
12. ___ I have a network of people in my life that I can count on for help.
13. ___ If I have habits that hinder my success, I'm not sure what they are.
14. ___ When I don't like the way an instructor teaches, I know how to learn the subject anyway.
15. ___ When I get very angry, sad, or afraid, I do or say things that create a problem for me.
16. ___ When I think about performing an upcoming challenge (like taking a test), I usually see myself doing well.
17. ___ When I have a problem, I take positive actions to find a solution.
18. ___ I don't know how to set effective short-term and long-term goals.
19. ___ I remember to do important things.
20. ___ When I have a difficult course in school, I study alone.
21. ___ I'm aware of beliefs I have that hinder my success.
22. ___ I don't know how to study effectively.
23. ___ When choosing between doing an important school assignment or something really fun, I usually do the school assignment.
24. ___ I break promises that I make to myself or to others.
25. ___ I make poor choices that keep me from getting what I really want in life.
26. ___ I have a written plan that includes both my short-term and long-term goals.
27. ___ I lack self-discipline.
28. ___ I listen carefully when other people are talking.
29. ___ I'm stuck with any habits of mine that hinder my success.
30. ___ When I face a disappointment (like failing a test), I ask myself, "What lesson can I learn here?"
31. ___ I often feel bored, anxious, or depressed.
32. ___ I feel just as worthwhile as any other person.

33. ____ Forces outside of me (like luck or other people) control how successful I will be.
34. ____ College is an important step on the way to accomplishing my goals and dreams.
35. ____ I spend most of my time doing unimportant things.
36. ____ When I encounter a challenging problem, I ask for help.
37. ____ I can be off course from my goals and dreams for quite a while without realizing it.
38. ____ I know how I learn best.
39. ____ My happiness depends mostly on what's happened to me lately.
40. ____ I accept myself just as I am, even with my faults and weaknesses.
41. ____ I am the cause of low grades I receive in school.
42. ____ If I lose my motivation in college, I don't know how I'll get it back.
43. ____ I use self-management tools (like calendars and to-do lists) that help me remember to do important things.
44. ____ I know very few people whom I can count on for help.
45. ____ I'm aware of the habits I have that hinder my success.
46. ____ If I don't like the way an instructor teaches, I'll probably do poorly in the course.
47. ____ When I'm very angry, sad, or afraid, I know how to manage my emotions so I don't do anything I'll regret later.
48. ____ When I think about performing an upcoming challenge (like taking a test), I usually see myself doing poorly.
49. ____ When I have a problem, I complain, blame others, or make excuses.
50. ____ I know how to set effective short-term and long-term goals.
51. ____ I forget to do important things.
52. ____ When I have a difficult course in school, I find a study partner or join a study group.
53. ____ I'm unaware of beliefs I have that hinder my success.
54. ____ I've learned to use specific study skills that work effectively for me.
55. ____ I often feel happy and fully alive.
56. ____ I keep promises that I make to myself or to others.
57. ____ I make wise choices that help me get what I really want in life.
58. ____ I live day to day, without much of a plan for the future.
59. ____ I am a self-disciplined person.
60. ____ I get distracted easily when other people are talking.
61. ____ I know how to change habits of mine that hinder my success.
62. ____ When I face a disappointment (like failing a test), I feel pretty helpless.
63. ____ When choosing between doing an important school assignment or something really fun, I usually do something fun.
64. ____ I feel less worthy than other people.

Transfer your scores to the scoring sheets on the next page. For each of the eight areas, total your scores in columns A and B. Then total your final scores as shown in the sample.

Self-Assessment Scoring Sheet

SAMPLE

A		B	
6.	8	29.	3
14.	5	35.	3
21.	6	50.	6
73.	9	56.	2

___28___ + 40 − ___14___ = 54

SCORE #1: Accepting Personal Responsibility

A		B	
1.		9.	
17.		25.	
41.		33.	
57.		49.	

_____ + 40 − _____ = _____

SCORE #2: Discovering Self-Motivation

A		B	
10.		2.	
26.		18.	
34.		42.	
50.		58.	

_____ + 40 − _____ = _____

SCORE #3: Mastering Self-Management

A		B	
3.		11.	
19.		27.	
43.		35.	
59.		51.	

_____ + 40 − _____ = _____

SCORE #4: Employing Interdependence

A		B	
12.		4.	
28.		20.	
36.		44.	
52.		60.	

_____ + 40 − _____ = _____

SCORE #5: Gaining Self-Awareness

A		B	
5.		13.	
21.		29.	
45.		37.	
61.		53.	

_____ + 40 − _____ = _____

SCORE #6: Adopting Lifelong Learning

A		B	
14.		6.	
30.		22.	
38.		46.	
54.		62.	

_____ + 40 − _____ = _____

SCORE #7: Developing Emotional Intelligence

A		B	
7.		15.	
23.		31.	
47.		39.	
55.		63.	

_____ + 40 − _____ = _____

SCORE #8: Believing in Myself

A		B	
16.		8.	
32.		24.	
40.		48.	
56.		64.	

_____ + 40 − _____ = _____

Carry these scores to the corresponding boxes in the chart on the next page, writing them in the "Your Score" column.

Choices of Successful Students

Your score	Successful students . . .	Struggling students . . .
Score _____	**accept self-responsibility,** seeing themselves as the primary cause of their outcomes and experiences.	see themselves as Victims, believing that what happens to them is determined primarily by external forces such as fate, luck, and powerful others.
Score _____	**discover self-motivation,** finding purpose in their lives by discovering personally meaningful goals and dreams.	have difficulty sustaining motivation, often feeling depressed, frustrated, and/or resentful about a lack of direction in their lives.
Score _____	**master self-management,** consistently planning and taking purposeful actions in pursuit of their goals and dreams.	seldom identify specific actions needed to accomplish a desired outcome. And when they do, they tend to procrastinate.
Score _____	**employ interdependence,** building mutually supportive relationships that help them achieve their goals and dreams (while helping others do the same).	are solitary, seldom requesting, even rejecting, offers of assistance from those who could help.
Score _____	**gain self-awareness,** consciously employing behaviors, beliefs, and attitudes that keep them on course.	make important choices unconsciously, being directed by self-sabotaging habits and outdated life scripts.
Score _____	**adopt lifelong learning,** finding valuable lessons and wisdom in nearly every experience they have.	resist learning new ideas and skills, viewing learning as fearful or boring rather than as mental play.
Score _____	**develop emotional intelligence,** effectively managing their emotions in support of their goals and dreams.	live at the mercy of strong emotions, such as anger, depression, anxiety, or a need for instant gratification.

Score	believe in themselves, seeing themselves capable, lovable, and unconditionally worthy as human beings.	doubt their competence and personal value, feeling inadequate to create their desired outcomes and experiences.
_____		

Interpreting your scores: A score of . . .

0–39	Indicates an area where your choices will **seldom** keep you on course.
40–63	Indicates an area where your choices will **sometimes** keep you on course.
64–80	Indicates an area where your choices will **usually** keep you on course.

In the next few months, you will learn how to choose all of these beliefs and behaviors more consistently. If you choose them as your daily habits, you will definitely get on course to achieving success both in college and in life. I wish you a great journey. Let us begin!

Journal Entry 1

I n this activity, you will take an inventory of your personal strengths and weaknesses as revealed by your self-assessment questionnaire.

1. In your journal, write the eight areas of the self-assessment and record your scores for each, as follows:

All glory comes from daring to begin.

Eugene F. Ware

_____ 1. Accepting personal responsibility

_____ 2. Discovering self-motivation

_____ 3. Mastering self-management

_____ 4. Employing interdependence

_____ 5. Gaining self-awareness

_____ 6. Adopting lifelong learning

_____ 7. Developing emotional intelligence

_____ 8. Believing in myself

Transfer your scores from the self-assessment to the appropriate lines above.

2. Write about the areas on the self-assessment in which you had your highest scores. Explain why you think you scored higher in these areas than in others. Also, explore how you feel about these scores. Your entry might begin, "By doing the self-assessment, I learned that I . . . ."

3. **Write about the areas on the self-assessment in which you had your lowest scores.** Explain why you think you scored lower in these areas than in others. Also, explore how you feel about these scores. Remember the saying, "If you keep doing what you've been doing, you'll keep getting what you've been getting." With this thought in mind, write about any specific changes you'd like to make in yourself during this course. Your entry might begin, "By doing the self-assessment, I also learned that I . . . ."

The five suggestions for creating a meaningful journal are printed on the inside back cover of *On Course.* Please review these suggestions before writing. **Especially remember to copy the directions for each step (bold print) into your journal before writing.**

Relax, think, write.

On Course Principles at Work

I think we have to appreciate that we're alive for only a limited period of time, and we'll spend most of our lives working.

Victor Kiam, Chairman, Remington Products

Applying the strategies you're about to explore in *On Course* will not only improve your results in college, they'll also boost your success at work. You're about to explore dozens of strategies that will help you achieve your goals both in college and in your career.

This is no small matter. Career success (or lack of it) affects nearly every part of your life: family, income, self-esteem, who you associate with, where you live, your level of happiness, what you learn, your energy level, your health, and maybe even the length of your life.

Some students think, "All I need for success at work is the special knowledge of my chosen career." All that nurses need, they believe, is good nursing skills. All that accountants need is good accounting skills. All that lawyers need is good legal skills. These skills are called HARD skills, the knowledge needed to perform a particular job. Hard skills include knowing where to insert an intravenous feeding tube, how to write an effective business plan, and what the current inheritance laws are. These are the skills you'll be taught in courses in your major field of study. They are essential to qualify for a job. Without them you won't even get an interview.

But, most people who've been in the work world a while will tell you this: Hard skills are necessary to get a job but often insufficient to keep it or advance. That's because nearly all employees have the hard skills necessary to do the job for which they're hired. True, some may perform these skills a little better or a little worse than others, but one estimate suggests that only 15 percent of workers who lose their jobs are fired because they can't do their job. That's why career success is often determined by SOFT skills, the same strategies you'll be learning in this book. As one career specialist put it, "Having hard skills gets you hired; lacking soft skills gets you fired."

A United States government study agrees that soft skills are essential to job success. In the early 1990s, the Secretary of Labor asked a blue-ribbon panel to determine what it takes to be successful in the modern employment world. This panel published a report called the Secretary's Commission on Achieving Necessary Skills (SCANS). The SCANS report presents a set of foundation skills and workplace competencies deemed essential for work world success today.

No one familiar with today's work world will find many surprises in the report, especially in the foundation skills. The report calls for employees to develop the same soft skills that are asked for in employment ads, that employers look for in reference letters and job interviews, and that supervisors assess in periodic evaluations of their work force.

The SCANS report identifies the following soft skills as necessary for work and career success: taking responsibility, making effective decisions, setting goals, managing time, prioritizing tasks, persevering, giving strong efforts, working well in teams, communicating effectively, having empathy, knowing how to learn, exhibiting self-control, believing in one's own self worth. The report identifies these necessary skills but doesn't suggest a method for developing them. *On Course* will show you how.

Learning these soft skills will help you succeed in your first career after college. And, because soft skills are portable (unlike most hard skills), you can take them with you in the likely event that you later change careers. Most career specialists say the average worker today can expect to change careers at least once during his or her lifetime. In fact, some 25 percent of workers in the United States today are in occupations that did not even exist a few decades ago. If a physical therapist decides to change careers and work for an Internet company, he needs to master a whole new set of hard skills. But the soft skills he's mastered are the same ones that will help him shine in his new career.

So, as you're learning these soft skills, keep asking yourself, "How can I use these skills to stay on course to achieving my greatest potential at work as well as in college?" Be assured, what you're about to explore can make all the difference between success and failure in your career.

AS SMART AS HE WAS, ALBERT EINSTEIN COULD NOT FIGURE OUT HOW TO HANDLE THOSE TRICKY BOUNCES AT THIRD BASE.

©2002 BY SIDNEY HARRIS

Believing in Yourself: Develop Self-Acceptance

FOCUS QUESTIONS	Why is high self-esteem so important to success? What can you do to raise your self-esteem?

Roland was in his forties when he enrolled in my English 101 class. He contributed wonderful ideas to class discussions, so I was perplexed when the first two writing assignments passed without an essay from Roland.

Both times, he apologized profusely, promising to complete them soon. He didn't want to make excuses, he said, but he was stretched to his limit: He worked at night, and during the day he took care of his two young sons while his wife worked. "Don't worry, though," he assured me, "I'll have an essay to you by Monday. I'm going to be the first person in my family to get a college degree. Nothing's going to stop me."

But Monday came, and Roland was absent. On a hunch, I looked up his academic record and found that he had taken English 101 twice before. I contacted his previous instructors. Both of them said that Roland had made many promises but had never written an essay.

I called Roland, and we made an appointment to talk. He didn't show up. During the next class, I invited Roland into the hall while the class was working on a writing assignment.

"Sorry I missed our conference," Roland said. "I meant to call, but things have been piling up."

"Roland, I talked to your other professors, and I know you never wrote anything for them. I'd love to help you, but you need to take an action. You need to write an essay." Roland nodded silently. "I believe you can do it. But I don't know if *you* believe you can do it. It's decision time. What do you say?"

"I'll have an essay to you by Friday."

I looked him in the eye.

"Promise," he said.

I knew that what Roland actually did, not what he promised, would reveal his deepest core beliefs about himself.

Self-esteem and core beliefs

So it is with us all. Our core beliefs—true or false, real or imagined—form the inner compass that guides our choices.

At the heart of our core beliefs is the statement *I AM_____*. How we complete that sentence in the quiet of our souls has a profound effect on the quality of our lives.

Self-esteem is the high-octane fuel that propels us into the cycle of success. Do we approve of ourselves as we are, accepting our personal weaknesses along with our strengths? Do we believe ourselves capable, admirable, lovable, and fully worthy of the best life has to offer? If so, our beliefs will make it possible for us to make wise choices and stay on course to a rich, full life.

The good news is that self-esteem is learned, so anyone can learn to raise his or her self-esteem. Much of this book is about how you can do just that.

Know and accept yourself

People with high self-esteem know that no one is perfect, and they accept themselves with both their strengths and weaknesses. To paraphrase philosopher Reinhold Niebuhr, successful people accept the things they cannot change, have the courage to change the things they can change, and possess the wisdom to know the difference.

Successful people have the courage to take an honest self-inventory, as you began in Journal Entry 1. They acknowledge their strengths without false humility; they admit their weaknesses without stubborn denial. They tell the truth about themselves and take action to improve what they can.

Fortunately for Roland, he decided to do just that. The Friday after our talk he turned in his English 101 essay. His writing showed great promise, and I told him so. I also told him I appreciated that he had let go of the excuse that he was too busy to do his assignments. From then on, Roland handed in his essays on time. He met with me in conferences. He visited the writing lab, and he did grammar exercises to improve his editing skills. He easily passed the course.

We cannot change anything unless we accept it.
      Carl Jung

A few years later, Roland called me. He had transferred to a four-year university and was graduating with a 3.8 average. He was continuing on to graduate school to study urban planning. What he most wanted me to know was that one of his professors had asked permission to use one of his essays as a model of excellent writing. "You know," Roland said, "I'd still be avoiding writing if I hadn't accepted two things about myself: I was a little bit lazy and I was a whole lot scared. Once I admitted those things about myself, I started changing."

Each of us is a unique combination of strengths and weaknesses. You can pretend you don't have any weaknesses, as struggling people typically do. Or you can acknowledge your weaknesses and start the process of change, as successful people typically do.

Journal Entry 2

In this activity, you will explore your strengths and weaknesses and the reputation you have with yourself. This exploration of your self-esteem will allow you to begin revising any limiting beliefs you may hold about yourself. By doing so you will take a major step toward your success.

1. **In your journal, write a list of ten or more of your personal strengths:** For example, Mentally: *I'm good at math;* Physically: *I'm very athletic;* Emotionally: *I seldom let anger control me;* Socially: *I'm a good friend;* and Others: *I am always on time.*

2. **Write a list of ten or more of your personal weaknesses:** For example, Mentally: *I'm a slow reader;* Physically: *I am overweight;* Emotionally: *I'm easily hurt by criticism;* Socially: *I don't listen very well;* and Others: *I'm a terrible procrastinator.*

3. **Using the information in Steps 1 and 2 and score #8 on your self-assessment, write about the present state of your self-esteem.** On a scale of 1 to 10 (with 10 high), how strong is your self-esteem? How do you think it got to be that way? How would you like it to be? What changes could you make to achieve your ideal self-esteem?

To create an outstanding journal, remember to use the five suggestions printed on the inside back cover of *On Course*. **Especially remember to dive deep!**

Relax, think, and write.

2 Accepting Personal Responsibility

I accept responsibility for creating my life as I want it.

SUCCESSFUL STUDENTS . . .	STRUGGLING STUDENTS . . .
adopt the Creator role, believing that their choices create the outcomes and experiences of their lives.	accept the Victim role, believing that external forces determine the outcomes and experiences of their lives.
master Creator language, accepting personal responsibility for their results.	use Victim language, rejecting personal responsibility by blaming, complaining, and excusing.
make wise decisions, consciously designing the future they want.	make decisions carelessly, letting the future happen by chance rather than by choice.

Adopting the Creator Role

> **FOCUS QUESTIONS** What is self-responsibility? Why is it the key to controlling the outcomes and experiences of your life?

I am the master of my fate;
I am the captain of my soul.
William E. Henley

When psychologist Richard Logan studied people who survived ordeals such as being imprisoned in concentration camps or lost in the Arctic, he found that all of these victors shared a common belief. They saw themselves as personally responsible for the outcomes of their lives.

Ironically, responsibility has gotten a bad reputation lately. Many see it as a heavy burden they must drag through life. Add a little chain gang music, and the picture is complete.

In fact, accepting responsibility is the only way to take maximum control over our lives. **The essence of being personally responsible is responding effectively to all of life's opportunities and challenges.**

Whether your challenge is surviving an Arctic blizzard or excelling in college, accepting personal responsibility moves you into cooperation with yourself and with the world. As long as you resist your role in creating the outcomes and experiences in your life, you will fall far short of your potential.

I first met Deborah when she was a student in my English 101 class. Deborah wanted to be a nurse, but before she could qualify for the nursing program, she had to pass English 101. She was taking the course for the fourth time.

"Your writing shows fine potential," I told Deborah after I had read her first essay. "You'll pass English 101 as soon as you eliminate your grammar problems."

"I know," she said. "That's what my other three instructors said."

"Well, let's make this your last semester in English 101, then. After each essay, make an appointment with me to go over your grammar problems."

"Okay."

"And go to the Writing Lab as often as possible. Start by studying verb tense. Let's eliminate one problem at a time."

"I'll go this afternoon!"

But Deboarah never found time: *No, really . . . I'll go to the lab just as soon as I. . . .*

The more we practice the habit of acting from a position of responsibility, the more effective we become as human beings, and the more successful we become as managers of our lives.
Joyce Chapman

Deborah scheduled two appointments with me during the semester and missed them both: *I'm so sorry . . . I'll come to see you just as soon as I. . . .*

To pass English 101 at our college, students must pass one of two essays they write at the end of the semester. Each essay, identified by social security number only, is graded by two other instructors. At semester's end, Deborah once again failed English 101.

"It isn't fair!" Deborah protested. "Those exam graders expect us to be professional writers. This is the only class that's keeping me from becoming a nurse!"

I suggested another possibility: "What if *you* are the only obstacle keeping you from becoming a nurse?"

Deborah didn't like that idea. She wanted to believe that her problem was "out there." The obstacle was her teachers. All her disappointments were their fault. She saw herself as helpless. The exam graders weren't fair. Life wasn't fair!

I reminded Deborah that it was *she* who had not studied her grammar. It was *she* who had not come to conferences. It was *she* who had not accepted personal responsibility for creating her life the way she wanted it.

"Yes, but . . ." she said.

Every time your back is against the wall, there is only one person that can help. And that's you. It has to come from inside.

Pat Riley,
Professional Basketball Coach

Victims and Creators

When people keep doing what they've been doing even when it doesn't work, they are acting as **Victims.** When people change their beliefs and behaviors to create the best results they can, they are acting as **Creators.**

When you accept personal responsibility, you believe that you create *everything* in your life. This idea upsets some people. Accidents happen, they say. People treat them badly. Sometimes they really are victims of outside circumstances.

This claim, of course, is true. At times, we *are* all affected by circumstances beyond our control. If a hurricane destroys my house, I am a victim (with a small "v"). But if I allow that event to ruin my life, I am a Victim (with a capital "V").

The essential issue is this: Would it improve your life to believe that you create all of the joys and sorrows in your life? Answer "YES!" and see that belief improve your life. After all, if you believe that someone or something out there causes all of your problems, then it's up to "them" to change. What a wait that can be! How long, for example, will Deborah have to wait for "those English teachers" to change?

If, however, you accept responsibility for creating your own results, what happens then? You will choose the beliefs and behaviors necessary to keep you on course to your best possible life.

Responsibility and choice

The key ingredient of personal responsibility is **choice.** Animals respond to a stimulus because of instinct or habit. For humans, however, there is a brief, critical moment of decision available between the stimulus and the response. In this moment, we make the choices—consciously or unconsciously—that influence the outcomes of our lives.

Suppose that while climbing into a friend's car, you realize she's had too much to drink. You could ignore her drunkenness or get out of the car. You could scream at her or calmly ask for the keys so you can drive. Which do you choose? Or suppose you have a test tomorrow and a friend calls with free tickets to a great concert. What are your options? Which do you choose?

Numerous times each day, you have opportunities to make a choice. Some choices have a very small impact: Shall I get my hair cut today or tomorrow? Some have a huge impact: Shall I stay in college or drop out? The results of the many choices you make create the outcome of your life.

The moment of choice looks like this:

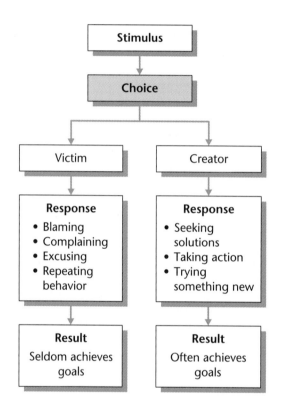

In that brief moment between stimulus and response, we can choose to be a Victim or a Creator. When we respond as a Victim, we complain, blame, make excuses, and repeat ineffective behaviors. When we respond as a Creator, we pause at each decision point and ask, "What are my options, and which option will propel me toward my greatest dreams, toward becoming my best, happiest self?"

Successful people are masters of their choices. In good times and bad, a Creator believes, *A better choice exists, and I am responsible for finding it.*

Believing that you always have a better choice motivates you to look for it, often leading to the discovery of options you would otherwise have missed. People with the richest lives consistently seek and find positive choices. For this reason, choosing to accept personal responsibility is the first step toward being an exceptional student and human being.

I am a Shawnee. My forefathers were warriors. Their son is a warrior. . . . From my tribe I take nothing. I am the maker of my own fortune.

Tecumseh

Personally responsible students (Creators) realize that college merely offers them an *opportunity* to learn. They pause at each decision point and consider their best alternative. They seek solutions. They act purposefully. They try something new. In this way, they create an education worth having and a life worth living.

Journal Entry 3

I n this activity, you will experiment with the Creator role. By choosing to take responsibility for your life, you will immediately gain an increased power to achieve your greatest potential.

1. **Write and complete each of the ten sentence stems below.** For example, someone might complete the first sentence stem as follows:
   1. IF I TAKE FULL RESPONSIBILITY FOR ALL OF MY ACTIONS, I won't be able to blame anyone else if I fail.

   1. IF I TAKE FULL RESPONSIBILITY FOR ALL OF MY ACTIONS . . .
   2. IF I TAKE FULL RESPONSIBILITY FOR ALL OF MY THOUGHTS . . .
   3. IF I TAKE FULL RESPONSIBILITY FOR ALL OF MY FEELINGS . . .
   4. IF I TAKE FULL RESPONSIBILITY FOR MY EDUCATION . . .
   5. IF I TAKE FULL RESPONSIBILITY FOR MY CAREER . . .
   6. IF I TAKE FULL RESPONSIBILITY FOR MY RELATIONSHIPS . . .
   7. IF I TAKE FULL RESPONSIBILITY FOR MY HEALTH . . .
   8. IF I TAKE FULL RESPONSIBILITY FOR ALL THAT HAPPENS TO ME . . .
   9. WHEN I AM ACTING FULLY RESPONSIBLE FOR MY LIFE . . .
   10. IF I WERE TO CREATE MY VERY BEST SELF . . .

2. **Write about what you have learned in this journal about personal responsibility and how you will use this awareness to improve your life.** You might begin, *By reading and writing about personal responsibility, I have learned. . . .*

Relax, think, write.

Mastering Creator Language

FOCUS QUESTION How can you create greater success by changing your vocabulary?

C reators and Victims speak different languages. They might as well be from different planets. Listen carefully to people's choice of words, especially when they are facing a challenge. You can tell immediately who accepts responsibility and who doesn't.

Your inner conversation

Have you ever noticed that there is almost always a conversation going on in your mind? If right now you're thinking, "What conversation? There's no conversation going on in my mind," well, that's the conversation I'm talking about. Whenever something happens, a cast of inner voices chatter away. Which voice we heed determines the quality of the choices we make next. Victims typically heed the voice of their Inner Critic or Inner Defender.

The Inner Critic.   This is the internal voice that criticizes us for all that goes wrong. The Inner Critic says, "Everything is my fault." Ironically, this self-reproach has a positive intention. By criticizing ourselves, perhaps we can correct our faults and be found acceptable by others. The Inner Critic's voice often sounds much like that of our parents or other authority figures when they were being judgmental of us or others when we were children.

PEANUTS reprinted by permission of United Feature Syndicate, Inc.

The world of self-criticism on the one side and judgment toward others on the other side represents a major part of the dance of life.

Hal Stone & Sidra Stone

The Inner Defender.   The flip side of the Inner Critic is the Inner Defender. Our Inner Defender tries to protect us by deflecting criticism outward, saying, "It's all their fault!" The blame for all troubles lies with someone else, or bad luck, so little money, a troubled childhood, not enough time, or too much time. The Inner Defender's voice sounds similar to our own voice when we were scared, confused children trying to figure out how to avoid criticism or punishment.

There is, fortunately, the voice of a Creator within us all.

The Inner Guide.   Creators resist the inner drama of their Inner Critic and their Inner Defender. Instead, they listen to the wisdom of their Inner Guide. The Inner Guide objectively observes events and simply asks, "Am I on course or off course? If I'm off course, how can I best get back on course?" Our Inner Guide tells us impartial truths, allowing us to be more fully conscious of the world, other people, and especially ourselves.

Whether we choose to listen to our Inner Critic, our Inner Defender, or our Inner Guide will change the outcome of our lives. Listen to the words of a Victim who is taking a challenging college course:

> *I hate this course. It's a stupid requirement, and I shouldn't have to take it.*
> *The professor is boring. All he does is read from his notes. How are you supposed to stay awake?*
> *Going to the support lab is no help. It's noisy in there every afternoon. I try to study, but my housemate is no help. Every time I open a book, he's got friends over.*
> *Worst of all, the tests are ridiculous. The professor gave me an F on the first one! No one's passing that class.*

Or listen to the words of a Victim who wants to lose weight:

> *I hate being overweight. I get tired and winded just walking up a flight of stairs. It's awful. I have to lose weight.*
> *It's easy to diet until you get depressed. I've tried going to the gym twenty different times, but it never lasts.*
> *I've tried every diet known to mankind. But you can hear that junk food calling you when you're trying to study. The next thing you know, you've got an empty bag of cheese puffs next to you. Plus, the TV is always bombarding you with food commercials. I try to ignore the food commercials, but it's no use.*

If these two Victims don't change their language, their futures are easy to predict. The first will still be trying to pass that course; the second will still be overweight. But, if they change their language, they can change their behavior and therefore the outcomes of their lives. And so can you.

The language of responsibility

Let's see what a difference it makes when we translate some Victim statements into the responsible language of Creators.

Victims make excuses

The professor is boring.

Creators seek solutions

I find this professor boring, so I'm going to tape-record his lectures. That way I can listen to them a little bit at a time.

It's easy to diet until you get depressed.

The next time I feel depressed, I'll take a walk instead of snacking.

Victims blame

The professor gave me an F on the first test.

The TV is always bombarding you with food commercials.

Creators accept responsibility

I got an F on the first test because I didn't read the assignments.

I'm going to tape my favorite shows so I can fast-forward through the commercials.

What you're supposed to do when you don't like a thing is change it. If you can't change it, change the way you think about it. Don't complain.

Advice to Maya Angelou
from her grandmother

Victims complain

It's a stupid requirement.

I hate being overweight.

Creators take action

I'm going to find out if there's a test I can take to be exempted.

I'm going to enroll in a weight reduction class.

Victims repeat ineffective behavior

Going to the support lab is no help. It's noisy in there every afternoon.

I've tried going to the gym twenty different times, but it never lasts.

Creators try something new

I'm going to visit the support lab when it first opens in the morning; I'll bet there's no crowd that early.

I'm going to jog along the lake this week; maybe I'll enjoy myself enough to stick with it.

Victims "have to" do things

I shouldn't have to take the course.

Creators "choose to" do things

I choose to take this course because it's required for my degree, and my degree will qualify me for the kind of work I've always wanted to do.

I have to lose weight.

I choose to lose weight so I'll look as good on the outside as I feel on the inside.

Victims pretend their problems belong to others. (They say "you" when they mean "I.")

How are you supposed to stay awake?

The next thing you know, you've got an empty bag of cheese puffs next to you.

Creators own their problems. (They say "I" when referring to their own problems.)

I find myself falling asleep when I listen to his lectures.

Sometimes I go unconscious, and I eat a whole bag of junk food. I will stay aware of what I'm eating.

Victims "try"

Creators commit and follow through

I have also stopped using the word try. . . . I either do something or I don't.
Wally "Famous" Amos

I try to study, but my house-mate is no help.

I've tried every diet known to mankind.

I'll study for two hours tonight; I'll tell my roommate not to bother me until I'm finished.

I'm going to make an appointment with a nutritionist and get some expert advice.

Most of all, Victims give up

Most of all, Creators take control of their choices and their lives

There's nothing I can do.

There's always something I can do.

I've always been that way.

I can choose to be different.

I can't . . .

I can . . .

I have to . . .

I choose to . . .

I should . . .

I will . . .

I quit.

I'll keep going.

Creators accept responsibility for creating their results, and their words reflect that ownership. Whenever you feel yourself slipping into the language of a Victim, ask yourself: What do I want in my life: excuses or results? What could I think and say that would get me the results that I want?

Journal Entry 4

In this activity you will practice the language of personal responsibility. By learning to translate Victim statements into Creator statements, you will master the language of successful people.

1. **Draw a line down the middle of a journal page. On the left side of the line, copy the ten Victim statements below.**

2. **On the right side of the line, translate the Victim statements into the words of a Creator.** The key to Creator language is taking ownership of a problem. When you respond as if you are responsible for a bad situation, then you are empowered to do something about it (unlike Victims who must wait for someone else to solve their problems). Use the translations in the journal article on pages 26–27 as models.

3. **Write what you have learned about how you use language: Is it your habit to speak as a Victim or as a Creator?** Be sure to give examples. What is your goal for language usage from now on? Specifically, how will you accomplish this goal? Your paragraph might begin, *While reading about and practicing Creator language, I learned that I. . . .*

Relax, think, write . . . and DIVE DEEP!

Excuses rob you of power and induce apathy.

Agnes Whistling Elk

VICTIM LANGUAGE

1. I can never find a parking place.

2. I failed because he's a lousy instructor.

3. It's not my fault that I'm late.

4. I've been too upset to get my work done.

5. I have to take Math 101.

6. I wish I could write better.

7. This textbook is so boring.

8. I'll try to do my best.

9. My parents drive me crazy.

10. I'd die if he/she ever left me.

CREATOR LANGUAGE

Making Wise Decisions

Life is a journey with many crossroads, and every one requires a choice. What we're experiencing in our lives today is the result of our past choices. More importantly, what we experience in the future will be fashioned by the choices we make from this moment on.

This is an exciting thought. If we can make wiser choices, we can more likely create the future we want.

On the road to a college degree, you will face important choices such as these:

Shall I . . .

- major in business, science, or creative writing?
- work full-time, part-time, or not at all?
- drop a boring course or stick it out?
- study for my exam or go out with friends?

The sum of these choices, plus thousands of others, will determine your degree of success in college and in life. Doesn't it seem wise, then, to develop an effective strategy for choice management?

Every choice we make allows us to manipulate the future.
John Luc Picard, "Star Trek, The Second Generation" *Television Series*

The Wise-Choice Process

In the face of any challenge, you can make a responsible decision by answering the six questions of the Wise-Choice Process. This process is a variation of a decision-making technique developed by Dr. William Glasser.

1. **WHAT'S MY PRESENT SITUATION:** The important information here is "What exists?" (not "Whose fault is it?"). Quiet your Inner Critic, that self-criticizing voice in your head. Ignore your Inner Defender, that judgmental voice that blames everyone else for your problems. Consider only the objective facts of your situation, including how you feel about them. Rely on your Inner Guide, your wise, impartial voice that tells the truth as best it can.

   For example: *I stayed up all night studying for my first history test. When I finished taking the test, I hoped for an A. At worst, I expected a B. When I got the test back, my grade was a D. Five other students got A's. I feel depressed and angry.*

A person defines and redefines who they are by the choices they make, minute to minute.

Joyce Chapman

2. **HOW WOULD I LIKE MY SITUATION TO BE?** You can't change the past, but if you could create an ideal outcome in the future, what would it look like?

I would like to get A's on all of my future tests.

3. **DO I HAVE A CHOICE HERE?** The answer is always "YES!" Don't fall into the Victim trap of believing you have no choices. Assume you can find a better choice and you probably will.

4. **WHAT ARE MY POSSIBLE CHOICES?** Create a list of possible choices that you *could* do, knowing that you aren't obligated to do any of them. Compile your list without judgment. Don't say, "Oh, that would never work." Don't even say, "That's a great idea." Judgment during brainstorming stops the creative flow. Move out of judgment into possibility and discover as many options as you can.

- *I could complain to my classmates and anyone else who will listen.*
- *I could drop the class and take it next semester with another instructor.*
- *I could complain to the department head that the instructor grades unfairly.*
- *I could ask my successful classmates for ideas.*
- *I could ask the instructor for suggestions about improving my grades.*
- *I could request an opportunity to retake the test.*
- *I could get a tutor.*

5. **WHAT'S THE LIKELY OUTCOME OF EACH POSSIBLE CHOICE?** Decide how you think each choice is likely to turn out. If you can't predict the outcome of one of your possible choices, stop this process and gather the information you need. Here are the possible choices from Step 4 and their likely outcomes:

- *Complain to classmates: I'd have the immediate pleasure of blasting the instructor and maybe getting others' sympathy.*
- *Drop the class: I'd lose three credits this semester and possibly have to make them up in summer school.*
- *Complain to the department head: Probably he'd ask if I've seen my instructor first, so I wouldn't get much satisfaction.*
- *Ask successful classmates for ideas: I might learn how to improve my study habits; I might also make new friends.*
- *Ask the instructor for suggestions: I might learn what to do next time to improve my grade; at least the instructor would learn that I want to do well in this course.*

- *Request an opportunity to retake the test: My request might get approved and give me an opportunity to raise my grade. At the very least, I'd demonstrate how much I want to do well.*
- *Get a tutor: This action wouldn't help my grade on this test, but it would probably improve my next test score.*

6. **WHICH CHOICE(S) WILL YOU COMMIT TO DOING?** In this final step, decide which choices will likely create the most favorable outcome and commit to acting on them. If no favorable options exist, consider which choice leaves you no worse off than before. If no such option exists, then ask which choice creates the least unfavorable outcome.

   I'll talk to my successful classmates, make an appointment with my instructor and have him explain what I could do to improve, and I'll request an opportunity to retake the test. If these choices don't raise my next test score to at least a B, I'll get a tutor.

The end result of your life here on earth will always be the sum total of the choices you made while you were here.
Shad Helmstetter

Each situation will dictate the best options. In the example above, if the student had previously failed four tests instead of one, the best choice might be to drop the class. Or, if everyone in the class were receiving D's and F's, and if the student had already met with the instructor, a responsible option might be to see the department head about the instructor's grading policies.

No matter what your final decision may be, the mere fact that you are making a choice is wonderfully empowering. By participating in the Wise-Choice Process, you demonstrate that you believe you *can* change the outcome of your life for the better.

Journal Entry 5

I n this activity you will apply the Wise-Choice Process to improve a difficult situation. Think about a current problem, one that you're comfortable sharing with your classmates and teacher. As a result of this problem, you may be angry, sad, frustrated, depressed, or afraid.

Perhaps this situation has to do with a grade you received, a teacher's comment, or a classmate's action. Maybe the problem relates to a relationship, a job, or your health.

1. **Write the six questions of the Wise-Choice Process, and answer each one as it relates to your situation.**

The Wise-Choice Process

1. WHAT'S MY PRESENT SITUATION? (Describe the problem objectively and completely.)
2. HOW WOULD I LIKE MY SITUATION TO BE? (What is your ideal future outcome?)

3. DO I HAVE A CHOICE HERE? (Yes!)
4. WHAT ARE MY POSSIBLE CHOICES? (Create a long list of specific choices that might create your preferred situation.)
5. WHAT'S THE LIKELY OUTCOME OF EACH POSSIBLE CHOICE? (If you can't predict the likely outcome of an option, stop and gather more information.)
6. WHICH CHOICE(S) WILL I COMMIT TO DOING? (Pick from your list of choices in Step 4.)

2. Write what you learned from doing the Wise-Choice Process. Be sure to Dive Deep. You might begin, *By doing the Wise-Choice Process, I learned that I. . . .*

When I see all the choices I really have, it makes the world a whole lot brighter.

Debbie Scott, student

Remember, you may wish to enliven your journal by adding pictures cut from magazines, drawings of your own, or quotations that appeal to you.

Relax, think, write.

CASE STUDY IN CRITICAL THINKING

The Late Paper

Professor Freud announced in her syllabus for Psychology 101 that final term papers had to be in her hands by noon on December 18. No student, she emphasized, would pass the course without a completed term paper turned in on time. As the semester drew to a close, **Kim** had an "A" average in Professor Freud's psychology class, and she began researching her term paper with excitement.

Arnold, Kim's husband, felt threatened that he had only a high school diploma while his wife was getting close to her college degree. Arnold worked at a bakery, and his coworker **Philip** began teasing that Kim would soon dump Arnold for a college guy. That's when Arnold started accusing Kim of having an affair and demanding she drop out of college. She told Arnold he was being ridiculous. In fact, she said, a young man in her history class had asked her out, but she had refused. Instead of feeling better, Arnold became even more angry. With Philip continuing to provoke him, Arnold became sure Kim was having an affair, and he began telling her every day that she was stupid and would never get a degree.

Despite the tension at home, Kim finished her psychology term paper the day before it was due. Since Arnold had hidden the car keys, she decided to take the bus to the college and turn in her psychology paper a day early. While she was waiting for the bus, **Cindy,** one of Kim's psychology classmates, drove up and invited Kim to join her and some other students for an end-of-semester celebration. Kim told Cindy she was on her way to turn in her term paper, and Cindy promised she'd make sure Kim got it in on time. "I deserve some fun," Kim decided, and hopped into the car. The celebration went long into the night. Kim kept asking Cindy to take her home, but Cindy always replied, "Don't be such a bore. Have another drink." When Cindy finally took Kim home, it was 4:30 in the morning. She sighed with relief when she found that Arnold had already fallen asleep.

When Kim woke up, it was 11:30 A.M., just 30 minutes before her term paper was due. She could make it to the college in time by car, so she shook Arnold and begged him to drive her. He just snapped, "Oh sure, you stay out all night with your college friends. Then, I'm supposed to get up on my day off and drive you all over town. Forget it." "At least give me the keys," she said, but Arnold merely rolled over and went back to sleep. Panicked, Kim called Professor Freud's office and told **Mary,** the secretary, that she was having car trouble. "Don't worry," Mary assured Kim, "I'm sure Professor Freud won't care if your paper's a little late. Just be sure to have it here before she leaves at 1:00." Relieved, Kim decided not to wake Arnold again; instead, she took the bus.

At 12:15, Kim walked into Professor Freud's office with her term paper. Professor Freud said, "Sorry, Kim, you're 15 minutes late." She refused to accept Kim's term paper and gave Kim an "F" for the course.

Listed below are the characters in this story. Rank them in order of their *responsibility for Kim's failing grade in Psychology 101.* Give a different score to each character. Be prepared to explain your choices.

Most responsible ← 1 2 3 4 5 6 → Least responsible

_____**Professor Freud, the teacher**   _____**Philip, Arnold's coworker**
_____**Kim, the psychology student**   _____**Cindy, Kim's classmate**
_____**Arnold, Kim's husband**   _____**Mary, Prof. Freud's
                                             secretary**

DIVING DEEPER: Is there someone not mentioned in the story who may also bear responsibility for Kim's failing grade?

Personal Responsibility at Work

I found that the more I viewed myself as totally responsible for my life, the more in control I seemed to be of the goals I wanted to achieve.

Charles J. Givens, Entrepreneur and Self-made Multimillionaire

A student once told me she'd had more than a dozen jobs in three years. "Why so many jobs?" I asked. "Bad luck," she replied. "I keep getting one lousy boss after another." Hmmmm, I wondered, twelve lousy bosses in a row? What are the odds of that?

Responsibility is about ownership. As long as I believe my career success belongs to someone else (like "lousy" bosses), I'm being a Victim, and my success is unlikely. Victims give little effort to choosing or preparing for a career. Instead, they allow influential others (like parents and teachers) or circumstances to determine their choice of work. They complain about the jobs they have, make excuses for why they haven't gotten the jobs they really want, and they blame others for their occupational woes. By contrast, Creators know that the foundation of success at work (as in college) is accepting this truth: *By our choices, we are each the primary creators of the outcomes and experiences of our lives.*

Accepting responsibility in the work world begins with consciously choosing your career path. You alone can decide what career is right for you. That's why Creators explore their career options thoroughly, match careers requirements with their own talents and interests, consider the consequences of choosing each career (such as how much education the career requires or what the employment outlook is), and they make informed choices. Choose your career wisely because few things in life are worse than spending eight hours a day, 50 weeks a year, working at a job you hate.

Taking responsibility for your work life also means planning your career path to keep your options open and your progress unobstructed. For example, you could keep your career options open in college by taking only general education courses while investigating several possible fields of work. Or you could eliminate a financial obstacle by getting enough education—such as a dental hygiene degree—to support yourself while pursuing your dream career—such as going to dental school.

In short, Creators make use of the power of wise choices. They believe that there is always an option that will lead them toward the careers they want, and they take responsibility for creating the employment they want. Instead of passively waiting for a job to come to them, they actively go out and look. One of my students lost a job when the company where she worked closed. She could have spent hours in the cafeteria complaining about her bad fortune and how she could no longer afford to stay in school. Instead she created employment for herself by going from store to store in a mall asking every manager for a part-time job until one said, "Yes." In the time she could have wasted in the cafeteria complaining about her money problems, she solved them with positive actions.

When it comes to finding a full-time career position, Creators continue to be proactive. They don't wait for the perfect job opening to appear in their local paper. They don't sit by the phone waiting for a call from an employment agency. They know that employers prefer to hire people they know and like, so Creators do all they can to get known and liked by employers in their career field. They start by researching companies that need their talents and for whom they might like to work. Then, they contact potential employers directly. They don't ask if the employer has a job opening. Instead, they seek an informational interview: "Hi, I've just gotten my degree in accounting, and I'd like to make an appointment to talk to you about your company. . . . What's that? You don't have any positions open at this time? No problem. I'm just gathering information at this point, looking for where my talents might make the most contribution. Would you have some time to meet with me this week? Or would next week be better?" Creators go to these information-gathering interviews prepared with knowledge about the company, good questions to ask, and a carefully prepared résumé. At the end of the meeting they ask if the interviewer knows of any other employers who might need their skills. They call all of the leads they get and use the referral as an opening for a job interview: "I was speaking with John Smith at the Ajax Company, and he suggested that I give you a call about a position you have open." A friend of mine got an information-gathering interview and wowed the personnel manager with her professionally prepared résumé and interviewing skills; even though the company "had no openings" when she called, two days after the interview, she was offered a position.

Accepting responsibility not only helps you *get* a great job, it makes it possible to *excel* on the job. Employers love responsible employees. Wouldn't you? Instead of complaining, blaming, making excuses, and thus creating an emotionally draining work environment, responsible employees create a positive work place where absenteeism is low and work production is high. Instead of repeating ineffective solutions to problems, proactive employees seek solutions, take new actions, and try something new. They pursue alternative routes instead of complaining about dead ends. Creators show initiative instead of needing constant direction, and they do their best work even when the boss isn't looking. As someone once said, "There is no traffic jam on the extra mile." Creators are willing to go the extra mile, and this effort pays off handsomely.

If you run into a challenge while preparing for a career, seeking a job, or working in your career, don't complain, blame, or make excuses. Instead, ask yourself a Creator's favorite question: "What can *I* do about it?"

Believing in Yourself: Change Your Inner Conversation

FOCUS QUESTIONS   How does your inner conversation affect your self-esteem? How can you raise your self-esteem by changing your self-talk?

It is the mind that maketh good or ill,

That maketh wretch or happy, rich or poor.

Edmund Spencer

Imagine this: Three students schedule an appointment with their professor to discuss a project they're working on together. They go to the professor's office at the scheduled time, but he isn't there. They wait forty-five minutes before finally giving up and leaving. As you watch what they do next, identify which student has the strongest self-esteem.

Student #1, feeling discouraged and depressed, spends the evening watching television while leaving homework in other subjects untouched. Student #2, feeling insulted and furious, spends the evening complaining to friends about the inconsiderate, incompetent instructor. Student #3, feeling confused about the mixup, decides to call the instructor the next day to see what happened and to set up another meeting; meanwhile, this student spends the evening studying for a test in another class.

Which student has the strongest self-esteem?

The curse of stinkin' thinkin'

Self-esteem can be defined as the state that exists when you are not arbitrarily haranguing and abusing yourself but choose to fight back against those automatic thoughts with meaningful rational responses.

Dr. Thomas Burns

How is it that three people can have the same experience and respond to it so differently? According to psychologists like Albert Ellis, the answer lies in what each person believes caused the event. Ellis suggested that our different responses could be understood by realizing that the activating event (A) plus our beliefs (B) equal the consequences (C). In other words, A + B = C. For example:

Activating Event	+ **B**eliefs	= **C**onsequence
Student #1: Instructor didn't show up for a scheduled conference.	My instructor thinks I'm dumb. I'll never get a college degree. I'm a a failure in life.	Got depressed and watched television all evening.
Student #2: Same.	My instructor won't help me. Teachers don't care about students. Life stinks.	Got angry and spent the night telling friends how horrible the instructor is.

| Student #3: Same. | I'm not sure what went wrong. Sometimes things just don't turn out the way you plan. There's always tomorrow. | Studied for another class. Planned to call the instructor the next day to see what happened and set up a new appointment. |

Ellis suggests that our upsets are caused not so much by our problems as by what we think about our problems. When our thinking is full of irrational beliefs, what Ellis calls "stinkin' thinkin'," we feel awful even when the circumstances don't warrant it.

Stinkin' thinkin' isn't based on reality. Rather, these irrational thoughts are the automatic chatter of the Inner Critic (keeper of Negative Beliefs about myself) and the Inner Defender (keeper of Negative Beliefs about other people and the world).

So what about our three students and their self-esteem? It's not hard to see that Student #1, who got depressed and wasted the evening watching television, has low self-esteem. This student is thrown far off course simply by the instructor's not showing up. A major cause of this self-defeating reaction is the Inner Critic's harsh self-judgments. Here are some common self-damning beliefs held by Inner Critics:

I'm dumb.	I'm not as good as other people.
I'm selfish.	I'm worthless.
I'm unattractive.	I'm not college material.
I'm lazy.	I'm weak.
I'm a failure.	I'm a lousy parent.
I'm incapable.	I'm unlovable.

A person dominated by his Inner Critic misinterprets events, inventing criticism that isn't there. A friend says, "Something came up, and I can't meet you tonight." The Inner Critic responds, "Did I do something wrong? I screwed up again, didn't I!"

The activating event doesn't cause the self-criticism; rather the judgmental chatter of the Inner Critic does. A strong Inner Critic is both a cause and an effect of low self-esteem.

What about student #2, the one who spent the evening telling friends how horrible the instructor was? Though perhaps less apparent, this student also demonstrates low self-esteem. The finger-pointing Inner Defender is merely the Inner Critic turned outward and is just as effective at getting the student off course. Here are some examples of destructive beliefs held by an Inner Defender:

People don't treat me right, so they're rotten.

People don't act the way I want them to, so they're awful.

The Inner Critic keeps us feeling insecure and childlike. When it is operating, we feel like children who have done something wrong and probably will never be able to do anything right.
Hal Stone and Sidra Stone

Replacing a negative thought with a positive one changes more than just the passing thought—it changes the way you perceive and deal with the world.
Dr. Clair Douglas

People don't live up to my expectations, so they're the enemy.

People don't do what I want, so they're against me.

Life is full of problems, so it's terrible.

Life is unfair, so I can't stand it.

Life doesn't always go my way, so I can't be happy.

Life doesn't provide me with everything I want, so it's unbearable.

A person dominated by her Inner Defender discovers personal insults and slights in neutral events. A classmate says, "Something came up, and I can't meet you tonight." The Inner Defender responds, "Who do you think you are, anyway? I can find someone a lot better to study with than you!"

The activating event doesn't cause the angry response; rather the judgmental chatter of the other-damning Inner Defender does. A strong Inner Defender is both a cause and an effect of low self-esteem.

Only student #3 demonstrates high self-esteem. This student realizes he doesn't know why the instructor missed the meeting. He doesn't blame himself, the instructor, or a rotten world. He considers alternatives: Perhaps the instructor got sick or was involved in a traffic accident. Until he can find out what happened and decide what to do next, this student turns his attention to an action that will keep him on course to another goal. The Inner Guide is concerned with positive results, not judging self or others. A strong Inner Guide is both a cause and an effect of high self-esteem.

Disputing irrational beliefs

How, then, can you raise your self-esteem?

First, you can become aware of the constant chatter of your Inner Critic and Inner Defender. Be especially alert when events in your life go sour and strong emotions get you off course.

Does it help to change what you say to yourself? It most certainly does. . . . Tell yourself often enough that you'll succeed and you dramatically improve your chances of succeeding and of feeling good.

Drs. Bernie Zilbergeld and Arnold A. Lazarus

Once you become familiar with your inner voices, you can begin a process of separating yourself from your Inner Critic and Inner Defender. To do this, practice disputing your irrational and self-sabotaging beliefs. Here are some effective ways to dispute:

- Offer a positive explanation of the problem: *My instructor may have missed the meeting because of a last-minute crisis.*

- Prove the accusations wrong by offering contrary evidence: *My instructor called me last week to see if I needed help with my project, so I'm confident he'll help me again.*

- Question the importance of the problem: *Even if my instructor won't help me, I can still go to the Writing Center to get help.*

- Offer a practical plan of action to solve the problem: *It's true that I haven't done well up until now. But I'm going to make some changes. I'm going to read my assignments two or three times, attend every class, take good notes, and create a study team.*

If all options fail, distract yourself from negative thoughts. Simply tell yourself, "STOP!" and replace your blaming, complaining, or excusing with something positive: Watch a funny movie, tell a joke, recall your goals and dreams, think about someone you love.

Wisely choose the thoughts that occupy your mind. Avoid letting automatic, negative thoughts undermine your self-esteem. Evict them and replace them, instead, with esteem-building thoughts.

Journal Entry 6

In this activity, you will practice disputing the harsh judgments of your Inner Critic and your Inner Defender. As you become skilled at seeing yourself and the world more realistically, your self-esteem will thrive.

1. **Write a sentence expressing a recent problem or event that upset you.** Think of something troubling that happened in school, at work, or in your personal life. For example, *I got a 62 on my math test.*

2. **Write a list of five criticisms your Inner Critic (IC) might level against you as a result of this situation. Have your Inner Guide (IG) dispute each one immediately.** For example,

   IC: You failed that math test because you're terrible in math.
   IG: It's true I failed the math test, but I'll study harder next time and do better. This was only the first test, and I now know what to expect next time.
   Review the methods of disputing illustrated on page 38.

3. **Write a list of five criticisms your Inner Defender (ID) might level against someone else or life as a result of this situation. Have your Inner Guide (IG) dispute each one immediately.** For example,

   ID: You failed that math test because you've got the worst math instructor on campus.
   IG: I have trouble understanding my math instructor, so I'm going to make an appointment to talk with him in private. John really liked him last semester, so I bet I'll like him, too, if I give him a chance.

4. **Write what you have learned about changing your inner conversation.** Wherever possible, offer personal experiences to explain your ideas. Your journal entry might begin, *In reading and writing about my inner conversations, I have discovered that. . . .*

Relax, think, write.

Entering college is like crossing the border into another country. Each has new customs to learn. Heed the following college customs and your stay in higher education will be not only more successful but more enjoyable as well.

1. Read your college catalogue. This resource contains most of the factual information you'll need to plot a great journey through higher education. It explains how your college applies many of the customs discussed in this section. Keep a college catalogue on hand and refer to it often.

2. See your advisor. Colleges provide an advisor who can help you make wise choices. Sometimes this person is a counselor, sometimes a teacher. Find out who your advisor is, make an appointment, and get advice on what courses to take and how to create your best schedule. Students who sidestep advisors often enroll in unnecessary courses or miss taking courses that are required for graduation. Your tuition has paid for a guide through college; use this valuable resource.

3. Understand prerequisites. A "prerequisite" is a course that must be completed before you can take another course. For example, colleges require the completion of calculus before enrollment in more advanced mathematics courses. Before you register, confirm with your advisor that you have met all the prerequisites. Otherwise you may find yourself registered for a course you aren't prepared to pass. Prerequisites appear within each course description in your college catalogue.

4. Complete your general education requirements. Most colleges require students to take a minimum number of general education courses such as freshman composition, speech, history, psychology, and mathematics. Find a list of these required courses in your college catalogue, and check each requirement when completed. Regardless of how many credits you earn, you can't graduate until you've completed the general education requirements.

5. Choose a major wisely. You usually choose a major area of study in your first or second year. Examples of majors include nursing, early childhood education, biology, teaching, mechanical engineering, and art. Even if you have a major picked out, you may want to visit the counseling center to discover what major might be a stepping-stone to your chosen career. For example, majoring in English is great preparation for a law degree. All majors and their required courses are listed in your college catalogue. Until you've entered a major, you're wise to concentrate on completing your general education requirements.

6. Take a realistic course load. I once taught a student who worked full-time, was married with three small children, and had signed up for six courses in her first semester. After five weeks, she was exhausted and withdrew from college. There are only 168 hours in a week. Be realistic about the number of courses you can handle given your other responsibilities.

7. Attend the first day of class (on time). Of course, it's wise to attend *every* day, but, whatever you do, be present on the first day! On this day professors usually lay the ground rules for the entire semester. If you're absent, you may miss something that will bite you later.

8. Sit in class where you can focus on learning. Many students focus best sitting up front. Others prefer sitting on the side about halfway back where they can see all of their classmates and the professor during a discussion. Experiment. Try different places in the room. Once you find the place that best supports your learning, sit there permanently, unless you find that changing seats every day is best for you.

9. Study the syllabus. In the first class, professors usually provide a syllabus (sometimes called a first-day handout). The syllabus is the single most important handout you will receive all semester. Typically, it contains the course objectives, the required books and supplies, all assignments and due dates, and the method for determining grades. This handout also presents any course rules you need to know. Your professor will assume that you've read and understood this document; be sure to ask questions about any part you don't understand.

10. Buy required course books and supplies as soon as possible. College instructors cover a lot of ground quickly. If you don't have your study materials from the beginning, you may fall too far behind to catch up. To get a head start, some students go to the bookstore weeks before classes begin and purchase course materials. Bookstores can usually tell you the required supplies and books for every class. If money is tight, check with the financial aid office to see if your college provides temporary book loans.

11. Introduce yourself to one or more classmates and exchange phone numbers. After an absence, contact a classmate to learn what you missed. Few experiences in college are worse than returning to class and facing a test that was announced in your absence.

12. Inform your instructor before an absence. Think of your class as your job and your professor as your employer. Professional courtesy dictates notifying your employer of anticipated absences. The same is true with instructors.

13. If you arrive late, slip in quietly. Don't make excuses. Just come in and sit down. If you want to explain your lateness, see the professor after class. Speak as a Creator: Offer reasons, not excuses.

14. Ask questions. If the question you don't ask shows up on a test, you're going to be upset with yourself. Your classmates are equally nervous about asking questions. Go ahead, raise your hand and ask one on the first day; after that, it'll be easier.

15. To hold an extended conversation with your professors, make an appointment during their office hours. Most college professors have sched-uled office hours. Ask your professor for his or her office hours and mention that you'd like to make an appointment to discuss a specific topic. Be sure to show up (or call beforehand to reschedule).

16. Get involved in campus life. Most colleges offer numerous activities that can broaden your education, add pleasure to your life, and introduce you to new friends. Consider participating in the drama club, school newspaper, intercultural counsel, student government, athletic teams, band or orchestra, literary magazine, yearbook committee, science club, or one of the many other organizations on your campus.

17. Know the importance of your grade point average (GPA). Your GPA is the average grade for all of the courses you have taken in college. GPAs range from 0.0 ("F") to 4.0 ("A"). Your GPA affects your future in many ways. At most colleges a minimum GPA (often 2.0, a "C") is required to graduate. Students who fall below the minimum GPA are usually ineligible for financial aid and cannot play intercollegiate sports. Academic honors (like the Dean's List) and some scholarships are based on your GPA. Finally, potential employers often note GPAs to determine if prospective employees have achieved success in college.

18. Know how to compute your grade point average (GPA). At most colleges, GPAs are printed on a student's transcript, which is a list of courses completed (with the grade earned). You can get a copy of your transcript from the registrar's office. Transcripts are usually free or available for a nominal charge. Computing your own grade point average is simple using the formula on p. 42.

19. If you stop attending a class, withdraw officially. For various reasons students stop attending classes. Some students think that when they do, the college administration will know to withdraw them from the course. That's not the way the system works. Students are enrolled in a course until

Formula for Computing Your Grade Point Average (GPA)

$$\frac{(G1 \times C1) + (G2 \times C2) + (G3 \times C3) + (G4 + C3) + \ldots (Gn + Cn)}{\text{Total number of credits attempted}}$$

In this formula, G = the grade in a course and C = number of credits for a course. For example, suppose you had the following grades:

"A" in Math 110 (4 credits)	G1 ("A") = 4.0	C1 = 4
"B" in English 101 (3 credits)	G2 ("B") = 3.0	C2 = 3
"C" in Sociology 101 (3 credits)	G3 ("C") = 2.0	C3 = 3
"D" in Music 104 (2 credits)	G4 ("D") = 1.0	C4 = 2
"F" in Physical Education 109 (1 credit)	G5 ("F") = 0.0	C5 = 1

Here's how to figure the GPA from the grades above:

$$\frac{(4.0 \times 4) + (3.0 \times 3) + (2.0 \times 3) + (1.0 \times 2) + (0.0 \times 1)}{4 + 3 + 3 + 2 + 1} = \frac{16 + 9 + 6 + 2 + 0}{13} = 2.5$$

they're *officially* withdrawn. A student who stops attending is still on the class role at semester's end when grades are assigned, and the instructor will very likely give the nonattending student an "F." That failing grade is now a permanent part of the student's record, lowering the GPA, and discouraging potential employers. If you decide to stop attending a class, go directly to the registrar's office and follow its official procedures for withdrawing from a class. Make certain that you withdraw before your college's deadline. This date is often about halfway through a semester or quarter.

20. **Talk to your instructor before withdrawing.** If you're going to fail a course, withdraw to protect your GPA. But don't withdraw without speaking to your instructor first. Sometimes students think they are doing far worse than they really are. (These students probably have strong Inner Critics.) Discuss with your instructor what you need to do to pass the course and make a step-by-step

plan. If you discover that failing is probable and can't be avoided, withdraw officially.

21. **Keep a file of important documents.** Forms get lost in large organizations like a college. Save everything that may affect your future: course syllabi, completed tests and assignments, approved registration forms, scholarship applications, transcripts, paid bills. If you're exempted from a college requirement or course prerequisite, get it in writing and add the document to your files.

22. **Finally, some college customs dictate what you should *not* do. Avoiding these behaviors shows respect to your classmates and professors.**

- Don't pack up your books or put on your coat until the class is over.

- After an absence, don't ask your professor, "Did I miss anything?" (Of course you did.)

- Don't wear headphones during class.

- Don't let a beeper or cellular phone disturb the class.
- Don't talk with a neighbor while the professor or a classmate is talking.
- Don't make distracting noises in class (clicking pen, popping gum, drumming fingers, and so on.)

College customs exercise

Ask an upperclassman, "What is the one thing you now know about college customs that you wish you had known on your first day?" Be prepared to report your findings.

3 Discovering Self-Motivation

Once I accept responsibility for creating my own life, I must choose the kind of life I want to create. In other words, I must choose the purpose of my life.

I am choosing all the goals and dreams for my life.

SUCCESSFUL STUDENTS . . .	STRUGGLING STUDENTS . . .
discover their dreams, providing them with a passionately felt life purpose and consistent motivation.	have little sense of purpose, passion, or drive in their lives.
commit to their dreams, visualizing the successful creation of their ideal future.	wander aimlessly from one activity to another.
design a compelling life plan, complete with purposeful long- and short-term goals.	tend to invent their lives as they live them.

Discovering Your Dreams

FOCUS QUESTIONS Do you want to feel more motivated, passionate, and alive? How can you increase and sustain your self-motivation?

Dreams vault us out of bed in the morning. They provide energy when we run headlong into an obstacle. Dreams give our lives purpose and meaning.

If you don't presently have a vision of a future you'd like to create, you're not alone. Many people search for years to find their purpose in life. Later, they realize that experiences that earlier seemed meaningless or even painful were, in fact, essential preparation for discovering their dreams. Be patient with yourself and trust that you'll discover your dreams at exactly the right moment. In the meantime, enjoy the quest!

College offers a wonderful opportunity to discover or expand your dreams. You'll be exposed to hundreds, even thousands, of new people, ideas, and experiences. With each encounter, be conscious of your energy. When your voltage rises, pay attention. Something within you is getting inspired.

Philosopher Joseph Campbell gave this wise advice for living a meaningful life: "Follow your bliss." Become conscious of times when you experience passion for life. Let this passion reveal your dreams.

Nothing happens unless first a dream.

Carl Sandburg

Life roles and dreams

Think about the roles you have chosen for your life. A life role is an activity to which we regularly devote large amounts of time and energy. For example, you're presently playing the role of college student.

How many of the following roles are you also playing: friend, employee, employer, athlete, brother, sister, church member, son, daughter, roommate, husband, wife, parent, grandparent, tutor, musician, neighbor, volunteer? Do you play other roles as well?

Most people identify four to seven major life roles. If you have chosen more than seven, you may be spreading yourself too thin. Consider combining or eliminating one or more of your roles for now. If you have identified fewer than four roles, assess your life again. You may have forgotten or overlooked a role. For example, if you spend many hours watching television, then that is one of your present life roles. Maybe an invisible role like this one is keeping you from spending more time in important roles.

Once you identify your life roles, ask yourself what dreams you have in each one. For example, what do you dream of accomplishing in your role as

The future belongs to those who believe in the beauty of their dreams.

Eleanor Roosevelt

a student? Twenty years from now will you have a two-year associate of arts (A.A.) degree? A four-year bachelor of arts (B.A.) or bachelor of science (B.S.) degree? Will you attend graduate school and earn a master of arts (M.A.) or master of science (M.S.) degree? Will you go even further and obtain a doctor of philosophy (Ph.D.) degree, a medical doctor (M.D.) degree, or a doctor of jurisprudence (J.D.) law degree? Any of these futures could be yours.

Whatever you do, don't be limited by puny dreams. Aspire to greatness. Dare to dream big! If you want to be a doctor, don't settle for being a nurse. If you want to be a nurse, don't settle for being a hospital clerk. If you really want to be a hospital clerk, don't settle for being a doctor. Go all out for what *you* want!

Creating inner motivation

I had no big dreams as a college freshman. I lacked a vision of what I wanted to accomplish, and my choices showed it. I remember the afternoon my advisor looked over my course selections for my first semester. He crossed out a course that I had picked and registered me for Latin.

Latin? What was I going to do with an ancient language? I guess my face shouted my doubt. My advisor scraped his desk chair a little closer to me, a fatherly smile spreading across his face. "Latin, you see, contains the roots of much of the English language," he said kindly. "Studying Latin will improve your vocabulary."

Well, what did I know? I wasn't sure why I was in college anyway. I didn't have any reason *not* to take Latin. I wanted to be agreeable. I wanted him to like me. "Okay," I said. And that's how I happened to take Latin.

A year later, in my sophomore year, I was still drifting. The time had come to declare my major. I thought I might choose English. My roommate thought that was a bad idea. He counted off on his fingers all the reasons he believed no one should major in English.

"Well, how about psychology, then?" I wondered aloud.

"Hmmmmm." My roommate was pondering my future. He had attended a private high school. I was impressed. Finally, he nodded. "Psychology is good," he said.

And that's how I happened to become an undergraduate psychology major. (As I later discovered what I wanted to create in my life, I returned to graduate school for advanced degrees in both English and psychology—so it's never too late to change course.)

Without a dream to guide my energy, I was like a Ping-Pong ball, bouncing back and forth between other people's ideas of what I should do. Worse, I didn't even realize I had another choice. I didn't know that I could be pursuing a motivating dream.

Years later, I wished my advisor (or anyone else) had said, "Hold it, young man. Have you considered what your life is all about? Have you considered discovering the dreams that will catapult you out of bed each morning, keep

Climb High
Climb Far
Your goal the sky
Your aim the star.
Inscription on the
Hopkins Memorial
Steps, Williams
College

your energy surging well into the evening, give you peaceful, contented sleep at night? Have you got at least one motivating dream? You deserve it, you know!"

I hope by now you're wondering to yourself, "So, what *are* my greatest dreams?" Or, if you believe you've already discovered your dreams, perhaps you're wondering, "Are there even *bigger* dreams for me?"

You are not here merely to make a living. You are here in order to enable the world to live more amply, with greater vision, with a finer spirit of hope and achievement. You are here to enrich the world, and you impoverish yourself if you forget the errand.
Woodrow Wilson

If you want to live a rich, personally fulfilling life, remember that you are responsible for choosing your destination. Years from now, when your life is nearly over, who will you be? What will you have? What will you have done? Who will be in your life? How will you feel about your life?

Through the years, I have had the joy of working with students who discovered wonderful and motivating dreams: becoming an operating room nurse, writing and publishing a novel, traveling around the world, operating a refuge for homeless children, marrying and raising a beautiful family, playing professional baseball, starting a private school, composing songs for Aretha Franklin, becoming a college professor, swimming in the Olympics, managing a mutual fund, having a one-woman art show, becoming a fashion model, owning a clothing boutique, holding political office, eliminating hunger on the planet, and more.

What is *your* dream? What will excite *you?* What is it that *you* want to have, do, and be? Once you know, you will have an inexhaustible supply of inner motivation to create a life worth living.

Journal Entry 7

In this activity, you will explore your dreams. People with motivating dreams make better choices, are better able to stay on course, and are more likely to live rich, personally fulfilling lives. Take a deep breath and relax. It's time for some no-limit dreaming.

By the way, some people think of dreams as unattainable fantasies, things to be wished for but never accomplished. Not so here. Here, *dreams* refer to your life's greatest aspirations, those marvelous accomplishments that you desire deep within you and that you are perfectly capable of achieving if you employ your full potential. Journal Entries 7, 8, and 9 offer you an opportunity to turn your dreams into attainable goals by making them ever more specific and by setting deadlines for their accomplishment. Get ready to create your future the way *you* want it to be!

1. **Write a list of the four to seven major roles that you have chosen in your life. Next to each role, write your biggest dream(s) for that role.** Ask yourself: "If I knew that I could not fail, what would I love to accomplish or experience in each role during my life?" Then describe specifically your future vision of what

you would like to have, do, and be in each role. State each dream in the present tense as if it already exists. For example . . .

Role: Student	DREAM: I have a Ph.D. in psychology.
Role: Partner	DREAM: I am happily married to someone I love and who loves me enough to support my personal growth.
Role: Worker	DREAM: I have my own counseling practice assisting children to develop high self-esteem.
Role: Self-nurturer	DREAM: I am in great shape, physically and emotionally; I have a beautiful four-bedroom house.

I started getting successful in school when I saw how college could help me achieve my dreams.

Bobby Marinelli, student

The four roles above are, of course, only examples. Be sure to use the actual roles that you play in your life. If you discover a dream that doesn't fit into any of your current roles, create a new one. For example, if one of your dreams is to write a book, create a new role of "Author."

2. **Write about WHY one of your dreams is important to you.** Begin by stating your dream (from Step 1): *One of my dreams is that I have my own counseling practice assisting children to develop high self-esteem.* Continue writing **why** you have chosen this dream. For now, don't worry about how you will create this dream.

3. **Repeat Step 2 for another of your dreams.** First tell **what** the second dream is; then tell **why** you have chosen this dream.

Remember, dive deep. When you explore your life and dreams at a deep level, you improve your chances of having an important insight that can change your life for the better. So dive deep into yourself!

Relax, think, write.

Committing to Your Dreams

FOCUS QUESTIONS Do you start new projects (like college) with great enthusiasm, only to lose motivation along the way? How can you keep your motivation strong?

Many people doubt they can achieve what they truly want. When a big, exciting dream creeps into their thoughts, they shake their heads. "Oh, sure," they mumble to themselves, "how am *I* going to accomplish that dream?" This is merely the voice of your Inner Critic, and you can choose to ignore it.

In truth, you don't need to know how to achieve a dream when you first think of it. What you do need is an unwavering commitment, fueled by a strong desire. Once you promise yourself that you will do whatever it takes to accomplish your dream, you often discover the method for achieving it in the most magical ways.

Commitment creates method

A commitment is an unbending intention, a single-mindedness of purpose that promises to overcome all obstacles regardless of how you may feel at any particular moment. During the summer between my sophomore and junior years in college, I made such a commitment.

That summer, I used all of my savings to visit Hawaii. While there, I met a beautiful young woman, and we spent twelve blissful days together.

Perhaps like you, one of my dreams has always been to have a wonderful love relationship. So I promised to return to Hawaii during Christmas break. Back in college, six thousand miles away, my commitment was sorely tested. I had no idea how, in just three months, I could raise enough money to return to Hawaii. Committed to my dream, however, I spent weeks inventing and rejecting one scheme after another.

Then one day, I happened upon a possible solution. I was glancing through *Sports Illustrated* when I noticed an article by a student-athlete from Yale University. Until that moment, all I'd had was a commitment. When I saw that article, I had a plan. A long shot, yes, but a plan, nonetheless: Maybe the editors of *Sports Illustrated* would buy an article about the sport I played, lightweight football. Every evening for weeks, I worked on an article. Finally, I dropped it in the mail and crossed my fingers.

A few weeks later, my manuscript came back, rejected. On the printed rejection form, however, a kind editor had handwritten, "Want to try a rewrite? Here's how you might improve your article. . . ."

I spent another week revising the article, mailed it directly to my encouraging editor, and waited anxiously. Christmas break was creeping closer. I had just about given up hope of returning to Hawaii in December.

Then one day my phone rang, and the caller identified himself as a photographer from *Sports Illustrated.* "I'll be taking photos at your football game this weekend. Where can I meet you?"

And that's how I learned that my article had been accepted. Better yet, *Sports Illustrated* paid me enough money to return to Hawaii. I spent Christmas on the beach at Waikiki, with my girlfriend on the blanket beside me.

Suppose I hadn't made a commitment to return to Hawaii? Would reading *Sports Illustrated* have sparked such an outrageous plan? Would I, at twenty years of age, have ever thought to raise money by writing a feature article for a national magazine? It is doubtful.

Don't be afraid of the space between your dreams and reality. If you can dream it, you can make it so.
Belva Davis

Always bear in mind that your own resolution to succeed is more important than any one thing.
Abraham Lincoln

When you have a clear intention, methods for producing the desired results will present themselves.
Student Handbook, University of Santa Monica

What intrigues me as I recall my experience is that the solution for my problem was there all the time; I just didn't see it until I made a commitment.

By committing to our dreams, we program our brains to look for solutions to our problems and to keep us going when the path gets rough. Whenever you're tempted to look for motivation outside yourself, remember this: Motivation surges up from a *commitment* to a passionately held purpose.

The key to making and keeping your commitment is visualizing the pleasure you'll derive when you achieve your dream.

Visualize your ideal future

Human beings seek pleasure and avoid pain. Use this psychological truth to your benefit.

To make or strengthen a commitment, visualize yourself accomplishing your dream and imagine the delight you'll experience when your dream becomes reality. Consider also the pleasures you'll experience along the way. Let these positive outcomes and feelings draw you like a magnet toward your dream. All of our accomplishments are created twice. Before we can create them in the world, we must create them in our minds.

Some years ago, I happened to glance at a three-ring notebook carried by one of my students. Taped to the cover was a photo showing her in a graduation cap and gown.

"Have you graduated?" I asked.

"Not yet. But that's what I'll look like when I do."

"How did you get the photo?"

From my own experience, there is no question that the speed with which you are able to achieve your goals is directly related to how clearly and how often you are able to visualize your goals.
Charles J. Givens

"My sister graduated from college a few years ago," she explained. "After the ceremony, I put on her cap and gown and had my mother take this picture. Whenever I get discouraged about school, I look at this photo and imagine myself walking across the stage to receive my diploma. I hear my family cheering for me, just like we did for my sister. Then I stop feeling sorry for myself and get back to work. This picture reminds me what all my efforts are for."

A few years later, at her graduation, I remember thinking, "She looks just as happy today as she did in the photo. Maybe happier."

Life will test our commitments. To keep them strong in times of challenge, we need a clear picture of our desired results. We need a motivating mental image that, like a magnet, draws us steadily toward our ideal future.

The power of visualizing makes sense when you remember that getting anywhere is difficult if you don't know where you're going. A vivid mental image of your chosen destination keeps you on course even when life's adversities conspire against you.

How to visualize

Here are four keys to an effective visualization.

1. **RELAX.** Visualizing seems to have the most positive impact when experienced during the *alpha* waves produced by deep relaxation.

2. **USE PRESENT TENSE.** Imagine yourself experiencing success *now*. Therefore, use the present tense for all verbs: *I am walking across the stage to receive my diploma.* OR *I walk across the stage.* (Not past tense: *I was walking across the stage;* and not future tense: *I will be walking across the stage.*)

3. **USE ALL FIVE SENSES.** Imagine the scene concretely and specifically. Use all of your senses. What do you see, hear, smell, taste, touch?

4. **FEEL THE FEELINGS.** Events gain power to motivate us when accompanied by strong emotions. Imagine your accomplishment to be just as grand and magnificent as you wish it to be. Then feel the excitement of your success.

> *I see a Chicago in which the neighborhoods are once again the center of our city, in which businesses boom and provide neighborhood jobs, in which neighbors join together to help govern their neighborhood and their city.*
> Harold Washington, Chicago's first black mayor

Psychologist Charles Garfield notes that athletes have used visualizations to win sports events; psychologist Brian Tracy writes about salespeople using visualizations to succeed in the business world; and Dr. Bernie Siegel, a cancer specialist, has even chronicled patients improving their health with visualizations.

Finally, consider this: Keeping your commitment may be even more important than actually achieving your dream. Life, someone has said, is a journey, not a destination. When you are on course to a personally meaningful dream, you will learn and grow in ways that you cannot imagine today.

So create lofty dreams. And, from deep within you, commit to their achievement.

Journal Entry 8

In this activity, you will visualize the accomplishment of one of your most important dreams. Once you vividly picture this ideal outcome, you will have strengthened your commitment to this dream, and you will know how to do the same thing with all of your dreams.

1. **Write a visualization of the exact moment in the future when you are experiencing the accomplishment of your biggest dream in your role as a *student*.** Describe the scene of your success as if it is happening to you *now*. For example, if your dream is to graduate from a four-year college with a 4.0 average, you might write, *I am dressed in a long, blue robe, the tassel from my graduation cap tickling my face. I look out over the thousands of people in the au-*

dience, and I see my mother, a smile spreading across her face. I hear the announcer call my name. I feel a rush of adrenaline, and chills tingle on my back as I take my first step onto the stage. I see the college president smiling, reaching her hand out to me in congratulations. I hear the announcer repeat my name, adding that I am graduating with highest honors, having obtained a 4.0 average. I see my classmates standing to applaud me. Their cheers flow over me, filling me with pride and happiness. I walk . . .

For visual appeal, consider also drawing a picture of your dream in your journal. Or cut pictures from magazines and use them to illustrate your writing. Allow your creativity to support your dream.

Remember the four keys to an effective visualization:

1. **Relax** and create *alpha* brain waves.

2. Use **present tense verbs** . . . the experience is happening now!

3. Use **all five senses.** What do you see, hear, smell, taste, and feel (touch)?

4. Include **emotion.** Imagine yourself feeling great in this moment of grand accomplishment. You deserve to feel fantastic!

Read your visualizations often. Ideal times are right before you go to sleep and when you first awake in the morning. You may even wish to record your visualizations on a cassette tape and listen to them often.

Relax, think, write . . . your ideal future.

Designing a Compelling Life Plan

FOCUS QUESTIONS Do you have a motivating vision for your life? How can you create such a vision or improve upon the one you have?

What is significant about a life plan is that it can help us live our own lives (not someone else's) as well as possible.

Harriet Goldhor Lerner

By committing to personally motivating dreams, we create destinations for our life's journey. By choosing purposeful short- and long-term goals, we continue designing a compelling life plan.

Short-term goals define the specific destinations we plan to reach within the next few months. Long-term goals define the specific destinations we plan to reach in a year or more. Each short-term goal realized is a steppingstone toward a long-term goal, and each long-term goal realized is a steppingstone toward one of our dreams.

Sadly, people typically spend more time planning a one-week vacation than they spend planning their lives. According to psychologist Brian Tracy, people don't set life goals for two reasons. First, they don't realize the importance of having these goals; second, they don't know how to set goals. Let's eliminate these two obstacles so you can experience the power of having goals.

We . . . believe that one reason so many high-school and college students have so much trouble focusing on their studies is because they don't have a goal, don't know what all this studying is leading to.

Muriel James and
Dorothy Jongeward

Why goals are important

People who don't realize the importance of goals probably haven't heard about a study done at Yale University. Researchers first asked members of the Yale class of 1953 if they had specific, written, long-term goals. Only 3 percent did. Twenty years later, the researchers contacted these same Yale graduates to see what had happened to them. They found that the 3 percent with goals had lives that were measurably better than the 97 percent without goals. In one area in particular, the results were quite remarkable: The 3 percent who had set specific goals had accumulated more personal wealth than had the other 97 percent put together.

One student I know greatly improved her life by setting goals. While growing up, Joan dreamed of becoming a famous singer, and following high school, she started performing in night clubs. She married her manager, and the two of them lived in a trailer, moving from town to town in pursuit of singing jobs. After exhausting years on the road, Joan recorded a song. It didn't sell, and her dreams began to unravel. Marital problems complicated her career. Career problems complicated her marriage. Joan grew tired of the financial and emotional uncertainty in her life. Finally, in frustration, she divorced her husband and gave up the dream of singing professionally.

Although disappointed, Joan started setting new goals. She needed to earn a living, so she set a short-term goal to become a hairdresser. After graduating from cosmetology school, Joan saved enough money to settle some debts, buy her first new car, and pay for a new long-term goal. She decided to go to a community college (where I met her) and major in dental hygiene.

Two years later, Joan graduated with honors and went to work in a dentist's office. Still lacking a dream that excited her, Joan chose another long-term goal: her bachelor's degree. Joan worked days in the dentist's office and at night she attended classes. A few years later, she again graduated with honors.

Then, she set another long-term goal: to earn her master's degree. Earlier in her life, Joan had doubted that she was "college material." With each academic success, her confidence grew. "One day I realized that, once I set a goal, it's a done deal," Joan said.

That awareness inspired her to begin dreaming again. As a child, Joan had always imagined herself as a teacher. Master's degree now in hand, she returned to our college to teach dental hygiene. A year later, she was appointed department chairperson. In only seven years, propelled by her goals and dreams, Joan had gone from a self-doubting freshman to head of the college's dental hygiene department.

How to set a goal

To be effective, a goal needs five qualities. You can remember them by applying the DAPPS rule. "DAPPS" is an acronym, a memory device in which each letter of the word stands for one of five qualities:

Dated.   Effective goals have specific deadlines. A short-term goal usually has a deadline within a few months. A long-term goal generally has a deadline of a year or more, maybe even five or ten years away. As this date approaches, your motivation typically increases. This energy helps you finish strong. If you don't meet your deadline, you have an opportunity to examine what went wrong and create a new plan. Without a deadline, you might stretch the pursuit of a goal over your whole life, never reaching it.

Achievable.   Effective goals are realistic. It's unrealistic to say you'll complete a marathon next week if your idea of a monster workout has been jogging around the block a few times a week. Still, if you're going to err, err on the side of optimism. When you set goals at the outer reaches of your present ability, stretching to reach them causes you to grow. Listen to other people's advice, but trust yourself to know what is achievable for you. Apply this guideline: "Is achieving the goal at least 50 percent believable to me?" If so, go for it.

Personal.   Effective goals are *your* goals, not someone else's. Ask yourself if your current goals contribute to *your* personal dreams. If not, trade them in for goals of your own. You don't want to be lying on your deathbed some day and realize you have lived someone else's life. Trust that you know better than anyone else which goals and dreams are right for you.

I wanted to be the greatest hitter who ever lived. A man has to have goals—for a day, for a lifetime—and that was mine, to have people say, "There goes Ted Williams, the greatest hitter who ever lived."
Ted Williams,
Hall-of-fame baseball player

I know many top managers and leaders in every field who review several goal cards each day and listen to audio cassette recordings in their own voice of those goals, on their way to and from their place of business every day.
Denis Waitley

Positive.   Effective goals focus your energy on what you *do* want rather than on what you *don't* want. So translate negative goals into positive goals. For example, a negative goal to stop being late to classes becomes a positive goal to arrive on time to every class. I recall a race car driver who explained how he miraculously kept his spinning car from smashing into the retaining wall: "I kept my eye on the track, not the wall." Focus your thoughts and actions on where you *do* want to go rather than on where you *don't* want to go, and you, too, will stay on course.

Specific.   Effective goals state outcomes in specific, measurable terms. It's not enough to say, "My goal is to do better this semester" or "My goal is to work harder at my job." How will you know if you've achieved these goals? What concrete evidence will you have? Revise your goals: "I will achieve a 3.5 or better grade average this semester. On my job, I will volunteer for all offerings of overtime." Being specific keeps you from fooling yourself into believing you've achieved a goal when, in fact, you haven't.

Your life plan

A life plan shows you the big picture of where you are headed and the step-pingstones necessary to get there.

SUCCESS

YOUR LIFE ROLES

YOUR DREAMS IN EACH LIFE ROLE

YOUR LONG-TERM GOALS FOR EACH DREAM

YOUR SHORT-TERM GOALS FOR EACH LONG-TERM GOAL

People who have unclear goals, unclear pictures of themselves, and make unclear choices, end up with an unclear future—and never a chance at reaching what they thought they had wanted.
Shad Helmstetter

Take a look at a page of a life plan that one student, Maria, designed for herself:

MY LIFE ROLE: College student

MY DREAM IN THIS ROLE: I have a master's degree in social work.

MY LONG-TERM GOALS IN THIS ROLE:

1. Associate of Arts degree from BCCC by June 2004.
2. Bachelor of Arts degree from University of Maryland by June 2006.

MY SHORT-TERM GOALS IN THIS ROLE (this semester):

1. Earn an A in ENG 101 by 5/20.
2. Write an essay of five hundred or more words with fewer than three grammar errors by 5/20.
3. Earn an A in PSY 101 by 5/20.
4. Learn and apply five or more psychological strategies that will help my family be happier and more loving by 5/1.

5. Earn an A in CSS 110 by 5/20.

6. Consciously adopt five or more new success behaviors and teach these strategies to my children by 4/15.

7. Learn to use a computer well enough to prepare all of my written assignments by 3/1.

8. Take at least one page of notes in every class period this semester.

9. Turn in every assignment on time this semester.

This is the first page of Maria's six-page life plan. She wrote a similar page for each of her other five life roles: parent, wife, employee, friend, and group leader for troubled teenagers.

Consciously designing your life plan, as Maria did, has many advantages. A life plan defines your desired destinations in life, and it charts your best route for getting there. Like a road map, a life plan constantly shows whether you are on course or off course. It gives your Inner Guide something positive to focus on when the chatter of your Inner Critic or Inner Defender attempts to distract you from your dream.

Perhaps most of all, a life plan is your personal definition of a life worth living. With it in mind, you'll be less dependent on something or someone else to give you motivation. Your most compelling motivation will be found within.

Journal Entry 9

I n this activity, you will design your life plan. To focus your mind, glance back at Maria's life plan and use it as a model.

When you're stuck in a dark place and you suddenly see a light, you immediately begin to follow it. That's why setting goals is important.
Rosalyn Mosley, student

1. **Title a clean page in your journal: MY LIFE PLAN. Below that, complete your life plan for your role as a student:**

   My Life Role: Student

   My Dream(s) in this Role: (Use the same dream you wrote in Journal Entry 7 unless it has changed.)

   My Long-Term Goals in this Role: (Remember, these goals are steppingstones to your dream as a student and may take years to achieve.)

   My Short-Term Goals in this Role: (Remember, these goals are steppingstones to your long-term goals as a student and will probably be completed by the end of this semester.)

As you write the long- and short-term goals for this part of your life plan, remember to apply the DAPPS rule. Make sure that each goal is **D**ated, **A**chievable, **P**ersonal, **P**ositive, and **S**pecific.

If you wish, repeat this process for one or more additional life roles. The more roles you consider, the more complete your vision of life will be. Taken together, these pages become your plan for a great life!

2. **Write about what you have learned by designing your life plan.** Remember, at this time you don't need to know *how* to achieve your goals and dreams. All you need to know is *what* you want to create in your life. In the next chapter, you will learn strategies for accomplishing your life plan.

For now, relax, think, and write your life plan.

CASE STUDY IN CRITICAL THINKING

Popson's Dilemma

Fresh from graduate school, **Assistant Professor Popson** was about halfway through his first semester of teaching college English. On this particular day he was sitting in his office awash with gloom because attendance in his classes had dropped from twenty-five to sixteen. Truthfully, only about twelve students were present at any one class.

At that very moment, Professor Popson's best student in freshman composition, nineteen-year-old **Robert Winkle,** entered the office. "Can I see you for a moment?" "Sure," Popson said, "What's up?" Winkle said, "Every day, I find it harder and harder to hang in here. I was really excited about college at the beginning of the semester. Now I've lost my motivation, and I don't know why. But if I drop out, my mom is going to be crushed. What should I do?" Popson didn't want to give bad advice to his best student. "Can you come back tomorrow?" Popson asked. "I'll ask around and see what other professors have to say."

Professor Assante said, "Motivate him with money. Give him the statistics that show college grads earning nearly a million dollars more in their lifetimes than nongrads. Tell him the choice is between driving a five-year-old Sentra or a brand new Lexus, between living in an apartment or a five-bedroom house. Remind him that a college degree is money in the bank."

Professor Buckley said, "Appeal to his sense of purpose. If he's as talented as you say, he's going to want to leave a legacy he can be proud of. Show him that going to college is his key to making a contribution to the future of humanity."

Professor Chen said, "I've been teaching for thirty years, and if there's one thing I've learned, it's this: You can't motivate someone else. If this young man isn't motivated to stay in college, let him go out and experience the world. If college is right for him, he'll discover it for himself, and he'll come back full of motivation."

Professor Donnely said, "He's too young to be making a life-changing decision like dropping out of school. He doesn't understand the consequences. You have to do whatever you can to keep him enrolled. I'd play up how disappointed his mother is going to be if he drops out. Lay the guilt on thick. He'll thank you years from now. And so will his mother."

Professor Egret said, "Make a personal appeal. Let him know he matters to you and that you'll be personally disappointed to see him drop out. Offer to mentor him even after he finishes your class. Let him understand he has a champion in you, and he'd be giving that up if he drops out."

Professor Fanning said, "You say he can easily earn an 'A' in your class, right? Well, tell him that. Urge him to hang in there to get his 'A.' After that he can decide what to do for next semester."

Listed below are the six professors in this story. Rank the quality of their advice on the scale below. Give a different score to each professor. Be prepared to explain your choices.

Best Advice ← 1   2   3   4   5   6 → Worst Advice

____ **Professor Assante**   ____ **Professor Donnely**
____ **Professor Buckley**   ____ **Professor Egret**
____ **Professor Chen**   ____ **Professor Fanning**

DIVING DEEPER: **Is there a response not mentioned by one of the six professors that would have been even more motivating for you?**

Self-Motivation at Work

Figure out what kind of job would make you happiest because the kind that would make you happiest is also the one where you will do your best and most effective work.

Richard Bolles, Career Expert, Author of *What Color is Your Parachute?*

One of the most important choices you will ever make is whether to seek a job or a career. When you have a job, you work for a paycheck. When you have a career, you work for the enjoyment and satisfaction you earn from your daily efforts . . . and you also get paid, possibly very well. I've had both, and I assure you, a career makes life a whole lot sweeter. If you want to feel motivated to get up and go to work 50 weeks a year, you'll definitely want to choose a career.

College is a great place to prepare for a career. But, to stay self-motivated, you'll want to match your career choice and college major with your unique interests, talents, and personality. I once had a student who was majoring in accounting because he'd heard that accountants make lots of money. He saw no problem with the fact that he hated math. He thought he was preparing for a career when in fact he was preparing for a job.

Some of the most motivated students in higher education are those who see college as the next logical step on the path to their goal. Sometimes these are younger students who are pursuing a life-long dream of working in a particular profession. More often they are older students who've grown tired of working at an uninspiring job and have returned to college to prepare for a career. These self-motivated students are the ones who not only make the most of their education but who also enjoy the journey.

If you have a dream of a particular career, stay open to the possibility of finding something even more suited for you. If you're not yet sure what you want to do, keep exploring. The answer will probably reveal itself to you, and when it does, your life will change. One student I knew went from barely getting C's and D's to earning straight A's when she discovered her passion to be a kindergarten teacher.

Use your life-planning skills to design a motivating career path for yourself, identifying the long- and short-term goals that will act as stepping-stones to your success. Using the DAPPS rule, you might create a career path like this:

2 years: I've received my A.A. degree in accounting with high honors and, by thoroughly researching accounting firms nationally, I've decided on five firms that look promising to work for after earning my B.A. degree.

5 years: I've earned my B.A. in accounting with high honors, and I'm employed in an entry-level accounting position in a firm of my choice earning $40,000 or more per year.

10 Years: I own my own accounting firm, and I'm earning $100,000 or more per year, contributing to the financial prosperity and security of my clients.

Keep in mind that there is more to choosing an employer than how much money you're offered. Choosing an employer whose purpose and values are compatible with your own will assist you greatly to stay motivated. By reading a company's mission statement, you can find out what it claims are its purpose and values. For example, suppose you wanted to work in retail sales or marketing for one of the giant office products companies. Here is the mission statement for Staples:

Slashing the cost and hassle of running your office! Our vision is supported by our core values: C.A.R.E.

- *Customers*—Value every customer
- *Associates*—Support them as valuable resources
- *Real Communications*—share information with people when they need it
- *Execution*—achieve our business goals

Now, here is the mission statement for a major competitor, Office Depot:

Office Depot's mission is to be the most successful office products company in the world. Our success is driven by an uncompromising commitment to:

- *Superior Customer Satisfaction:* A company-wide attitude that recognizes that customer satisfaction is everything.
- *An Associate-Oriented Environment:* An acknowledgment that our associates are our most valuable resource. We are committed to fostering an environment where recognition, innovation, communication and the entrepreneurial spirit are encouraged and rewarded.
- *Industry Leading Value, Selection and Services:* A pledge to offer only the highest-quality merchandise available at everyday low prices, providing customers with an outstanding balance of value, selection and services.
- *Ethical Business Conduct:* A responsibility to conduct our business with uncompromising honesty and integrity.
- *Shareholder Value:* A duty to provide our shareholders with superior Return-On-Investment.

Based on their mission statements, which company do you think has a purpose and value system that would create a more motivating work environment for you?

Once you actually begin your search for a position in your chosen career, your goal-setting abilities and visualizing skills will help you stay motivated. You can expect to make dozens of contacts with potential employers for each one that responds with interest to your inquiry. One way to keep yourself motivated during your search is to set a goal of making a specific number of contacts each week. *Goal: I will send a letter of inquiry and my résumé to 10 or more potential employers each week.* In this way, you focus your energy on what you have control over—your own actions.

Additionally, take a few minutes each day to visualize yourself already in the career of your choice; see your office, your co-workers, and imagine yourself doing the daily activities of your career. This mental movie will reduce anxieties and remind you of the purpose for your hard work. Visualizing yourself in your ideal career will help keep you motivated when you encounter delays and disappointments on the path to your goal.

When you actually begin your career, self-motivation strategies will become extremely important to your success. You can't read many employment ads without noticing how many businesses are seeking employees who are "self-motivated." The ad might say "Must work well on own," or "Seeking a self-starter," but you know what such buzz words really mean. These employers want a worker who is able to take on a task and stick with it until completion despite obstacles or setbacks. Who wouldn't want a self-motivated worker? If you were an employer, wouldn't you?

Finally, your ability to set goals in your career is critical to your success. Goals and quotas are inevitable for those in sales positions, but many employers require all of their workers to set goals and create work plans. Your ability to set effective goals will not only help you excel at achieving goals for yourself, but also for your team, office, and company. As you move up in responsibility, your ability to coach others to set goals will be a great asset to the entire organization.

You will likely be working 30, 40, or even more years. Your ability to discover inner motivation will have a great deal to do with the quality of the outcomes and experiences you create during all of these years.

Believing in Yourself: Write a Personal Affirmation

> **FOCUS QUESTIONS**   What personal qualities will you need to achieve your dreams? How can you strengthen these qualities?

Certain personal qualities will be necessary to achieve your dreams. For example, if your dream is a happy family life, you'll need to be loving, supportive, and communicative. If your dream is discovering the cure for cancer, you'll need to be creative, persistent, and strong-willed.

We are what we imagine ourselves to be.
Kurt Vonnegut, Jr.

Think of the dream you have for your education. What are the personal qualities you'll need to accomplish it? Will you need to be intelligent, optimistic, articulate, responsible, confident, goal-oriented, mature, focused, motivated, organized, hard-working, curious, honest, enthusiastic, self-nurturing?

The potential for developing all of these personal qualities, and more, exists in every healthy human being. Whether a particular person fulfills that potential is another matter.

During childhood, a person's judgment of his or her personal qualities seems to be based mostly on what others say. If your friends, family, or teachers told you as a child that you're smart, you probably internalized this quality and labeled yourself "smart." But if no one said you're smart, perhaps you never realized your own natural intelligence. Worse, someone important

"Mother, am I poisonous?"

may have told you that you're dumb, and thus began the negative mind chatter of your Inner Critic.

I was saying "I'm the greatest" long before I believed it.
Muhammad Ali

How we become the labels that others give us is illustrated by a mistake made at a school in England. A group of students at the school were labeled "slow" by scores on an achievement test. Because of a computer error, however, their teachers were told these children were "bright." As a result, their teachers treated them as having high potential. By the time the error had been discovered, the academic scores of these "slow" students had risen significantly. Having been treated as if they were bright, the kids started to act bright. Perhaps, like these children, you have positive qualities waiting to blossom.

As adults we can choose what we believe about ourselves. As one of my psychology professors used to say, "In your world, your word is law." If you say something is true, that thought becomes your truth. Your self-talk defines your reality. Suppose, for example, you want to be more organized. If you tell yourself over and over, "I am organized, I am organized, I am organized," you increase the likelihood of taking actions to get organized. Your words are the parent to both your new beliefs and new actions.

Claiming your desired personal qualities

An effective way to strengthen desired qualities is to create a personal affirmation, a statement in which we claim desired qualities as if we already had them in abundance. Here are some examples:

- I am a bold, joyful, loveable man.
- I am a confident, creative, selective woman.
- I am a spiritual, wise, and curious man, finding happiness in all that I do.
- I am a supportive, organized, and secure woman, and I am creating harmony in my family.

We continue to be influenced by our earliest interactions with our parents. We hear their voices as our own internal self-talk. Those voices function like posthypnotic suggestions. They often govern our lives.

John Bradshaw

Affirmations help us breathe life into personal qualities that were smothered by what important adults told us when we were children. One of my colleagues recalls that whenever she made a mistake as a child, her father would say, "I guess that proves you're NTB." "NTB" was his shorthand for "not too bright." Imagine her challenge of feeling intelligent when she kept getting that message from her father! Today, she doesn't even need her father around; her Inner Critic is happy to remind her that she's NTB. She could benefit from an affirmation that says, "I am VB (very bright)." An affirmation, then, is a method for weakening the negative influences of your Inner Critic and replacing them with positive qualities.

What limiting messages did you receive as a child? Perhaps others said you were "homely," "stupid," "clumsy," or "always screwing up." If so, today you can create an affirmation that strengthens your desired positive qualities. For example, you could say, "I am a beautiful, intelligent, graceful woman, turning any mistake into a powerful lesson."

Some people report that their positive affirmations seem like lies. The negative messages from their childhood (chanted today by their Inner Critics) feel more like the truth. If so, try thinking of your affirmation as prematurely telling the truth. You may not feel beautiful, intelligent, or graceful when you first begin to claim these qualities, but, just as the "slow" children at the English school responded to being treated as bright, with each passing day you will grow into the truth of your chosen qualities. Using affirmations is like becoming your own parent: You acknowledge the positive qualities that no one has thought to tell you about . . . until now.

Living your affirmation

To adopt new beliefs, we can now systematically choose affirming statements, then consciously live in them.

Joyce Chapman

Of course, simply creating an affirmation is insufficient to offset years of negative programming. Affirmations need reinforcement to gain influence in your life. Here are six ways to empower your affirmation.

1. **Realize that you already possess the qualities you desire.**
   You already *are* creative, persistent, loving, intelligent . . . whatever.
   These are your natural human qualities waiting to be rediscovered. To
   confirm this reality, simply recall a specific event in your past when
   you displayed a desired quality. This quality may presently be hidden, but you can call it forth. You simply have to remember your true
   identity.

2. **Give power to your affirmation by repeating it over and
   over until it becomes as familiar to you as your name.** One
   student repeated her affirmation during regular workouts on a rowing
   machine. The steady pace of the exercise provided the rhythm to
   which she repeated her affirmation. What would be a good occasion
   for you to repeat your affirmation?

3. **Say your affirmation while looking at yourself in the mirror.** This approach helps you take personal ownership of the positive
   qualities.

4. **Be vigilant about other words you use to describe yourself.**
   Your self-perceptions define who you believe you are; thus, how you
   describe yourself defines your future. If you want to be intelligent,
   keep your Inner Critic from saying things like, "Boy, am I stupid. I
   never do anything right." Keep your Inner Defender from claiming,
   "It's not my fault. She's the worst instructor in the whole college." Instead, consciously choose to say, "I got a 50 on the math test. I'm intelligent, so I'll learn from my mistakes." Let your Inner Guide
   describe what you did, what your positive quality is, and what you'll
   do differently in the future.

5. **Use your affirmation when life tests you.** In the midst of life's
   many challenges, let your affirmation remind you of the personal
   qualities that will help you stay on course to your dreams.

6. **Record your affirmation on a loop tape.** These ever-repeating
   tapes are made for telephone answering machines and are sold at
   many electronics stores. You can listen to your affirmation tape as
   you commute to work, eat lunch alone, or wait for a friend. Another
   great time to listen to or repeat your affirmation is before doing an
   assignment or taking a test.

Decide which personal qualities will help you stay on course to your
dreams. Your personal affirmation will help to bring them forth!

*The practice of doing
affirmations allows us to
begin replacing some of our
stale, worn out, or negative
mind chatter with more
positive ideas and concepts. It
is a powerful technique, one
which can in a short time
completely transform our
attitudes and expectations
about life, and thereby totally
change what we create for
ourselves.*

Shakti Gawain

Journal Entry 10

In this activity, you will create a personal affirmation. If you repeat your affirmation often, it will help you develop the personal qualities needed to achieve your dreams.
First, take a moment to breathe deeply and relax.

1. **Write a one-sentence statement of your greatest dream in your role as a student.** Simply copy the dream you wrote in Journal Entry 9 for your role as a student.

2. **Write a list of personal qualities that would help you achieve this educational dream.** Use adjectives like *persistent, intelligent, hard-working, loving, articulate, organized, friendly, confident, relaxed,* and so on. Write as many qualities as possible.

3. **Circle the three qualities on your list that seem the *most essential* for you to achieve your dream as a student.**

4. **Write three versions of your personal affirmation.** Do this by filling in the blanks in sentence formats A, B, and C below. Fill the blanks with the three personal qualities you circled in Step 3 above. NOTE: Use the same three personal qualities in each of the three formats.

My "Born to Lose" tattoo was on my mind long before it was on my arm. Now I'm telling myself I'm "Born to Win."
Steve R., student

Format A: I am a _____, _____, _____ man/woman.
Example: I am a strong, intelligent, persistent woman.

Format B: I am a _____, _____, _____ man/woman, _____ing _____.
Example: I am a strong, intelligent, persistent woman, creating my dreams.

Format C: I am a _____, _____, _____ man/woman, and I _____.
Example: I am a strong, intelligent, persistent woman, and I love life.

Don't copy the examples; create your own unique affirmation.

5. **Choose the one sentence from Step 4 that you like best and write that sentence five or more times.** This repetition helps you to begin taking ownership of your affirmation and desired qualities.

6. **Write three paragraphs—one for each of the three qualities in your affirmation.** In each of these paragraphs, write about a specific experience when you displayed your desired quality. For example, if one of your desired qualities is persistence, tell a story about a time in your life when you were persistent (even a little bit!). Write the story like a scene from a book, with enough specific details that

readers will feel as though they are seeing what you experienced. Your paragraph might begin, *The first quality from my affirmation is. . . . A specific experience in my life when I demonstrated that quality was. . . .*

You can add creativity to your journal by writing your affirmation with colors, maybe adding pictures or key words cut from magazines, drawings of your own, or quotations that appeal to you.

Relax, think, write.

In college you'll be asked to write essays, journals, research papers, lab reports, and tests in almost every class. In your career, too, you'll probably write more than you can now imagine. Even to get most jobs, you'll need to write a cover letter and résumé. Most writing today is done on computers because they simplify revising and editing your work. You can add, delete, and move text, easily printing out drafts as you go along. Here, then, are some great strategies to help you write better in college and on your job.

Before Writing

1. Create a positive affirmation about writing. Create an affirming statement, like *"I write well, clearly expressing the important ideas I have to say."* Along with your personal affirmation, repeat this writing affirmation to reprogram your beliefs about your ability to write well.

2. If you get to choose the topic, pick one that truly interests you. You'll enjoy researching and writing about something meaningful to you, and your grades will probably improve as well.

3. Begin immediately. Even if you only think of a few ideas, write something to get your mind focused on the topic. Your unconscious mind will then begin mulling over the issues even when you're engaged in something else. Along with the next five suggestions, this step will prepare you for a productive brainstorming session (described in 9 below).

4. Create motivating focus questions. Continue the initial exploration of the topic by deciding what question(s) you have about your topic. For example, the central question of this book is "How do some people succeed in college and in life while others, with the same apparent potential, struggle?" I've been seeking and writing about the answer to that question for over ten years. If a question truly intrigues you, motivation will be plentiful and the focus of your inquiry will become clear.

5. Seek answers to your questions in the library. If your topic calls for research, go to your library

and search for sources of information that can answer your focus questions. Learn to use the computer catalogue to find books, periodicals, journals, and other reference material. Don't forget about electronic sources, such as CD-ROMs. Be sure to write down the source of your information for later inclusion in your essay and your list of references. Cards (3″ × 5″) are convenient for recording sources.

6. Search for answers to your questions on the Internet. Internet search engines are computer programs that search out Web pages containing information of interest to you. One of the most popular search engines on the Internet is Yahoo. I have heard that Yahoo stands for You Always Have Other Options, which suggests it was developed by Creators who know the value of having choices. Yahoo can be reached by clicking your browser's net search button or entering the following URL address: *http://www.yahoo.com*. Type in the key words for your search, submit your query, and review your returns. Other powerful search engines include Excite (*http://www. excite.com*), Infoseek (*http://www.infoseek.com*), Alta Vista (*http://altavista.digital. com*), and Lycos (*http://www.lycos.com*).

7. Ask other people to answer your questions. Say, *"I was wondering how you'd answer this question. . . ."* Engage anyone who'll talk to you, including participants of computer listservs (on-line discussion groups) to which you belong. At the least, having a conversation about your topic will get your creative juices flowing. At best, you may get fascinating answers that will suggest a whole new slant on your topic.

8. Carry and use 3″ × 5″ cards for notes. Once you begin thinking about a subject, ideas will come to you at the strangest moments. You may be ordering French fries in the cafeteria when a great idea hits you. Don't think you'll remember it later. Pull out a 3″ × 5″ card and make a note. Keep your cards rubber-banded together for organizing later.

9. Brainstorm. After you have taken the previous steps, your mind should be overflowing with ideas.

Set aside a special time to brainstorm in depth about your topic. Some people call this a "brain dump." You can brainstorm on paper, but using a computer is even better because you can later delete or move ideas easily. Write down every idea that comes into your head with no effort to evaluate its worth—such judgment stifles creativity. If you have notes on 3″ × 5″ cards, add them as well.

10. Organize your thoughts. Use an organizing strategy that feels right to you. The following two strategies offer ways to create a blueprint for writing.

Outline. The table of contents of this book is an outline that shows the major (flush left) and supporting (indented) categories of *On Course*. An outline is a great organizing strategy if your preferred way of learning requires a linear, left-brained approach. In Journal Entry 23 you will discover if this is how you prefer to organize information. (See an additional outline in Wise Choices in College: Effective Note Taking, on page 120.)

Concept map. A concept map (depicted on the next page) shows the connections between key elements in a complex idea. Suppose you were going to write an essay about your long-term goal as a student and how you planned to achieve it. You would write the key idea or question in the center of a page and add subideas (or subquestions). This is a great brainstorming and organizing strategy if your preferred way of learning is holistic and right-brained (which you'll explore in Journal Entry 23).

If you find that one of these methods works well for you, look for computer programs designed specifically to help you create outlines and concept maps.

11. Incubate your ideas. Let your ideas grow without your conscious intervention. As you work on other things, your conscious and unconscious minds will transform your ideas into concepts you might never have thought of. Again, have 3″ × 5″ cards or note paper to capture ideas as they come to your awareness.

During Writing

12. Create a thesis that expresses your main idea. This sentence or group of sentences states the main idea you most want your readers to remember. Everything else you write exists to expand and explain your thesis. You may need to write for a while before your thesis emerges. It may even change as you write further. But eventually you need a clearly stated thesis, because an essay without one is like a body without a spine—nothing holds it together. If you're composing on a computer, you will appreciate the ease with which you can revise and move your thesis where it fits best.

13. Write a hook. The first few sentences or paragraphs should hook your readers' attention. You can capture your reader with strategies such as an intriguing story (anecdote), a question, humor, a quotation, or a shocking statement. A good hook grabs your reader because it makes a promise about what you will deliver and the style with which you will write it. You don't have to write the hook first. In fact, the best hook may only become apparent after you've written the first draft of your essay.

14. Use transitions. A transition is a bridge between ideas. Help your reader follow your flow of ideas by using transitional words or phrases. When you offer support, signal with phrases such as *For example, As an illustration,* or *For instance.* When you point out similarities, signal with *Likewise* or *Similarly.* When you point out differences, signal with *By contrast, But, However,* or *On the contrary.* When you summarize or conclude, signal with *In other words, In summary, In conclusion,* or *Finally.* Treat your readers like tourists in a strange land. As their guide, you don't want to confuse or lose them.

15. Answer reader questions. Good writing anticipates and answers questions that an interested reader would ask. Even if you created questions before you began writing, be alert for new questions that emerge as you write. Two questions

CONCEPT MAP

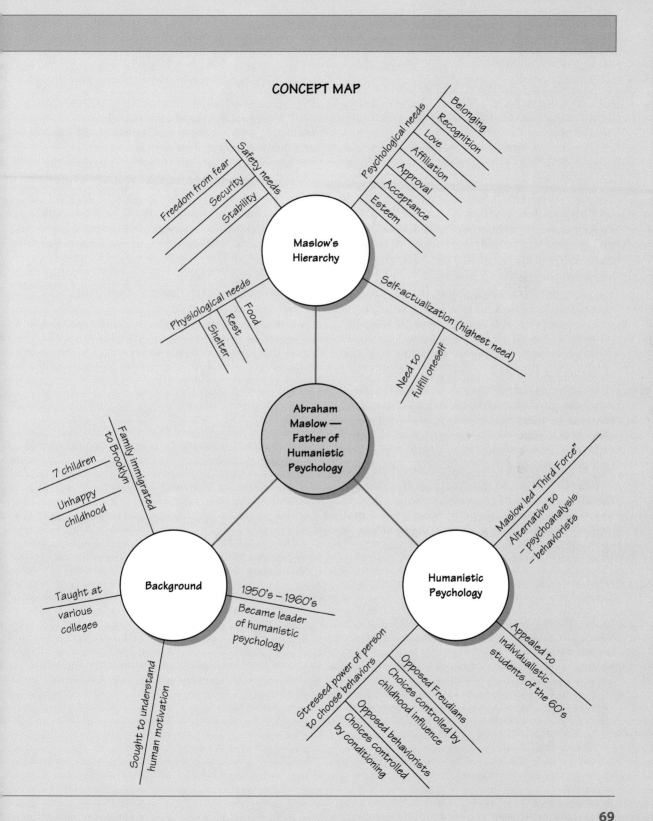

that almost always need answering are *"Why?"* and *"How do you know?"* Other important questions begin with *What? When? Who? Where? How?* and *What if?*

16. Use the 4 E's to generate specific and sufficient support. The 4 E's represent four questions that almost always need answering as you write: Can you give an **EXAMPLE** of that? Can you give an **EXPERIENCE** to illustrate that? Can you **EXPLAIN** that further? Can you give **EVIDENCE** to support that? If you fully answer one or more of the questions represented by the 4 E's, you will begin writing more effectively.

17. Cite sources. If you quote or paraphrase an idea that belongs to someone else, give your source. Not to do so is plagiarism or intellectual theft. In a research paper, add a bibliography of works cited. For an example, see the bibliography at the end of this book (pages 215–217).

18. Write a satisfying conclusion. One easy way to conclude is to summarize the main points you have made. To add a nice touch, end with an echo of something you wrote earlier. For example, suppose your hook was "Do you realize that college graduates earn nearly a million dollars more in their lives than do nongrads?" You might echo this thought in your conclusion: "So, if you want to raise your lifetime earnings by nearly a million dollars, learn the beliefs and behaviors of successful students and earn your college degree."

After Writing

19. Incubate your ideas again. Set your writing aside. When you return to revise your writing, you'll find that you often have a new perspective on what you wrote.

20. Revise your writing. Re-vision means to "see again." When you revise, look for major changes that will improve the quality of your communication: a new thesis statement, better organization, additional support (examples, experiences, explanation, evidence), improved transitions, a catchier beginning, a stronger conclusion.

21. Edit carefully. Writing filled with errors is distracting to readers. At best, they're likely to think less of what you have to say because of the errors. At worst, they may misunderstand your meaning. Here's a trick to improve your proofreading: Begin at the end of your essay and read one sentence at a time backward. By reading from the end to the beginning, you can focus on the details of grammar, spelling, and punctuation rather than the thoughts. If writing on a computer, do a spellcheck. Remember that a computer's spellcheck will not pick up words incorrectly used but correctly spelled (like *there* for *their*).

Writing Exercise

Compare the quality of your writing in journal entries 1–5 with the quality of your writing in journal entries 6–10. Be prepared to explore the following questions:

- Has the quality of your writing improved? If so, how? Please offer examples.

- If your writing has not improved, why do you suppose it hasn't?

- Which of your journal entries do you think is the best written?

- What could you do to improve the writing in your remaining journal entries?

- How did you feel about writing when you began this course?

- Have your feelings about writing changed while keeping your journal? If so, how?

4 Mastering Self-Management

Once I accept responsibility for creating my life and discovering my purpose, the next step is to take purposeful actions that will turn my dreams into reality.

I am taking all of the actions necessary to achieve my goals and dreams.

SUCCESSFUL STUDENTS . . .	STRUGGLING STUDENTS . . .
act on purpose, choosing deeds that move them on course to their goals and dreams.	wait passively or wander from one unpurposeful activity to another.
employ self-management tools, regularly planning and carrying out purposeful actions.	live disorganized, unplanned lives, constantly responding to whims of the moment.
develop self-discipline, showing commitment, focus, and persistence in pursuing their goals and dreams.	quit or change course when their actions don't lead to immediate success.

Acting on Purpose

FOCUS QUESTIONS   Have you ever noticed how much highly successful people accomplish? How do they make such good use of their time?

Creators do more than dream. They consistently take purposeful actions that move them toward their goals and dreams.

Do not confuse a creator with a dreamer. Dreamers only dream, but creators bring their dreams into reality.
    — Robert Fritz

Thomas Edison did more than dream of inventing the light bulb; he performed more than ten thousand experiments before achieving his goal. Martin Luther King did more than dream of justice and equality for people of all races; he spoke and organized and marched and wrote. College graduates did more than dream of their diplomas; they attended classes, read books, wrote essays, conferred with instructors, rewrote essays, formed study groups, did library research, asked questions, went to support labs, sought out tutors, and more!

When we consider the accomplishments of successful people, we may forget that these people weren't born successful. Most achieved their success through the persistent repetition of purposeful actions. Creators apply a powerful strategy for turning dreams into reality: Do important actions first, *before* they become urgent.

Harness the power of Quadrant II

The significance of **importance** and **urgency** in choosing our actions is illustrated in the chart of the Quadrant II Time Management System® on the next page (from Stephen Covey's book *The 7 Habits of Highly Effective People*). This chart shows that our actions fall into one of four quadrants, depending on their importance and urgency. As you read about the four quadrants, ask yourself, "In which quadrant am I choosing to spend most of my time?"

QUADRANT I ACTIONS (Important and Urgent)   are important activities done under the pressure of deadlines. One of my college roommates began his junior paper (the equivalent of two courses) just three days before it was due. His writing was important and *very* urgent. He worked on the paper for seventy-two hours straight, finally turning it in without proofreading. He fell deeper and deeper into this pattern of procrastination, until in our senior year he failed out of college. People who spend their lives in Quadrant I are constantly dashing about putting out brush fires

NOTICE

This evening, the sturdy Levis
I wore every day for over a year
& which seemed to the end in perfect condition,
suddenly tore.
How or why I don't know.
But there it was—a big rip at the crotch.
A month ago my friend Nick
walked off a racquetball court,
showered,
got into his street clothes,
& halfway home collapsed & died.
Take heed you who read this
& drop to your knees now & again
like the poet Christopher Smart
& kiss the earth & be joyful
& make much of your time
& be kindly to everyone,
even to those who do not deserve it.
For although you may not believe it will happen,
you too will one day be gone.
I, whose Levis ripped at the crotch
for no reason,
assure you that such is the case.
Pass it on.

    —*Steve Kowit*

	Urgent	**Not Urgent**
Important	**Quadrant I** *Example:* Staying up all night cramming for an 8:00 A.M. test.	**Quadrant II** *Example:* Creating a study group in the first week of the semester.
Not Important	**Quadrant III** *Example:* Attending a hastily called meeting that has nothing to do with your goals.	**Quadrant IV** *Example:* Mindlessly watching television until 4:00 A.M.

I am personally persuaded that the essence of the best thinking in the area of time management can be captured in a single phrase: organize and execute around priorities.

Stephen Covey

in their lives. They frantically create modest achievements in the present while sacrificing extraordinary success in the future. Worse, Quadrant I is the quadrant in which people experience stress, develop ulcers, and flirt with nervous breakdowns.

QUADRANT II ACTIONS (Important and Not Urgent)   are important activities done *without* the pressure of looming deadlines. When you engage in an important activity with time enough to do it well, you can create your greatest dreams. Lacking urgency, Quadrant II actions are easily postponed. Almost all of the suggestions in this book belong in Quadrant II. For example, you could postpone forever keeping a journal, using the Wise-Choice Process, adopting the language of Creators, discovering and visualizing your dreams, designing a life plan, and creating personal affirmations. However, when you do take purposeful actions such as these, you create a rich, full life. Quadrant II is where you will find Creators.

QUADRANT III ACTIONS (Not Important and Urgent)   are unimportant activities done with a sense of urgency. How often have you responded to the demand of your ringing phone only to be trapped in long, unwanted conversations? Or you agree to do something only because you can't bring yourself to say "no"? Anytime we allow someone else's urgency to talk us into an activity unimportant to our own goals and dreams, we have chosen to be in Quadrant III.

It is not enough to be busy . . . the question is: What are we busy about?

Henry David Thoreau

QUADRANT IV ACTIONS (Not Important and Not Urgent)   are simply time wasters. Everyone wastes some time, so it's not something to judge yourself for, though your Inner Critic will probably try. Instead, listen to your Inner Guide, become more conscious of your choices, and minimize wasting the irreplaceable hours of each day. A college professor I know surveyed his classes and found that many of his students regularly watch more than forty hours of television per week. That's the equivalent of a full-time job without pay or benefits!

What to do in Quadrant II

Creators spend as much time as possible in Quadrant II. In college, Creators schedule conferences with their instructors. They organize study groups. They tape-record summaries of their class notes and listen at every opportunity. They predict questions on upcoming tests and carry the answers on 3″ × 5″ study cards. No external urgency motivates them to take these purposeful actions. They create their own urgency by a strong commitment to their dreams.

While it is true that without a vision the people perish, it is doubly true that without action the people and their vision perish as well.

Johnetta B. Cole, president, Spelman College

By contrast, Victims spend much of their time in Quadrants III and IV, where they repeat unproductive actions like complaining, excusing, blaming, and wasting time. Not surprisingly, they move farther and farther off course.

If you want to know which quadrant you are in at any moment, ask yourself this question: "Will what I'm doing now positively affect my life one year from today?" If the answer is "yes," you are in Quadrant I or II. If the answer is "no," you are probably in Quadrant III or IV.

Creators say "no" to Quadrant III and Quadrant IV activities. Sometimes the choice requires saying "no" to other people: *No, I'm not going to be on your committee this semester. Thank you for asking.* Sometimes this choice requires saying "no" to themselves: *No, I'm not going to sleep late Saturday morning. I'm going to get up early and study for the math test. Then I can go to the movies with my friends without getting off course.*

When we say "no" to Quadrants III and IV, we free up time to say "yes" to Quadrants I and II. Imagine spending just thirty additional minutes each day taking purposeful actions. Think how dramatically that one small choice could change the outcome of your life!

Journal Entry 11

In this activity, you will assess the degree to which you are acting with purpose. As you spend more time in Quadrants I and II, you will notice a dramatic improvement in the results you are creating.

1. **Write a list of fifteen or more specific actions you have taken in the past two days.** (The actions will be *specific* if someone could have videotaped you doing them.)

2. **Using an entire journal page, draw a four-quadrant chart like the example on page 73.**

3. **Write each action from your list in Step 1 in the appropriate quadrant on your chart.** After each action, put the approximate amount of time you spent in the activity. For example, Quadrant IV might be filled with actions such as these:

1. Watched TV (2 hours)
2. Phone call to Terry (1 hour)
3. Watched TV (3 hours)
4. Went to the mall and wandered around (2 hours)
5. Hung out in the cafeteria (2 hours)
6. Played video game (2 hours)

4. **Write about what you have learned concerning your use of time.** Effective writing anticipates questions that a reader may have and answers these questions clearly. To dive deeper in this journal entry, answer questions such as the following:

- What exactly did you discover after analyzing your time?
- In which quadrant do you spend the most time?
- What specific evidence did you use to draw this conclusion?
- If you continue using your time in this way, are you likely to reach your goals and dreams? Why or why not?
- What most often keeps you from taking purposeful actions?
- How do you feel about your discoveries?
- What different choices, if any, do you intend to make about how you use time?

Choose to relax before undertaking this journal activity. Relaxation, by the way, is a Quadrant II activity; it is important but not urgent. You could postpone it forever. But then you'd miss out on its benefits.

Relax, think, write.

Remember to reread the visualization of your dream (Journal Entry 8) often to help you stay motivated. Also, remember to say your affirmation (Journal Entry 10) each day to enhance the personal qualities that will keep you on course to your dreams!

Employing Self-Management Tools

FOCUS QUESTION — How can you devote more time to the people and activities that matter most to you?

Time is the coin of your life. It is the only coin you have, and only you can determine how it will be spent.

Carl Sandburg

At the beginning of class one day, I asked my students to pass in their assignments. A look of panic came over one man's face. "What assignment?" he moaned. "You mean we had an *assignment* due today?"

At lunch, I heard one student ask another: "Did you study for the math test today?" "No," the other replied, "I didn't have time."

Do these situations sound familiar? Do the 168 hours in your week seem to slip away? Do you wonder how some people always seem to be more efficient, effective, and organized than you are? Do you wonder how to better manage your time?

If so, here's some bad news: You *can't* manage time. No matter what we mortals do, time just keeps on ticking. You can't manage minutes, hours, days, or weeks.

But there is also good news: You *can* manage yourself. **The secret of mastering effective self-management is maximizing your time spent in Quadrants I and II.**

In this section you will learn about three tools that can help you take purposeful actions: a monthly calendar, a daily actions list, and a tracking form. Experiment with all three until you discover which one or combination of these tools helps you maximize your time in Quadrants I and II. Variations are included in most planners sold in office or stationery supply stores. Commercial planners often contain *weekly calendars,* but a monthly planner will suffice for most college students.

Monthly calendars

I think that learning about and using time is a very complicated kind of learning. Many adults still have difficulty with it.

Virginia Satir

The first self-management tool, a **monthly calendar** (page 80), provides an overview of upcoming commitments, appointments, and assignments. Use it to record the hours of all classes, work, labs, doctor's appointments, family responsibilities, parties, and other commitments such as job interviews and conferences with your instructors. Also include the due dates of all tests, research papers, final exams, projects, lab reports, and quizzes. A monthly planner is an easy and effective self-management tool to use all by itself.

By scheduling purposeful actions on a calendar, Creators plan to spend most of their time doing what is important to accomplish their goals and dreams. However, scheduling purposeful actions is one thing; actually doing them is quite another. Once you have chosen your priorities, let nothing keep you from them except a rare emergency or special opportunity. Make a habit of saying "no" to unscheduled, low-priority alternatives. Avoid options not written on your calendar.

Daily actions lists

The second self-management tool, a **daily actions list** (page 81), records everything you want to do that day. Complete the list in three steps.

1. Write your life roles and corresponding goals, which you defined in Chapter 3, in the shaded boxes. This first step makes your daily actions list more than just a to-do list and ensures that your actions are directed at one or more of your chosen goals.

2. List Quadrant I (Important and Urgent) actions for each of your goals. For example, if your short-term goal for Math 107 is to earn an A, your list might contain actions like these:

Role: Math 107 student
Goal: Grade A

- Attend classes on time (MWF).
- Read pages 29–41 and do problems 1–10 on page 40.
- Study 2 hours or more for Friday's test on Ch's 1–3.

Each of these three actions is **important,** and each is relatively **urgent.** Notice that each action is written to heed the DAPPS rule, just as your goals are. Each action is Dated, Achievable, Personal, Positive, and Specific. Especially be specific. Vague items such as *Do homework* provide little help when the time comes to take action. Much more helpful are specifics, such as *Read pages 29–41 and do problems 1–10 on page 40.*

3. List Quadrant II (Important and Not Urgent) actions under each of your goals. For example, your list for Math 107 might continue with actions like these:

- *Make appointment with Prof. Finucci and ask her advice on preparing for Friday's test.*
- *Attend appointment with math lab tutor.*
- *Meet with study group and compare answers on practice problems.*

These Quadrant II behaviors are the sorts of activities that struggling students seldom do. You could go through the entire semester without taking any of these purposeful actions because none of them is urgent. But when you consistently choose Quadrant II actions, your decision will make a big difference in the results you create.

Whenever you have free time during the day, instead of slipping unconsciously into Quadrants III or IV, check your daily actions list for purposeful actions. As you complete an action, cross it off your list. As you think of important new actions for each role, add them to your corresponding list. In this way, each daily-actions-list form will usually last a week or more. At that time, copy any remaining actions to a clean form.

Tracking forms

The third self-management tool, a **tracking form** (page 82), is effective for scheduling actions that need to be done repeatedly to reach a short-term goal. The tracking form will help you take one small step after another until you have successfully reached your destination.

Fill out a tracking form for each short-term goal on which you want to focus. For example, suppose your short-term goal is to get an "A" in sociology. One outer action step might be "Read the textbook one or more hours." Additionally, an inner action step that you might plan to repeat often is "Say my affirmation five or more times." Write these two actions in the appropriate left-hand column. Put the dates of the next fourteen days at the top of the check-box columns.

Each day that you take these actions, check the appropriate box. At the end of fourteen days, you will discover how many times you actually completed the actions you planned. One of my students commented, "Before I used the tracking form, I thought I was studying a lot. Now I realize I'm not studying enough." She started studying more, and her grades improved dramatically. A tracking form keeps your Inner Defender from fooling you into thinking you're doing what's necessary to stay on course when, in fact, you're not.

The rewards of effective self-management

You'll rarely meet a successful person who doesn't use some sort of written self-management system. That's because these tools offer so many benefits. You stay conscious of your goals and dreams. You keep your life in balance by working on all of your priorities. You discover how you use and abuse time. You're encouraged to break large projects into smaller, easier-to-manage chunks. You're more likely to keep commitments to yourself and others. You're less likely to be tempted by distractions. And most important, a written self-management system helps you carry out the persistent, purposeful actions necessary to achieve your goals and dreams.

When the seniors in the College Board study were asked what contributed to a successful and satisfying career in college, 73 percent said the "ability to organize tasks and time effectively."
Tim Walter and Al Siebert

Researchers at the University of Georgia found that effective self-management activities affected grades positively. In fact, self-management attitudes and skills predict grades in college better than the Scholastic Aptitude Test (SAT) does.

Some people resist using self-management tools such as calendars, daily actions lists, tracking forms, or any printed forms for planning and carrying out purposeful actions. A few people can even be quite vocal about their dislike for such tools: "These things are for the anally retentive," one student objected. "Everything I need to do, I keep right here in my head." There is no right or wrong self-management system. What matters is whether or not you're getting the outcomes and experiences that you desire. If you are, keep doing what you've been doing. If not, consider that your life goals may be too grand and complex to keep all of the necessary steps listed and organized in your head. You may be spending too much time in Quadrants III and IV doing what isn't important to your goals and dreams. When this is the case, experiment with something new—like a written self-management system.

Consistently using a written self-management system is a habit that takes time to establish. You may begin with great energy, then find that a week has gone by without using your planner. Without self-judgment, simply examine where you went astray and begin your planning anew. Experiment until you find the system that works best for your personal style. In time, your skills in using a written self-management system will improve.

Journal Entry 12

I n this activity, you will experiment with three tools of a written self-management system. Keep in mind that you can adapt these self-management tools to suit your own style.

1. **Place a copy of each of the three self-management tools in your journal.** Tape photocopies of the monthly calendar, the daily actions list, and the tracking form onto three separate pages in your journal. Draw them if you prefer.

2. **Fill out each of the three tools.**

3. **Write your personal evaluation of each of the three tools.** As you write, once again keep in mind that good communication answers questions that an interested reader would ask about your topic. Develop your journal paragraphs by asking and answering questions such as the following:

   • What are the strengths and weaknesses of each tool?

   • Which tool is most appealing to you and why?

   • Which is least appealing to you and why?

   • What self-management system do you honestly intend to use?

   • If you presently use a self-management system, you can describe it and discuss changes, if any, that you intend to make in it.

Relax, think, write.

I used to wonder how other students got so much done. Now that I'm using a planner, I wonder how I settled for doing so little.

John Simmons, student

Monthly Calendar

Monday	Tuesday	Wednesday	Thursday	Friday	Saturday	Sunday

Month _____

Daily Actions List

Role:
Goal:

Role:
Goal:

Role:
Goal:

Role:
Goal:

Role:
Goal:

Telephone calls

Miscellaneous actions

Role:
Goal:

Tracking Form

Role:

Dream:

Long-term goal:

Short-term goals (to be accomplished this semester):

    1.

    2.

    3.

    4.

OUTER Action Steps

    Dates:

INNER Action Steps

    Dates:

CALVIN AND HOBBES ©1992 Watterson. Reprinted with permission of UNIVERSAL PRESS SYNDICATE. All rights reserved.

Developing Self-Discipline

> **FOCUS QUESTIONS** Do you find yourself procrastinating, even on projects that mean a great deal to you? How can you keep taking purposeful actions even when you don't feel like it?

Every semester I watch perfectly capable students abandon their goals and dreams. Somewhere along the path, they get distracted and stop or wander off in another direction.

"Hey," I want to shout, "the goals and dreams you say you want are over here! Keep coming this way. You can do it!"

Maybe they believe college is a sprint, over in a flash. Like most grand victories, college is a marathon. Graduates may cross the finish line in a flash, but thousands of small steps got them there.

Self-discipline is self-caring.
Dr. M. Scott Peck

In a word, success takes self-discipline—the willingness to do whatever has to be done, whether you feel like it or not, until you reach your goals and dreams. Every January, America's athletic clubs are wall-to-wall with people who made New Year's resolutions to get in shape. A month later, the crowds are gone, reminded that getting and staying in shape takes commitment, focus, and persistence.

So it goes with every important goal we set. Our actions reveal whether we have the self-discipline to stay on course in the face of tempting alternatives. Most students want to be successful, but *wanting* and *doing* are worlds apart. Going out with friends is easier than going to class . . . day after day. Talking on the phone is easier than reading a challenging textbook . . . hour after hour. Watching television is easier than doing research at the library . . . night after night.

Many people choose instant gratification. Few choose the far-off rewards of persistent and purposeful actions. Many begin the journey to their dreams; few finish. Yet all we need to do is put one foot in front of the other . . . again and again and again. A journey of a thousand miles may begin with a single step, but many more better follow.

Self-discipline has three essential ingredients: **commitment, focus,** and **persistence.** You explored how to strengthen your commitment in Journal Entry 8. Now, take a look at focus and persistence.

Staying focused

Distractions constantly tug at our minds, and, like a child, the unfocused mind dashes from one distraction to another. To be successful, we must be able to focus our attention.

A baseball game, like life, presents many distractions: the crowd, teammates, opposing players, nagging injuries, even one's own wandering thoughts. But one player developed a strategy to focus his attention. In the dugout, he would hold his baseball cap in front of his face to block out all distractions; then, peeking through one of the cap's air holes, he would focus solely on the pitcher. In this ingenious way, he concentrated on what he had to do later to get a hit. That's one of the skills that helped Baseball Hall-of-Famer Henry Aaron hit more home runs than any other baseball player in history. Like Aaron, you'll hit more home runs in life when you focus.

Everyone has experienced losing focus for a minute, an hour, even a day. But struggling students often lose focus for days and weeks at a time. They start arriving late, skipping classes, doing sloppy work, ignoring assignments. They forget why they're in college.

For many students, the time to beware losing focus is about halfway into the semester. That's when your Inner Defender starts giving you all of those great excuses to quit: *I've got boring teachers, my schedule stinks, I'm still getting over the flu, next semester I could start all over.* And your Inner Critic chimes in with practiced self-criticism: *I never could do math, I'm not as smart as my classmates, I'm too old, I'm too young, I'm not really college material.*

Your Inner Guide can help you regain focus by addressing one question: "What are my goals and dreams?" As a reminder, reread the visualization of your dream (Journal Entry 8) and your life plan (Journal Entry 9). If your goals and dreams don't motivate you to keep taking purposeful actions, then perhaps you need to rethink where you want to go in life.

Being persistent

If focus is self-discipline in thought, then persistence is self-discipline in action. Here's the question your Inner Guide can ask when you slow down or quit: "Do I love myself enough to keep going?" You are the one who'll ben-

To be disciplined or nondisciplined is a choice you make every minute and every hour of your life. Discipline is nothing more than the process of focusing on any chosen activity without interruption until that activity is complete.

Charles J. Givens

You always have to focus in life on what you want to achieve.

Michael Jordan

efit most from the accomplishment of your goals and dreams . . . and you're the one who will pay the price of disappointment if you fail.

When Luanne enrolled in my English 101 class, she had taken the course six times before. She needed to master standard English to pass the course, and that effort would sorely test her self-discipline.

Early in the semester, we had a conference, and I asked Luanne about her dreams. As she told me her dream to work in television, her eyes sparkled. I asked if mastering standard grammar would be a steppingstone to her success. She hesitated. She knew that agreeing would commit her to many hours of study.

Finally she said, "Yes."

"Great! So, what's one action that, if repeated daily for a month or more, would improve your grammar?" She needed to discover a Quadrant II activity and make it a new habit.

"Probably studying my grammar book."

I handed her a thirty-two-day commitment form (see page 88). "Okay, then, I'm inviting you to make a commitment to study your grammar book for thirty-two days in a row. You can put a check on this form each day that you keep your promise to yourself. This is how you can develop self-discipline. Will you do it?"

"I'll try."

"C'mon, Luanne. You've been *trying* for six semesters. My question is, 'Will you commit to studying grammar for thirty minutes every day for the next thirty-two days?'"

She paused again. Her choice at this moment would surely affect her success in college, and probably the outcome of her life.

"Okay," she said, "I'll do it."

And she did. Each time I passed the writing lab, I saw Luanne working on grammar. The tutors joked they were going to start charging her rent.

But that's not all Luanne did. She attended every English class. She completed every writing assignment. She met with me to discuss her essays. She created flash cards, writing problem sentences on one side and corrections on the other. In short, Luanne was taking the actions of an exceptional student. Luanne was finally demonstrating the persistence of self-discipline.

As mentioned earlier, English 101 students at our college must pass one of two exit exam essays that are graded by other instructors. The first exam this semester brought some good news: Luanne had gotten her highest scores ever. But there was the usual bad news as well: Both exam readers said her grammar errors kept them from passing her.

Luanne was at another important choice point. Did she have the self-discipline to persist in the face of discouraging news? Would she quit or continue?

"Okay," she said finally, "show me how to correct my errors." We reviewed her essay, sentence by sentence. The next day she went to the writing lab earlier; she left later. She rewrote the exam essay for practice, and we went over

Perhaps the most valuable result of all education is the ability to make yourself do the thing you have to do, when it ought to be done, whether you like it or not; it is the first lesson that ought to be learned; and however early a man's training begins, it is probably the last lesson that he learns thoroughly.

Thomas Henry Huxley

The major difference I've found between the highly successful and the least successful is that the highly successful stick to it. They have staying power. Everybody fails. Everybody takes his knocks, but the highly successful keep coming back.

Sherry Lansing, chairman, Paramount Pictures

it again. Applying self-discipline, Luanne's mastery of standard grammar continued to improve.

That semester, the second exam was given on the Friday before Christmas. In order to finalize grades, all of the English 101 instructors met that evening to grade the essays. I promised to call Luanne with her results.

The room was quiet except for rustling papers as two dozen English instructors read one essay after another. At about ten o'clock that night, I received my students' graded essays. I looked quickly through the pile and found Luanne's. She had passed! As I dialed the phone to call her, Luanne's previous instructors told others about her success.

"Merry Christmas, Luanne," I said into the phone, "you passed!"

I heard her delight, and at that moment, two dozen instructors in the room began to applaud.

Journal Entry 13

In this activity, you will apply self-discipline by planning and carrying out a thirty-two-day commitment. Behavioral psychologists suggest that breaking an old habit or starting a new one requires about thirty-two days.

1. **From your life plan in Journal Entry 9, copy one of your most important and challenging short-term goals from your role as a *student*.**

2. **Write and complete the following sentence stem five or more times: I WOULD MOVE STEADILY TOWARD THIS GOAL IF EVERY DAY I . . .**

   Write actions that *others can see you do* and that you can do every day of the week, including weekends. So you wouldn't write, "be motivated" or "attend class." Others cannot see your motivation, and you can't attend class every day for thirty-two days straight. Instead, if your short-term goal is to earn an "A" in English, you might complete the sentence with specific actions such as these:

   1. **I WOULD MOVE STEADILY TOWARD THIS GOAL IF EVERY DAY** *I spent at least fifteen minutes doing exercises in my grammar book.*

   2. **I WOULD MOVE STEADILY TOWARD THIS GOAL IF EVERY DAY** *I wrote at least two hundred words in my journal.*

   3. **I WOULD MOVE STEADILY TOWARD THIS GOAL IF EVERY DAY** *I revised one of my previous essays, correcting the grammar errors that my teacher marked.*

   Chances are, all of these actions will fall in Quadrant II.

A dream doesn't become reality through magic; it takes sweat, determination, and hard work.
        General Colin Powell

Becoming a world-class figure skater meant long hours of practice while sometimes tolerating painful injuries. It meant being totally exhausted sometimes, and not being able to do all the things I wanted to do when I wanted to do them.

Debi Thomas

3. **On a separate page in your journal, create a thirty-two-day commitment form or attach a photocopy of the one on page 88. Complete the sentence at the top of the form ("Because I know . . .") with ONE action from your list in Step 2.** For the next thirty-two days, put a check beside each day that you keep your commitment.

4. **Write your thoughts and feelings as you begin your thirty-two-day commitment.** Develop your journal paragraphs by asking and answering readers' questions, such as, What is your goal? What were some possible actions you considered? What action did you choose? How will this action, when performed consistently, help you reach your goal? What challenges might you experience in keeping your commitment? How will you overcome these challenges? How do you feel about undertaking this commitment? What other questions might someone possibly ask you about your thirty-two-day commitment?

IMPORTANT: If you miss a day on your thirty-two-day commitment, don't judge yourself or offer excuses. Simply ask your Inner Guide what got you off course, renew your commitment to yourself, and start over at Day 1.

Relax, think, write.

The Procrastinators

Two students from Professor Hallengren's English composition class sat in the cafeteria discussing the approaching deadline for their fourth essay.

"There's no way I can get this essay done on time," **Tracy** said. "I've turned in every essay late, and I still owe him a rewrite on the second one. Professor Hallengren is going to be furious!"

"You think you're in trouble!" **Ricardo** said. "I haven't even turned in the last essay. Now I'm going to be two essays behind."

"How come?" Tracy asked. "I would have thought a young guy right out of high school would have all the time in the world."

"Don't ask me where my time goes," Ricardo answered, shrugging. "Deadlines keep sneaking up on me, and before I know it, I'm weeks behind. I live on campus, and I don't even have to commute. But something always comes up. Last weekend I was going to write that other essay and study for my sociology test, but I had to go to a wedding out of state on Saturday. I was having such a good time, I didn't drive back until Monday morning. Now I'm even further behind."

32-Day Commitment

Because I know that this commitment will keep me on course to my goals, I promise myself that every day for the next 32 days I will take the following action: _____

_____

_____

Day 1		Day 17	
Day 2		Day 18	
Day 3		Day 19	
Day 4		Day 20	
Day 5		Day 21	
Day 6		Day 22	
Day 7		Day 23	
Day 8		Day 24	
Day 9		Day 25	
Day 10		Day 26	
Day 11		Day 27	
Day 12		Day 28	
Day 13		Day 29	
Day 14		Day 30	
Day 15		Day 31	
Day 16		Day 32	

"So that's why you missed English class on Monday," Tracy said. "Professor Hallengren lectured us because so many students were absent."

"I know I miss too many classes. One time I stayed home because I didn't have my essay ready. And sometimes I stay up late talking to my girlfriend on the phone or watching television. Then I can't get up in the morning."

"My situation is different," Tracy said. "I'm in my thirties and I'm a single mother. I have kids ages five, seven, and eight. I work twenty hours a week, and I'm taking four courses. I just can't keep up with it all! Every time I think I'm about to catch up, something goes wrong. Last week one of my kids got sick. Then my refrigerator broke, and I had to work overtime to get it fixed. Two weeks ago they changed my schedule at work, and I had to find new day care. If anything can go wrong, it happens to me. Every professor acts like his class is all I have to do. I wish! The only way I could do everything is give up sleeping, and I'm only getting about five hours a night as it is."

"What are you going to do?" Ricardo asked.

"I don't think I can make it this semester. I'm considering dropping all of my classes."

"Maybe I should drop out, too."

1. **Who do you think has the more challenging self-management problem, Ricardo or Tracy? Be prepared to explain your choice.**

2. **If this person asked for your advice on how to do better in college, what specific self-management strategies would you recommend that he or she adopt?**

DIVING DEEPER: **Which person, Ricardo or Tracy, is most like you in the way you manage your life? Explain the similarity.**

Self-Management at Work

Success in business requires training and discipline and hard work. But if you're not frightened by these things, the opportunities are just as great today as they ever were.

David Rockerfeller, Former Chairman, The Chase Manhattan Bank

As in college, success in the workplace means converting your goals into a step-by-step plan and having the self-discipline to spend the majority of your time doing what is important, preferably before it becomes urgent. Here in the realm of action, doers separate themselves from dreamers. Folks in business often refer to this aspect of success as "doing diligence."

In college, "doing diligence" is wise because the effort usually nets you good grades, and a high GPA impresses potential employers with both your intelligence and your work ethic. But getting good grades isn't all you can do in college to stand out in a job interview. Here are some other Quadrant II actions that will look great on your résumé: gain experience in your career field through part-time jobs, volunteer work, internships, or cooperative-education experiences; demonstrate leadership qualities through your involvement with the student government; create a portfolio of your best college work; or join clubs or activities that relate to your future career. Wise choices like these offer employers something that distinguishes you from all the other applicants for the job.

When it comes time to search for a position in your field, your effective self-management skills will once more serve you well. Consider using the Tracking Form to direct your outer and inner action steps towards your employment goal. The Daily Actions List is a great tool for keeping track of essential one-time actions like returning calls or sending thank-you notes after an interview. Monthly Planners help you avoid the embarrassment of arriving late or having to cancel a job interview because of a scheduling conflict. All of these tools will allow you to monitor your use of time, assuring that you spend the bulk of your time productively in Quadrants I and II.

As you begin your career search, consider doing the following outer action steps. Develop a list of careers that interest you. Make a list of potential employers in each career. Attend a résumé-writing workshop. Write a résumé and cover letter to showcase the talents and experiences you offer an employer. Personalize each cover letter to fit the job you're applying for. Develop your telephone skills. Participate in mock interviews where others ask you likely questions. Your college career center or a career development course can help you take these job-search actions effectively.

Searching for employment can get discouraging, and you would be wise to take some inner actions to maintain a positive attitude. You could create an affirmation as a mental pick-me-up. For example, "I am enthusiastically taking all of the actions necessary to find the ideal position to start my career." Or "I optimistically send out ten job inquiries each week." If you find an important action difficult to do (like calling employers to see if they have unadvertised openings), you could visualize yourself doing it and having the experience go extraordinarily well.

Once you move into your career, your self-management skills will become essential for accomplishing all you have to do. Notice how many people at your workplace carry planners, either paper or electronic. If you don't already have a planner that works for you, experiment to see if one will help you to manage the avalanche of tasks that will come your way in a new position.

At the beginning of your career, tasks will likely take you twice as long to do as they will after a few years of practice. So not only do you need to manage your Daily Actions List, you'll also need to make some sacrifices to get them all done. People with a "job" mentality sometimes stop short of getting all of their work done because work inevitably leaks into their personal time. They work until their "shift" is over. On the other hand, people with a "career" mentality know that sometimes they'll need to stay late or take work home. They have the discipline to work until the task is done. Of course, these folks have to find a balance that allows them to have a personal life as well. The important thing to know is that the workload is always heavy at the beginning of a career, and this is the time when you establish your reputation as someone who can be counted on to get the job done.

Believing in Yourself: **Develop Self-Confidence**

FOCUS QUESTIONS   In which life roles do you feel most confident? In which do you experience self-doubt? What can you do to increase your overall self-confidence?

O n the first day of one semester, a woman intercepted me at the class-room door.

"Can I ask you something?" she said. "How do I know if I'm cut out for college?"

"What's your opinion?" I asked.

"I think I'll do okay."

"Great," I said.

She stood there, still looking doubtful. "But . . . my high school counselor said. . . ." She paused.

"Let me guess. Your counselor said you wouldn't do well in college? Is that it?"

She nodded. "I think he was wrong. But how do I know for sure?"

Indeed! How *do* we know? There will always be others who don't believe in us. What matters, however, is that we have confidence in ourselves. Self-confidence is the core belief that *I CAN*, the unwavering trust that I can successfully do whatever is necessary to achieve my goals and dreams.

Ultimately, it matters little whether someone else thinks you can do something. It matters greatly whether *you* believe you can. Luck aside, you'll probably accomplish just about what you believe you can. In this section we'll explore three effective ways to develop greater self-confidence.

If people don't feel good about themselves and believe that they'll win a championship, they never will.
Tara VanDerveer, head coach of the 1990 NCAA Championship Stanford women's basketball team

Create a success identity

Are you confident that you can tie your shoes? Of course. And yet there was a time when you weren't. So how did you move from doubt to confidence? Wasn't it by practicing over and over? You built your self-confidence by stacking one small victory upon another. As a result, today you have confidence that you can tie your shoes every time you try. By the same method, you can build a success identity in virtually any endeavor.

Success brings its own self-confidence.
Lillian Vernon Katz

The life of Nathan McCall illustrates the creation of a success identity under difficult circumstances. McCall grew up in a Portsmouth, Virginia, ghetto where his involvement with crimes and violence led to imprisonment. After his release, McCall attended college and studied journalism. As you might imagine, one of his greatest challenges was self-doubt. But he persevered, taking each challenge as it came—one more test passed, one more course completed. After graduation, he got a job with a newspaper, and over the years he steadily rose to the position of bureau chief. Recalling his accumulated successes, McCall wrote in his journal, "These experiences solidify my belief that I can do anything I set my mind to do. The possibilities are boundless." Boundless indeed! McCall went from street-gang member and prison inmate to successful and respected reporter for the *Washington Post,* and his book, *Makes Me Wanna Holler,* climbed to the *New York Times* bestseller's list.

Genuine self-confidence results from a history of success, and a history of success results from persistently taking purposeful actions. That's why a thirty-two-day commitment (Journal Entry 13) is not only an effective self-management tool but also a great way to start building a success identity. After we experience success in one area of our life, self-confidence begins to seep into every corner of our being, and we begin to believe *I CAN.*

Research studies show that people who have high self-esteem regularly reward themselves in tangible and intangible ways. . . . By documenting and celebrating their successes, they insure that these successes will reoccur.

Marsha Sinetar

Celebrate your successes and talents

A friend showed me a school assignment that his eight-year-old daughter had brought home. At the top of the page was written: *Nice job, Lauren. Your spelling is very good. I am proud of you.* What made the comments remarkable is this: The teacher had merely put a check on the page; Lauren had added the compliment herself.

At the age of eight, Lauren has much to teach us about building self-confidence. It's great when someone else tells us how wonderful our successes and talents are. But it's even more important that we tell ourselves.

One way to acknowledge success is to keep a record of daily victories. Another way is to create a success wall: Every day write a success on a 3″ × 5″ card and post it on a wall where you'll see it often. Soon your wall will be covered with reminders of your accomplishments: *Got an 86 on history test . . . Attended every class on time this week . . . Exercised for 2 hours at gym.* In addition to acknowledging your successes, you can celebrate them by rewarding yourself with something special—a favorite dinner, a movie, a night out with friends.

Peak performers develop powerful mental images of the behavior that will lead to the desired results. They see in their mind's eye the result they want, and the actions leading to it.

Charles Garfield

Visualize purposeful actions

We can also strengthen our self-confidence by visualizing purposeful actions done well, especially actions outside our comfort zone. Psychologist Charles Garfield once performed an experiment to determine the impact of visualizations on a group of people who were afraid of public speaking. These nervous speakers were divided into three subgroups:

Group 1 read and studied how to give public speeches, but they delivered no actual speeches.

Group 2 read about speechmaking and also gave two talks each week to small audiences of classmates and friends.

Group 3 read about effective speaking and gave one talk each week to small groups. This group also watched videotapes of effective speakers and, twice a day, *mentally rehearsed* giving effective speeches of their own.

Experts on public speaking, unaware of the experiment, evaluated the effectiveness of these speakers both before and after their preparation. Group 1 did not improve at all. Group 2 improved significantly. Group 3, the group that had visualized themselves giving excellent speeches, improved the most.

Mentally rehearsing purposeful actions will not only help you improve your ability to do the action but will also reduce associated fears. Suppose you're feeling anxious about an upcoming test. Your Inner Critic is probably visualizing a disaster: *As soon as I walk into the exam room, my pulse starts racing, I start sweating, I start feeling weak, and my mind goes totally blank. I fail!*

If we picture ourselves functioning in specific situations, it is nearly the same as the actual performance. Mental practice helps one to perform better in real life.

Dr. Maxwell Maltz

What if you visualized a more positive future? You could imagine yourself taking the test confidently, creating an ideal outcome. Your revised mental movie might look like this: *I walk into the exam fully prepared. I've attended all of my classes on time, done my very best work on all my assignments, and studied effectively. Feeling confident, I find a comfortable seat and take a few moments to breathe deeply, relax, and focus myself. I concentrate on the subject matter of this test. I release all my other cares and worries, feeling excited about the opportunity to show how much I have learned. The instructor walks into the room and begins handing out the exams. I know that any question the instructor asks will be easy for me to answer. I glance at the test and see questions that my study group and I have prepared for all semester. Alert and aware, I begin to write. Every answer I write flows easily from the storehouse of knowledge I have in my mind. I work steadily and efficiently, and, after finishing, I check my answers thoroughly. I hand in the exam with a comfortable amount of time remaining, and as I leave the room, I feel a pleasant weariness. I am confident that I have done my very best.*

You choose the movies that play in your mind, so why not choose to star in a movie in which you successfully complete purposeful actions?

Creators know there are many choices that will strengthen self-confidence. When we consciously choose options like keeping a thirty-two-day commitment, celebrating our successes and talents, and visualizing the successful completion of purposeful actions, we will soon be able to say with supreme confidence: *I CAN.*

Journal Entry 14

In this activity, you will practice ways to increase your self-confidence. People with strong self-confidence take the steps necessary to achieve their goals and dreams despite their fears.

1. **List the successes you have created in your life.** The more successes you list, the more you will strengthen your self-confidence. Include small victories as well as big ones.

I wanted to be the best dentist that ever lived. People said, "But she's a woman; she's colored," and I said, "Ha! Just you wait and see."

Bessie Delany,
Dentist and Author

2. **List your personal skills and talents.** Again, the longer your list, the more you will strengthen your self-confidence. What are you good at doing? Don't overlook talents that you use daily. No talent is too insignificant to acknowledge.

3. **List positive risks that you have taken in your life.** When did you stretch your comfort zone and do something despite your fear?

4. **List important actions that you presently have some resistance about doing.** What purposeful actions cause anxious rumblings in the pit of your stomach? Maybe you fear asking a question in your biology lecture or you're nervous about going to a scheduled job interview.

5. **Write a visualization of yourself successfully doing one of the actions you listed in Step 4.** Remember to use the four keys to effective visualizing discussed in Journal Entry 8:

   1. **Relax.**
   2. **Use present tense verbs.**
   3. **Be specific** and use many senses.
   4. **Feel the feelings.**

As a model for your writing, reread the positive visualization on page 93.

Relax, think, write.

Reading well is one of the most critical skills for succeeding in college and in life. A time-honored system for effective reading is called the SQ3R Method: Survey, Question, Read, Recite, and Review. In this section you'll learn these techniques and more. Experiment with new reading strategies, and soon you will find that you are reading faster and with greater understanding.

Before Reading

1. Create a positive affirmation about reading. Do you have negative beliefs about your ability to understand and/or enjoy what you read? Create an affirming statement about reading, such as *"I enjoy reading books and articles of all kinds."* Along with your personal affirmation, repeat this reading affirmation in order to reprogram any negative beliefs about reading.

2. Create a reading plan. Make a plan to read often for short periods of time rather than in one marathon reading session. This approach keeps you current with your assignments and helps you remember more of what you read.

3. Do a survey of your reading assignment. Like observing a valley from a high mountain, a quick survey of your reading assignment gives you the big picture of what to expect. Thumb through the book, taking in chapter titles, chapter objectives, focus questions, text headings, charts, graphs, illustrations, previews, and summaries. Especially note any unusual type (capitals, bold, italics, and so on.) In a few minutes, you will have an overview of what you are about to read.

4. Turn text headings into questions. For example, suppose a computer book has a heading within the text that reads: **HTML Tags.** Turn this heading into one or more questions: *What is an HTML Tag? How are HTML Tags created?* (See additional examples in Wise Choices in College: Effective Studying in Chapter 7.) If you write your ques-

tions on notebook paper, leave room to insert answers. If you create your questions on 3" × 5" cards, write your answers on the backs.

During Reading

5. Read for the answers to your questions. Record the answers, the source, and the page number. These questions and answers make good study materials. If you write the questions and answers on 3" × 5" cards, you can conveniently carry them with you to study during otherwise wasted time (like waiting for a class to begin).

6. Write questions in the margins. As you come across answers to your questions, write the questions in the margin. Later, while studying, you can ask yourself the questions in the margins and compare your answers to those found in the text.

7. Read in chunks. Poor readers read one word at a time, sometimes moving their lips while reading. Good readers don't read words; they read ideas, and ideas are found in chunks of words. For example, try reading all of the words between the diamonds at once:

> ♦ *If you read* ♦ *the chunks* ♦ *you will increase* ♦ *your speed* ♦ *and your comprehension* ♦

Like any new habit, this method will initially feel awkward. As you practice, you'll find you can scan bigger and bigger chunks of information at increasingly faster rates of speed, like this:

> ♦ *If you read the chunks* ♦ *you will increase your speed* ♦ *and your comprehension* ♦

8. Concentrate on reading faster. In one experiment, students increased their reading speed by 25 to 50 percent simply by concentrating on reading faster while still understanding what they were reading. You, too, can probably read faster by consciously deciding to increase your speed.

9. Read for main ideas and supporting details. An essay or a chapter in a book usually has one main idea called the *thesis statement,* which typically appears in the first or last paragraph. The rest of the reading expands and supports the thesis. An individual paragraph usually has one main idea called the *topic sentence,*which is typically found in the first or last sentence of the paragraph. For each main idea, authors will usually offer support consisting of examples, experiences, explanations, and/or evidence.

10. Mark main ideas and supporting details. Create your own system for marking what you want to remember. Some readers use double underlining to indicate a thesis statement and single underlining to indicate a topic sentence. Others like to highlight main ideas with one color and supporting ideas with another. Read a whole paragraph before marking; it's easier to see what's important that way. Mark only 10 to 15 percent of your text, selecting only what is truly important.

11. Take notes. Paraphrase main ideas and supporting details in your notebook. Expressing the author's ideas in your own words anchors important ideas in your memory and allows you to add your own thoughts and questions.

12. Try to predict what's next. As you read, guess what the author will say in the next paragraph, page, or chapter. Making predictions keeps your mind alert.

13. Pause to recite. At the end of a section, stop for a moment to recall what you have just been reading. Write or say aloud what you think are the main ideas and the most convincing support. State the answers to any questions you created earlier. This minireview will help you clarify and remember the important ideas.

14. Reread difficult passages or chapters. Some subjects are difficult to understand, and some authors don't always write clearly. Reread challenging sections until the main ideas become clear.

Trust yourself that, with enough effort, you will comprehend.

15. Look up the definition of key words. Use a dictionary when you don't know the meaning of a key word. Consider starting a vocabulary list in your journal. Or create a deck of $3'' \times 5''$ flash cards with new words on one side and definitions on the other. Use your new words in conversations to lock them in your memory. Developing a large and eloquent vocabulary is a great success strategy.

16. Read critically. Not all ideas in print are true. Learn to read critically by analyzing the validity of the text. Look for red flags that may suggest a credibility problem. Who is the author? What are his or her credentials? Is the support sufficient, or is the article mostly opinions and generalizations? Are the author's opinions supported by logic or by emotion? Are sources of information identified? Are they believable? Current? Does the author stand to gain (e.g., money, status, revenge) by your acceptance of his or her opinion? Are various sides of an issue presented or only one?

After Reading

17. Review what you read. Ask yourself the following:

- What was the main idea?
- Why does the author think so? What are the reasons?
- How does the author know? What is the supporting evidence?
- What do you personally think of the author's main idea and support?
- What emotion (if any) does the reading stir in you?

18. **Answer end-of-chapter questions.** If the text provides review questions, see how well you can answer them. If one stumps you, skim the chapter for the answer.

19. **Reread the marked text.** A great way to review is to reread the text you have underlined or highlighted.

20. **Read another book on the same subject.** Sometimes another author will express the same idea in a way that makes more sense to you. Ask your instructor or a librarian to suggest supplemental reading.

21. **Discuss or teach what you have read.** Conversing about a reading assignment strengthens memory pathways that will help you remember key points. A powerful alternative is teaching the information to a friend or family member.

22. **Seek assistance.** If you continue to have difficulties understanding what you read, ask your instructor to explain the key points in the reading. For additional help, most colleges provide a reading center, a tutoring program, or both. If you continue to have problems understanding your reading assignments, see if your college has a diagnostician who can test you for a possible reading disability. Reading specialists may be able to help you improve your comprehension skills.

Reading Exercise

Experiment with one or more of these reading strategies and be prepared to discuss your results with classmates.

5 Employing Interdependence

Once I accept responsibility for taking purposeful actions to achieve my chosen goals and dreams, I then develop mutually supportive relationships that make the journey easier and more enjoyable.

I am developing mutually supportive relationships, helping both others and myself reach our goals and dreams.

SUCCESSFUL STUDENTS . . .	STRUGGLING STUDENTS . . .
develop mutually supportive relationships, recognizing that life is richer when giving to and receiving from others.	remain dependent, co-dependent, or independent in relation to others.
create a support network, using an interactive team approach to success.	work alone, seldom cooperating with others for the common good of all.
strengthen relationships with active listening, showing their concern for the other person's thoughts and feelings.	listen poorly, demonstrating little desire to understand another person's perspective.

Developing Mutually Supportive Relationships

FOCUS QUESTION   How could you make accomplishing your success a little easier and much more fun?

One semester, in the eleventh week, Martha made an announcement. "This is the last time I'll be in class. I'm withdrawing from college. I just wanted to say how much I'll miss you all."

A concerned silence followed Martha's announcement. Her quiet, solid presence had made her a favorite with classmates.

"My babysitter just moved," Martha explained, "and I've been trying to find someone I trust to look after my one-year-old . . . with no luck. My husband took his vacation this week to take care of her, but he has to go back to work. I have to drop out of school to be with my baby. Don't worry," she added weakly, "I'll be back next semester. Really, I will."

"But there are only a few more weeks in the semester. You can't drop out now!" someone said. Martha merely shrugged her shoulders, clearly defeated.

Then one of the other women in the class said, "My kids are grown and out of the house, and this is the only class I'm taking this semester. I'd be willing to watch your child for the next few weeks if that would help you get through the semester. The only thing is, you'll need to bring your baby to my house because I don't have a car."

"I don't have a car either," Martha said. "Thanks anyway."

"Wait a minute," a young man in the class said. "Not so fast. Aren't we learning that we're all in this together? I have a car. I'll drive you and your child back and forth until the semester's over."

Martha sat for a moment, stunned. "Really? You'd do that for me?" In three minutes Martha's fate had changed from dropping out of school to finishing her courses with the help of two classmates.

All of us decide whether we'll go for our dreams alone or if we'll seek and accept assistance from others along the way. In Western culture we often glorify the solitary hero, the strong individual who stands alone against all odds. This script makes good cinema, but does it help us stay on course to our dreams?

After all, who of us actually goes unaided by others? We eat food grown *by others*. We wear clothes sewn *by others*. We live in houses built *by others*. We work at businesses owned *by others*. And so it goes.

No man is an island, entire of itself; every man is a piece of the continent, a part of the main.

John Donne

Nobody but nobody can make it out here alone.

Maya Angelou

Even the Lone Ranger had help

Loners are fooled by the illusion of independence. Actually our lives are intertwined with the lives of many other people. Creators both give and ask for assistance. They know that life can be easier and more enjoyable when people cooperate.

When it comes to relating to others, there are four kinds of people:

Dependent people believe: *I can't achieve my goals by myself. I need other people to do most of the work for me.*

Co-dependent people believe: *I'll pursue my goals as soon as I've helped others get their goals.*

Independent people believe: *By working hard, I can get some of what I want all by myself. I'll just do without the rest.*

Interdependent people believe: *I know I can get some of what I want by working alone, but I'll accomplish more and have more fun if I give and receive help.*

Which belief do you hold? Which belief will best help you stay on course to your dreams?

We are all interdependent. Do things for others—tribe, family, community—rather than just for yourself.

Chief Wilma Mankiller

A sign of maturity

Moving from dependence to independence is a major step toward maturity. But moving from independence to *inter*dependence demonstrates the greatest maturity of all.

Interdependent students maximize their results in college by seeking assistance from instructors, study partners, librarians, academic advisors, counselors, community services, and family members. Interdependent students know that it's a lot easier getting to graduation with a supportive team than by themselves.

Interdependence will help you stay on course in college and support your success in ways you can't even imagine now. A friend of mine who buys old houses, remodels them, and resells them for a tidy profit ran into difficult times. His completed houses weren't selling, he was short of money to begin new projects, and bankers were unwilling to lend him additional money. Creditors began to harass him, and for a few weeks he considered declaring bankruptcy. Then he created an ingenious plan to raise capital: He asked friends to contribute money to his "investment fund," agreeing to pay them higher interest rates than banks were paying at the time. Within two weeks, he had accumulated enough money not only to sustain himself until his properties sold, but also to buy two new houses to remodel. With help, he was back in business.

Don't be fooled into thinking you are alone on your journey. You're not. Your struggle is everyone's struggle. Your pain is everyone's pain. Your power is everyone's power. It is simply that we take different paths along our collective journey toward the same destination.

Benjamin Shield

Among the most destructive relationships are those based on co-dependence. Co-dependent people are motivated not by their own successes, but by someone else's approval or dependence upon them. *I am worthwhile,* the co-dependent believes, *only if someone else can't get along without me.* Co-dependent people abandon their own dreams and even endure abuse to keep the approval of others.

John was a bright fellow who had been in college for seven years without graduating. During a class discussion, he related an experience that he said was typical of him: He had been studying for a midterm test in history when a friend called and asked for help with a test in biology, a course John had already passed. John set aside his own studies and spent the evening tutoring his friend. The next day John failed his history exam. In his journal, he wrote, "I've learned that in order to be successful, I need to make my dreams more important than other people's approval. I have to learn to say 'no.'" Co-dependent people like John often spend time in Quadrant III, engaged in activities that are urgent to someone else but unimportant to their own goals and dreams.

With co-dependence, dependence, and independence, giving and receiving are out of balance. The co-dependent person *gives* too much. The dependent person *takes* too much. The independent person seldom gives or receives. By contrast, the interdependent person finds a healthy balance of giving and receiving, and everyone benefits. That's why building mutually supportive relationships is one of the most important Quadrant II behaviors you'll ever undertake.

Giving and receiving

Surround yourself with only people who are going to lift you higher.

Oprah Winfrey

A story is told of a man who prayed to know the difference between heaven and hell. An angel came to take the man to see for himself. In hell, the man saw a huge banquet table overflowing with beautifully prepared meats, vegetables, drinks, and desserts. Despite this bounty, the prisoners of hell bore withered, sunken looks. Then the man saw why. The poor souls in hell could pick up all the food they wanted, but their elbows would not bend, and they could not place the food into their mouths. Living amidst all that abundance, the citizens of hell were starving.

Then the angel whisked the man to heaven where he saw another endless banquet table heaped with a similar bounty of splendid food. Amazingly, just as in hell, the citizens of heaven could not bend their elbows to feed themselves.

"I don't understand," the man said. "Is heaven the same as hell?"

The angel only pointed. The residents of heaven were healthy, laughing, and obviously happy as they sat together at the banquet tables. Then the man saw the difference.

The citizens of heaven were feeding each other.

Journal Entry 15

In this activity, you will explore your beliefs and behaviors regarding giving and receiving.

1. **Write and complete the following ten sentence stems:**

    1. A specific situation when someone assisted me was . . .
    2. A specific situation when I assisted someone else was . . .
    3. A specific situation when I made assisting someone else more important than my own success and happiness was . . .
    4. When someone asks me for assistance I usually feel . . .
    5. When I think of asking someone else for assistance I usually feel . . .
    6. What usually gets in the way of my asking for help is . . .
    7. If I often asked other people for assistance . . .
    8. If I joyfully gave assistance to others . . .
    9. If I gratefully accepted assistance from others . . .
    10. One goal that I could use assistance with today is . . .

2. **Write about what you discovered by completing the sentence stems in Step 1: Is your typical relationship to others (1) dependent, (2) co-dependent, (3) independent, or (4) interdependent?** Describe how you have most often related to others in the past and how you intend to relate to others in the future.

Here's a reminder from the section on effective writing strategies (p. 70). To dive deeper: **Use the 4 E's.** The 4 E's represent four questions that readers often wanted answered:

- Can you give an **EXAMPLE** of that?
- Can you give an **EXPERIENCE** to illustrate that?
- Can you **EXPLAIN** that further?
- Can you give **EVIDENCE** to support that?

As you fully answer one or more of these questions, you will begin writing more effectively.

Relax, think, write.

Creating a Support Network

FOCUS QUESTION How could you create and sustain an effective support network to help achieve your greatest dreams in college and in life?

For solving most problems, ten brains are better than one and twenty hands are better than two. Although Victims typically struggle alone, Creators know the incredible power of a network of mutually supportive people.

This ingredient of success has been called **OPB: Other People's Brains** or **Other People's Brawn.** College provides a great place to develop the habit of using OPB to achieve maximum success. Let's consider some choices you could make to create a support network, one that will help you not only achieve your goals in college but enjoy the experience as well.

To reach your goals you need to become a team player.
Zig Ziglar

Seek help from your instructors

Building positive relationships with your college instructors is a powerful Quadrant II action that can pay off handsomely. Your instructors have years of specialized training. You've already paid for their help with your tuition, and all you have to do is ask.

Find out your professors' office hours and make appointments. Come to your conferences prepared with questions or requests. You'll likely get very good help. As a bonus, by getting to know your instructors, you may find a mentor who will help you in college and beyond.

Get help from college resources

Nearly every college spends a chunk of tuition money to provide support services for students, but these services go to waste unless you use them. Do you know what support services your college offers, where they are, and how to use them?

Alone we can do so little; together we can do so much.
Helen Keller

Academic problems? Get help at one of your college's tutoring labs. Many colleges have a writing lab, a reading lab, and a math lab. Other sources of academic assistance might include a science learning center or a computer lab. Your college may also have a diagnostician who tests students for learning disabilities and suggests ways of overcoming them.

Money problems? Get help from your college's financial aid office. Money is available in grants and scholarships (which you don't pay back), loans (which you do pay back, usually at low interest rates), and student work programs (which offer jobs on campus). Your college may also have a service that can locate an off-campus job, perhaps one in the very career field you want to enter after graduation.

Personal problems? Get help from your college's counseling office. Trained counselors are available at many colleges to help students through times of emotional upset. It's not unusual for students to experience some sort of personal difficulty during college; Creators seek assistance.

Health problems? Get aid from your college's health service. Many colleges have doctors who see students at little or no cost. Health-related products often may be purchased inexpensively. Your college may even offer special health insurance for students.

Problems deciding on a career? Get help from your college's career office. There you can take aptitude tests, discover job opportunities, learn to write or improve your résumé, and practice effective interviewing skills.

Problems getting involved socially at your college? Request assistance from your college's student activities office. Here you'll discover athletic teams, trips, choirs, dances, service projects, student professional organizations, the college newspaper and literary magazine, and clubs just waiting for you to join them.

Create a project team

If you're tackling a big project, why not create a team to help? A project team accomplishes one particular task. In business, when a project needs attention, an ad hoc committee is formed. *Ad hoc* in Latin means "toward this." In other words, an ad hoc committee comes together for the sole purpose of solving one problem. Once the task is complete, the committee disbands.

One of my students created a project team to help her move. More than a dozen classmates volunteered, including a fellow who provided a truck. In one Saturday morning, the team packed and delivered her possessions to a new apartment.

What big project do you have that would benefit from the assistance of a group? The only barrier standing between you and a project team is your willingness to seek help.

My driving belief is this: great teamwork is the only way to reach our ultimate moments, to create the breakthroughs that define our careers, to fulfill our lives with a sense of lasting significance.

Pat Riley,
Professional Basketball Coach

Start a study group

One of the very best strategies for success in college is forming a study group. A study group differs from a project team in two ways. First, a study group is created to help everyone on the team excel in a particular course. Second, a study group meets many times throughout a semester. Occasionally a study group is so helpful that its members stay together throughout college. Here are three suggestions for maximizing the value of your study group:

©ED ARNO/*SCIENCE 80*

1. **Choose only Creators.** As the semester begins, make a list of potential members: classmates who attend regularly, come prepared, and participate actively. Also watch for that quiet student who doesn't say much but whose occasional comments reveal a special understanding of the subject. After the first test or essay, find out how the students on your list performed and invite three or four of the most successful to study with you.

2. **Choose group goals.** Regardless of potential, a study group is only as effective as you make it. Everyone should agree upon common goals. You might say to prospective study group members, "My goal in our math class is to master the subject and earn an A. Is that what you want, too?" Team up with students whose goals match or exceed your own.

3. **Choose group rules.** The last step is establishing team rules. Pat Riley, one of the most successful professional basketball coaches ever,

has his players create a "team covenant." Before the season, they agree on the rules they will follow to stay on course to their goal of a championship. Your team should do the same. Decide where, how often, and what time you'll meet. Most important, agree on what will happen during the meetings. Many study groups fail because they turn into social gatherings. Yours will succeed if you adopt rules like these:

Rule 1: *We meet in the library every Thursday afternoon from one o'clock to three o'clock.*

Rule 2: *Each member brings twenty new questions with answers, including the source (textbook page or class date).*

Rule 3: *All written questions are asked, answered, and understood before any socializing.*

Many people collaborate only with others who are like them. One of the greatest benefits of your college experience is meeting people of diverse backgrounds, with different ideas, skills, experiences, abilities, and resources. Be sure to network with those who are older or younger than you, who are from different states or countries, who are of different races or cultures, and who have different religions or political preferences.

Start a telephone list of the people you meet in college. You might even want to write a few notes about them: their major or career field, names of family members, hobbies, interests, and especially their strengths. Keep in touch with these people during and after college.

Creators develop mutually supportive relationships in college that continue to support them for years—even for a lifetime. Don't get so bogged down with the daily demands of college that you fail to create a support network.

> *Until recently, the "old girls" did not know how the "old boys" network operated. . . . Women now know that, besides hard work and lots of skill, the move to the top requires a supportive network.*
>
> June E. Gabler

Journal Entry 16

In this activity, you will explore the creation of a support network. Afterward, you may decide to start networking more, using OPB to help you achieve your greatest goals and dreams.

1. **Write and complete the following sentence stems:**

   1. An outer obstacle that stands between me and my success in college is . . . (examples might be a lack of time to study or a teacher you don't understand)

   2. Someone who could help me overcome this outer obstacle is . . .

   3. How this person could help me is by . . .

   4. An inner obstacle that stands between me and my success in college is . . . (examples might be shyness or a tendency to procrastinate)

5. Someone who could help me overcome this obstacle is . . .

6. How this person could help me is by . . .

7. The most challenging course I'm taking in college this semester is . . .

8. This course is challenging for me because . . .

9. Someone who could help me overcome this challenge is . . .

10. How this person could help me is by . . .

2. **Write about two (or more) choices you could make to create a stronger support network for yourself in college.** Consider the choices you could make to overcome the challenges and obstacles to your success mentioned in Step 1. Consider also any resistance you may have about taking steps to create a support network. Dive deep as you explore each choice fully.

Relax, think, write.

Strengthening Relationships with Active Listening

FOCUS QUESTIONS   Do you know how to strengthen a relationship with active listening? What are the essential skills of being a good listener?

Once we have begun a mutually supportive relationship, we naturally want the relationship to grow. Books on relationships abound, suggesting untold ways to strengthen a relationship. At the heart of all of these suggestions is a theme: We must show that we value the other person professionally, personally, or both.

When people talk, listen completely. Most people never listen.
Ernest Hemingway

Many ways exist to demonstrate another's value to us. Some of the most powerful methods include keeping promises, giving honest appreciation and approval, resolving conflicts so that both people win, staying in touch, and speaking well of someone when talking to others. However, for demonstrating the high esteem with which you value another person, there may be no better way than active listening.

Few people are truly good listeners. Too often, we're thinking what we want to say next. Or our thoughts dash off to our own problems, and we ignore what the other person is saying. Or we hear what we *thought* the person was going to say rather than what he actually said.

Good listeners, by contrast, clear their minds and listen for the entire message, including words, tone of voice, gestures, and facial expressions. No matter how well one person communicates, unless someone else listens actively, both the communication and the relationship are likely to go astray. Imagine the potential problems created if good listening skills are absent when an employer says to an employee: "I want you to include last year's sales figures in the report for comparison," but the employee assumes otherwise because previous years' sales figures have never been included before.

In some cases, the immediate problem caused by poor listening can be fixed—the employee can rewrite the sales report, for example. But the relationship may be injured beyond repair—the employer may never again trust the employee, even passing him over for future promotions.

Listening actively means accepting 100 percent responsibility for receiving the same message that the speaker sent, uncontaminated by your own thoughts or feelings. That's why active listening begins with empathy, the ability to understand the other person as if, for that moment, you *are* the other person. To empathize doesn't mean that you necessarily agree. Empathy means understanding what the other person is thinking and feeling. And you actively reveal this understanding.

With empathetic listening, you send this message: *I value you so much that I am doing my very best to see the world through your eyes.*

For the lack of listening, billions of losses accumulate: retyped letters, rescheduled appointments, rerouted shipments, breakdowns in labor management relations, misunderstood sales presentations, and job interviews that never really get off the ground.

Michael Ray and
Rochelle Myers

How to listen actively

Active listening is a learned skill. You will become an excellent listener if you master the following four steps:

Step 1: Listen to understand.   Change your purpose for listening. Listening isn't effective when you're simply waiting for the first opportunity to insert your own opinion. Instead, activate your empathy and listen with the intention of fully understanding what the other person thinks and feels.

Active listening, sometimes called reflective listening, involves giving verbal feedback of the content of what was said or done along with a guess at the feeling underneath the spoken words or acts.

Muriel James and
Dorothy Jongeward

Step 2: Clear your mind and remain silent.   Don't be distracted by judgmental chatter from your Inner Critic and Inner Defender. Clear your mind, stay focused, and be quiet. Let your mind listen for thoughts. Let your heart listen for the undercurrent of emotions. Let your intuition listen for a deeper message hidden beneath the words. Let your companion know that you are actively listening. Sit forward. Nod your head when appropriate. Offer verbal feedback that shows you are actively listening: "Mmmmm . . . I see . . . Uh huh . . ."

Step 3: Ask the person to expand or clarify.   Don't fill in the blanks with your own experience. Invite the speaker to share additional information and feelings.

- *Tell me more about that.*
- *Could you give me an example?*

- *Can you explain that a different way?*
- *How did you feel when that happened?*
- *What happened next?*

Step 4: Reflect the other person's thoughts and feelings.   Don't assume you understand. In your own words, restate what you heard, both the ideas and the emotions. Then verify the accuracy of your understanding.

- To a classmate: *Sounds like you're really angry about the instructor's feedback on your research paper. His comments seem more sarcastic than helpful. Is that it?*
- To a professor: *I want to be clear about this essay that you're assigning. The outline is due October third and the final draft is due November first. Have I got it right?*

Notice that reflecting adds nothing new to the conversation. Don't offer advice or tell your own experience.

Use active listening in your college classes

If I were to summarize in one sentence the single most important principle I have learned in the field of interpersonal relations, it would be this: Seek first to understand, then to be understood.

Stephen Covey

Active listening not only strengthens relationships with people, it strengthens our understanding of new concepts. In class, successful students clear their minds and prepare to hear something of value. They reflect the instructor's ideas, confirming the accuracy of what they heard. When confused, they ask the instructor to expand or clarify, either in class or during the instructor's conference hours. As Creators, these students actively listen to understand.

Choose today to master active listening. You'll be amazed at how much this choice will improve your relationships and your life.

Journal Entry 17

I n this activity, you will explore the power of active listening. With practice, active listening will become a habit that strengthens your relationships and supports your success.

1. **Write a conversation between you and your Inner Guide (IG) about a problem you are facing in college. Label each of your IG's responses with the listening skill it uses: silence, expansion, clarification, reflection (be sure to reflect feelings as well as thoughts).** Let your IG demonstrate the skills of active listening without giving advice.

Here's an example of how your dialogue might sound:

Me: I've been realizing what a difficult time I have asking for assistance.

IG: Would you like to say more about that? **(expansion)**

Me: Well, I have been having trouble in math. I know I should be asking more questions in class, but . . . I don't know, I guess I feel dumb because I can't do the problems myself.

IG: You seem frustrated that you can't solve the math problems without help. **(reflection)**

Me: That's right. I've always resisted that sort of thing.

IG: What do you mean by "that sort of thing?" **(clarification)**

Me: I mean that ever since I can remember, I've had to do everything on my own. When I was a kid, I used to play alone all the time.

IG: Uh huh . . . **(silence)**

Me: I never had anyone to help me as a kid. And I don't have anyone to help me now.

IG: So, no one is available to help you? Is that how it seems? **(reflection)**

Me: Well, I guess I could ask Robert for help. He seems really good in math, but I'm kind of scared to ask him.

IG: What scares you about asking him? **(expansion)** etc.

Imagine that the conversation you create here is taking place over the phone. Don't hang up until you've addressed all aspects of the problem and know what your next action step will be. Let your Inner Guide demonstrate how much it values you by being a great listener.

2. **Write what you learned about active listening during this conversation with your Inner Guide.** Remember to dive deep to discover a powerful insight. When you think you have written all you can, see if you can write at least one more paragraph.

Relax by clearing your mind and becoming silent, **think** of an important problem that you'd like to discuss with a good listener, and **write** a dialogue with your Inner Guide.

> *Dr. Eliot's listening was not mere silence, but a form of activity. Sitting very erect on the end of his spine with hands joined in his lap, making no movement except that he revolved his thumbs around each other faster or slower, he faced his interlocutor and seemed to be hearing with his eyes as well as his ears. He listened with his mind and attentively considered what you had to say while you said it. . . . At the end of an interview the person who had talked to him felt that he had his say.*
>
> Henry James
> about Charles W. Eliot, former
> president of Harvard

CASE STUDY IN CRITICAL THINKING

Professor Rogers' Trial

Professor Rogers thought her Speech 101 students would enjoy role-playing a real court trial as their last speech for the semester. She also hoped the experience would teach them to work well in teams, a skill much sought after by employers. So, she divided her students into groups of six—a team of 3 defense attorneys and a team of 3 prosecuting attorneys—providing each group with court transcripts of a real murder case. Using evidence from the trial, each team would present closing arguments for the case, after which a jury of classmates would render a verdict. Each team was allowed a maximum of 24 minutes to present its case, and all three team members would receive the same grade.

After class, **Anthony** told his teammates, **Silvie** and **Donald**, "We'll meet tomorrow at 4:00 in the library and plan a defense for this guy." Silvie felt angry about Anthony's bossy tone, but she just nodded. Donald said, "Whatever," put his earphones on, and strolled away singing louder than he probably realized.

"Look," Anthony said to Silvie at 4:15 the next day, "we're not waiting for Donald any more. Here's what we'll do. You go first and take about 10 minutes to prove that our defendant had no motive. I'll take the rest of the time to show how it could have been the victim's brother who shot him. I want an 'A' out of this."

Silvie was furious. "You can't just decide to leave Donald out. Plus, what about the defendant's fingerprints on the murder weapon! We have to dispute that evidence or we'll never win. I'll do that. And I'll go last so I can wrap up all the loose ends. I want to win this trial."

The defense team met twice more before the trial. Donald came to only one of the meetings and spent the entire time reading the case. He said he wasn't sure what he was going to say, but he'd have it figured out by the day of the trial. Anthony and Silvie argued about which evidence was most important and who would speak last. At one point, the college librarian had to "shush" them when Silvie lost her temper and started shouting at Anthony that no one had elected him the leader.

The day before the trial, Anthony went to Professor Rogers. "It's not fair that my grade depends on my teammates. Donald could care less what happens, and Silvie is always looking for a fight. I'll present alone, but not with them." "If you were an actual lawyer," Professor Rogers replied, "do you think you could go to the judge and complain that you aren't getting along with your partners? You'll have to figure out how to work as a team. The trial goes on as scheduled, and all three of you will get the same grade."

On the day of the trial, the three student prosecutors presented one seamless and persuasive closing argument. Then Anthony leapt up, saying, "I'll go first for my team." He spoke for 21 minutes, talking as fast as he could to present the entire case, including an explanation of how the defendant's fingerprints had gotten on the murder weapon. Silvie, greatly flustered, followed with a seven-minute presentation in which she also explained how the defendant's fingerprints had gotten on the murder weapon. At that point, Professor Rogers announced that the defense was already four minutes over their time limit. Donald promised to be brief. He assured the jury that the defendant was innocent and then read three unconnected passages from the transcript as "proof." His presentation took 75 seconds. The jury deliberated for five minutes and unanimously found the defendant guilty. Professor Rogers gave all members of the defense team a "D" for their speeches.

Listed below are the characters in this story. Rank them in the order of their responsibility for the group's grade of "D." Give a different score to each character. Be prepared to explain your answer.

Most responsible ← 1 2 3 4 → Least responsible

_____**Professor Rogers**   _____**Silvie**
_____**Anthony**   _____**Donald**

Interdependence at Work

Over 90 percent of us who work for a living do so in organizations, and the ability to function effectively as a member of a team is usually an imperative of success.

Nathaniel Branden, Psychologist

You may have noticed that many employment ads say, "Looking for a team player" or "Must relate well to others." Few abilities have more impact on your success at work than your ability to interact well with supervisors, peers, subordinates, suppliers, and customers. And enhancing this ability starts now.

Someday you'll probably ask a former professor or employer to write you a letter of recommendation. What they write on that future day will depend on the relationships you're building with them now. Are you someone who works well with others? Someone who completes assignments and does them with excellence? Attends regularly and on time? Is respectful? Self-aware? Responsible? A former student called me with a request that I write her a recommendation. After much thought, I said no. Based on her performance in my class, I could not honestly write anything that would help her chances of getting hired. Sadly, when she was "blowing off" my course, she hadn't anticipated the day when she would need me to speak well of her to a potential employer.

In the work world, most people must interact well with others to keep their jobs or to advance. In college, one way to continue developing effective interdependence is by participating actively in study groups. Learning to work collaboratively now will contribute to your success tomorrow (not to mention that your grades will likely be higher).

As you begin a search for your ideal job, one of the best sources of information about what a career is *really* like is someone who is now doing it. By conducting information-gathering interviews with enough people who are working in your chosen profession, you learn about qualifications, employment outlook, work conditions, and salaries. If you don't know anyone in the career of your choice, be a Creator and ask people you know for referrals. If that fails, try the Yellow Pages. Call a company you find there, ask for the Public Information Office, and explain the information you're seeking. Besides the information you may uncover, who knows who might be impressed with your professional approach to job hunting?

The same information gathering strategy is helpful when it comes to learning important information about a particular employer you may be considering. Talk to people who work there and find out from the inside what it's really like. For example, if you find the company's mission statement appealing, ask employees if the company backs up those words with actions. Of course, it's important to talk to a number of people to avoid being swayed by one or two biased opinions.

Many people limit their job search to employment agencies and advertised positions, jobs listed in the "visible" market place. However, some career specialists estimate that as many as 85–90 percent of the available jobs are unlisted and found only by uncovering them in the "invisible" market place. Creators discover these unpublished openings by networking. Do that by seeking informational interviews with possible employers, and ask them if they know of others who might have a job for which you'd qualify, as described in Chapter 2. Additionally, you can ask friends and acquaintances if they know of positions that are available where they work. Ask professors if they've heard of job openings. Ask at church and club meetings. Ask all of these folks to spread the word that you're looking for a position. You never know who might help you discover an opening that would be ideal for you. A great job might become visible only because you asked a friend who asked a co-worker who asked his sister who asked her boss who said, "Sure, we've got a job like that. Have the person call me."

Another great strategy during a job search is to develop a support group, especially one made up of other job seekers. Support groups not only provide emotional support when disappointments (and your Inner Critic) strike, they can also give you helpful suggestions and practice at essential skills. For example, support groups can critique your résumé and cover letters. They can help you practice your interviewing skills. Someone in your support group may share an experience that can teach you a valuable lesson. For instance, if someone reports going blank when an interviewer asked, "Do you have any questions for me?" you'll learn to prepare questions to ask at your own interviews.

Okay, you've gotten your dream position in the company you wanted. Teamwork continues to have a big impact on your work life. The *Harvard Business Review* reported a study that discovered why some scientists at Bell Labs in New Jersey were considered "stars" by their colleagues. Interestingly, the stars had done no better academically than their less successful colleagues. In fact, the study found that the stars and their coworkers were very similar when measured on IQ and personality tests. What distinguished the stars was their strong networks of important colleagues. When problems struck, the stars always had someone to call on for advice, and their requests for help were responded to quickly. Interdependence transformed good scientists into stars.

One last suggestion about interdependence could apply anywhere on your career path, but is particularly important once you are in your job. Find a mentor. A mentor is someone further along in his or her career development and willing to guide and help newer employees like you. Keep your eyes open for someone successful whose qualities you admire. You can create an informal mentoring relationship by making choices that put you into frequent contact with this person, or you can create a formal relationship by actually asking the person to be your mentor. With the wisdom of experience, a mentor can keep you on course to career success.

Believing in Yourself: **Be Assertive**

| FOCUS QUESTION | How can you communicate in a style that strengthens relationships, creates better results, and builds strong self-esteem? |

O ccasionally, we run into people who don't want us to achieve our goals and dreams. More often, though, we meet folks who are too busy, too preoccupied, or couldn't care less about helping us. Encountering such people is especially likely in a bureaucracy like a college. How we communicate our desires has a profound impact not only on the quality of the relationships and results we create, but on our self-esteem as well.

Once a human being has arrived on this earth, communication is the largest single factor determining what kinds of relationships she or he makes with others and what happens to each in the world.

Virginia Satir

According to family therapist Virginia Satir, the two most common patterns of ineffective communication are **placating** and **blaming.** Both perpetuate low self-esteem.

Placating: Victims who placate are dominated by their Inner Critic. They place themselves below others, protecting themselves from the sting of criticism and rejection by saying whatever they think will gain approval. Picture placators on their knees, looking up with a pained smile, nodding and agreeing on the outside, while fearfully hiding their true thoughts and feelings within. *"Please, please approve of me,"* they beg as their own Inner Critic judges them unworthy. Satir estimated that about 50 percent of people use placating as their major communication style.

Blaming: Victims who blame are dominated by their Inner Defender. They place themselves above others, protecting themselves from disappointment and failure by making others fully responsible for their problems. Picture them glowering down, a finger jabbing furiously in judgment at those below. Their Inner Defender snarls, *"You never . . .   Why do you always . . . ? Why don't you ever . . . ?   It's your fault that . . ."* Satir estimated that about 30 percent of people use blaming as their major communication style.

Either passively placating or aggressively blaming keeps Victims from developing mutually supportive relationships, making the accomplishment of their dreams more difficult. The inner result is damaged self-esteem.

Leveling

What, then, is the communication style of Creators? Some have called this style assertiveness: boldly putting forth opinions and requests. Satir calls this communication style *leveling*. Leveling is characterized by a simple, yet profound, communication strategy: asserting the truth as you see it.

Learning to perceive the truth within ourselves and speak it clearly to others is a delicate skill, certainly as complex as multiplication or long division, but very little time is spent on it in school.

Gay and Kathlyn Hendricks

Creators boldly express their personal truth without false apology or excuse, without harsh criticism or blame. Leveling requires a strong Inner Guide and a commitment to honesty. Here are three strategies that promote leveling:

1. Communicate purposefully.   Creators express a clear purpose even in times of emotional upset. If a Creator goes to a professor to discuss a disappointing grade, she will be clear whether her purpose is to (1) increase her understanding of the subject, (2) seek a higher grade, (3) criticize the instructor's grading ability, or whatever. By knowing her purpose, she has a way to evaluate the success of her communication. The Creator states purposefully, *When I saw my grade on this lab report, I was very disappointed. I'd like to go over it with you and learn how to improve my next one.*

We should replace our alienating, criticizing words with "I" language. Instead of, "You are a liar and no one can trust you," say, "I don't like it when I can't rely on your words—it is difficult for us to do things together."

Ken Keyes

2. Communicate honestly.   Creators candidly express unpopular thoughts and upset feelings in the service of building mutually supportive relationships. The Creator says honestly, *I'm angry that you didn't meet me in the library to study for the sociology test as you agreed.*

3. Communicate responsibly.   Because responsibility lies within, Creators express their personal responsibility with I-messages. An I-message allows Creators to take full responsibility for their reaction to anything another person may have said or done. An effective I-message has four elements:

A statement of the situation:	*When you . . .*
A statement of your reaction:	*I felt/thought/decided . . .*
A request:	*I'd like to ask that you . . .*
An invitation to respond:	*Will you agree to that?*

Let's compare Victim and Creator responses to the same situation. Imagine that you feel sick one day and decide not to go to your history class. You phone a classmate, and she agrees to call you after class with what you missed. But she never calls. At the next history class, the instructor gives a test that was announced the day you were absent. Afterward, your classmate apologizes: "Sorry I didn't call. I was swamped with work." What response do you choose?

Placating: *Oh, don't worry about it. I know you had a lot on your mind. I probably would have failed the test anyway.*

Blaming: *You're the lousiest friend I've ever had! After making me fail that test, you have some nerve even talking to me!*

Leveling: *I'm angry that you didn't call. I realize that I could have called you, but I thought I could count on you to keep your word. If we're going to be friends, I need to know if you're going to keep your promises to me in the future. Will you?*

Notice that the leveling response is the only one of the three that positively addresses the issue, nurtures a relationship of equals, and demonstrates high self-esteem.

> *I speak straight and do not wish to deceive or be deceived.*
>
> Cochise

Making requests

Making effective requests is another demonstration of both assertiveness and high self-esteem. Creators know they can't reach their greatest goals and dreams alone, so they ask for help. The key to making effective requests is applying the DAPPS rule. Whenever possible, make your requests <u>D</u>ated, <u>A</u>chievable, <u>P</u>ersonal, <u>P</u>ositive, and (above all) <u>S</u>pecific. Here are some translations of vague Victim requests to specific, clear Creator requests:

> *If you go to somebody and say, "I need help," they'll say, "Sure, honey, I wish I could," but if you say, "I need you to call so-and-so on Tuesday, will you do that?" they either will say yes or they'll say no. If they say no, you thank them and say, "Do you know someone who will?" If they say yes, you call on Wednesday to see if they did it. You wouldn't believe how good I've gotten at this, and I never knew how to ask anybody for anything before.*
>
> Barbara Sher

Victim Requests	**Creator Requests**
1. I'm going to be absent next Friday. It sure would be nice if someone would let me know if I miss anything.	1. John, I'm going to be absent next Friday. Would you be willing to call me Friday night and tell me what I missed?
2. I don't suppose you'd consider giving me a few more days to complete this research paper?	2. I'd like to request an extension on my research paper. I promise to hand it in by noon on Thursday. Would that be acceptable?

When you make specific requests, the other person can respond with a clear "yes" or "no." If the person says "no," all is not lost. Try negotiating:

1. *If you can't call me Friday night, could I call you Saturday morning to find out what I missed?*

2. *If Thursday noon isn't acceptable to you, could I turn my paper in on Wednesday by 5:00?*

A Creator seeks definite yes or no answers. Victims often accept "maybe" or "I'll try" for fear of getting a "no," but it's better to hear a specific "no" and be free to move on to someone who will say "yes."

One of my mentors offered a valuable piece of advice: "If you go through a whole day without getting at least a couple of 'no's,' you aren't asking for enough help in your life."

Saying "no"

Saying "no" is another tool of the assertive Creator. When I think of the power of saying "no," I think of Monique. One day after class she took a deep breath, sighed, and told me she was exhausted. She complained that everyone at her job kept bringing her tasks to do. As a result, she had virtually no social life, and she was falling behind in college. She wanted advice on how to manage her time better.

"Sounds like you're working 60 hours a week and doing the work of two people," I observed.

She nodded modestly.

When two people are relating maturely, each will be able to ask the other for what he or she wants or needs, fully trusting that the other will say "no" if he or she does not want to give it.

Edward Deci

"Here's an outrageous thought: The next time someone at work brings you more to do, say 'no'."

"That sounds so rude."

"Okay then, say, 'I'm sorry, but my schedule is full, and I won't be able to do that.'"

"What if my boss asks? I can't say 'no' to her."

"You can say, 'I'll be glad to take that on. But since I have so many projects already, I'll need you to give one of them to someone else. That way I'll have time to do a good job on this new project.'"

Monique agreed to experiment with saying "no." The next time I saw her, she was excited. "I wrote my boss a memo and told her I had too much work and I couldn't take on the latest project she had assigned me. Before I'd even talked to her about the memo, one of my co-workers came by. He said our boss had sent him to take over some of my projects. Not only didn't I get the new project, I got rid of two others. I just might be able to finish this semester after all."

Monique's voice had a power that hadn't been there before. With one "no" she had transformed herself from exhausted to exhilarated. That's the power of a Creator being assertive.

Journal Entry 18

In this activity, you will explore assertiveness. This powerful way of being creates great results, strengthens relationships, and builds self-esteem.

1. **Write three different responses to the instructor described in the following situation.** Respond to the instructor by (1) placating, (2) blaming, and (3) leveling. For an example of this exercise, refer to the journal article.

   Situation: You register for a course required in your major. It is the last course you need to graduate. When you go to the first class meeting, the instructor tells you that your name is NOT on the roster. The course is full, and no other sections of the course are being offered. You've been shut out of the class. The instructor tells you that you'll have to postpone graduation and return next semester to complete this required course.

   Remember, in each of your three responses, you are writing what you would actually say to the instructor—first as a placator, second as a blamer, and third as a leveler.

2. **Now, think about one of your most challenging academic goals. Decide who could help you with this goal. Write a letter to this person and request assistance.** You can decide later if you actually want to send the letter.

   Here are some possibilities to include in your letter:

   - Tell the person your most challenging academic goal for this semester.
   - Explain how this goal is a steppingstone to your dream.
   - Describe your dream and explain its importance to you.
   - Identify your obstacle, explaining it fully.
   - Discuss why you believe this person is ideally qualified to help you overcome your obstacle.
   - Admit any reluctance or fear you have about asking for assistance.
   - Request *exactly* what you would like this person to do for you and persuade him or her to give you helpful assistance.

   Remember, for effective requests, use the DAPPS rule.

3. **Write what you have learned about being assertive.** How assertive have you been in the pursuit of your goals and dreams? How has this choice affected your self-esteem? What changes do you intend to make in communicating (placating, blaming, leveling), making requests, and saying "no"? Be sure to use the 4 E's (Experiences, Examples, Explanation, and Evidence) to support what you say.

   Relax, think, write.

Effective note taking is your memory's good friend. Taking notes promotes listening actively, improving what you recall later. Well-organized notes also allow you to review what you heard and decide what to study and remember. Successful college students take notes in nearly every class. Successful professionals use note taking to record important meetings, agreements, projects, results, and concerns. The following strategies will help you take better notes in both academic and professional settings.

Before Note Taking

1. Create a positive affirmation about taking notes. Many students hold negative beliefs about their ability to take good notes or the value of doing so. Create an affirming statement about taking notes, such as, *I take notes that capture all of the important concepts and make learning easy.* Along with your personal affirmation, repeat this note-taking affirmation to reprogram your beliefs.

2. Get note-taking supplies that fit your style. Experiment and decide on your best note-taking supplies. Do you prefer pens or pencils? Do you like color ink or the rainbow look? Do you prefer three-ring binders, composition books, spiral binders, or 3" × 5" cards?

3. Bring your note-taking supplies to every class and use them. A student once told me during class, "I just can't take good notes." Her desk-top was empty. "Well," I suggested, "you might want to start by putting a pen in your hand and a piece of paper in front of you." That's one approach. Some prefer taking notes on 3" × 5" cards, later organizing them in a card box. Others like to take notes in three-ring binders where they can add and remove pages easily. All effective note-taking systems keep notes well organized and easily accessible for study.

4. Read homework assignments before class. By doing so, you are better prepared to assess what information from the lecture or class discussion belongs in your notes.

5. Prepare a list of questions based on homework assignments. As you read your assignments, write questions you would like answered in class. If you write them on binder paper, leave space after each question to write the answer. If you write them on 3" × 5" cards, you can put the answers on the back, thus creating great study cards. Bring the questions with you to class.

During Note Taking

No single method of note taking is best. Experiment with the strategies below and personalize a system that works well for you.

6. Use the outline method: An outline (depicted on page 120) shows the relationship of various ideas. Ideas that reach to the left-hand margin are major topics and are usually numbered. Subtopics are indented about one-half inch. Sub-subtopics are indented about one inch. Outlining is a good method when the information presented is well organized.

7. Use a concept map. A concept map (see example in Wise Choices in College: Effective Writing in Chapter 3) graphically shows the connections between key elements in a complex idea. Write the key idea in the center of a page; then, by placing satellites around the center, add subideas, and sub-subideas. Concept maps are especially helpful for taking notes when the professor leaps from idea to idea. When the professor returns to an idea already mentioned, you can add these new thoughts to the concept map in their proper relationship to ideas already recorded.

8. Use the Cornell Method: This method divides the page into three sections (depicted on page 121). The largest section (A) on the right is for taking notes during class or while reading. You can use your preferred note-taking method here: an outline, a concept map, or your own invention. The second section (B) is filled in later as you review; write questions that are answered in your notes in section A. When reviewing, simply cover your notes with your hand and quiz yourself with

Course: Psychology 101
Date: October 5
Topic: Abraham Maslow

1. Abraham Maslow (1908–1970)
    — Family immigrated to Brooklyn
        — One of seven children
        — Unhappy, neurotic child
    — Taught at Teachers College, Brooklyn College, Brandeis
    — Sought to understand human motivations
    — Became leader of humanistic psychology movement of the
      1950's and 1960's

2. Maslow's Hierarchy: Theory of Human Motivation (like a pyramid)
    — Physiological needs (the foundation)
        — Food, rest, shelter, etc.
    — Safety needs
        — Security, stability, freedom from fear
    — Psychological needs
        — Belonging, love, affiliation, acceptance, esteem, approval,
          recognition
    — Self-actualization (top of the pyramid)
        — Need to fulfill oneself
            — Maslow: "to become everything that one is capable of
              becoming."

3. Humanistic psychology
    — Maslow led the "Third Force" in psychology
        — Alternative to...
            — Freudian psychoanalysis
            — Behaviorist psychology
    — Stressed the power of a person to choose how to behave
        — As opposed to...
            — Freudians: Choices controlled by childhood influences
            — Behaviorists: Choices controlled by conditioning
    — Appealed to the individualistic, rebellious college students of the
      1960's

the questions in the left margin. The third section (C) allows space for summarizing the main points on that page of notes. As a variation, using a spiral binder for each subject, you can take class notes on the right page and write notes from your corresponding reading on the left (facing) page.

9. Record only important ideas in your notes. Some students try to write everything a professor says. Don't. Become skilled at ignoring digressions and recording only important points. The ideas that follow will help you perfect this skill.

10. Listen and look for cues. Professors may *tell* you what information belongs in your notes. If you hear your professor say any of the following phrases, start writing: *"The main point here is . . . In other words . . . In conclusion . . . Obviously . . . Most importantly . . . To summarize . . . The key here is . . . This will*

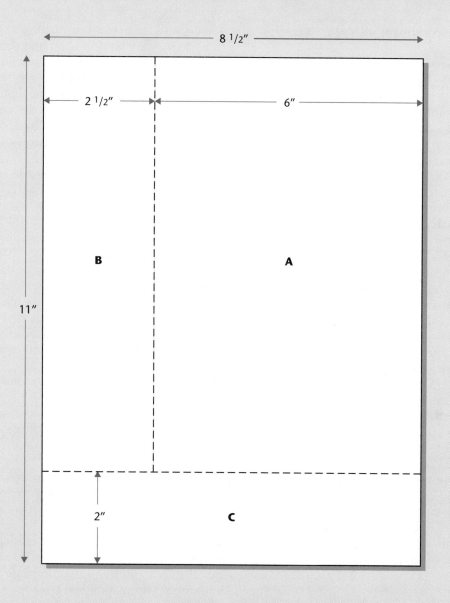

8 1/2"

2 1/2"   6"

B   A

11"

2"   C

definitely be on the final exam." Professors will also *show* you nonverbally what is important. Start writing if you see your professor do any of the following: write on the blackboard, show a transparency, emphasize an idea on a handout, read or point out a passage in your textbook, look carefully at lecture notes before speaking, become emotionally excited about an idea, lavishly praise a student's question or answer.

11. Listen for answers to your prepared questions. You've brought questions to class about your reading assignments. Now listen to the lecture or class discussion through the filter of those questions. When you hear an answer, jot it down. If the class is ending without one of your questions being answered, try to ask it, adding the answer to your notes. If your questions go unanswered, schedule an appointment with your instructor to get the answers.

12. Use abbreviations: Create your own personal abbreviations to make note taking go faster. For example:

ex	example
&	and
con't	continued
dept	department
imp	important
→	leads to
#	number
=	equals
1st	first
vs	versus
w/	with
w/o	without
nec	necessary
etc.	and other things

13. If you can't keep up, leave spaces. Some professors talk with the speed of a freight train. Don't panic. Leave space in your notes. After class, confer with a classmate or the professor to fill in the blanks.

14. Tape-record the class. Ask your instructor if you can record the class. In this way, when you miss something, you can refer to the tape later to fill in the gaps. You can review lessons by listening to the tapes while commuting or doing mindless activities. However, beware of the danger of depending on tape recordings. Some students think taping their classes replaces taking notes. Then they wait until the last minute to study and realize they have 45 hours of tapes to listen to before tomorrow's exam.

After Note Taking

15. Do an immediate data dump. As soon after class as possible, and without looking at your class notes, write down all you can remember. Record both concepts and examples used by the instructor. Compare your data dump with your class notes, verifying or supplementing ideas in your notes.

16. Review your notes. As soon after a class as possible, read over your notes and fill in any missing information. If there is something you don't understand, ask a classmate or the professor to clarify your confusion. Make sure you understand everything you recorded. As you design your semester schedule, you may wish to provide breaks between classes to allow for an immediate review of your notes.

17. Compare notes. Compare your notes with those of a competent classmate or study group members. Not only will you have an opportunity to correct errors and resolve any blanks in your notes, but reciting your notes will also help you remember them.

18. Revise your notes as appropriate. As you review your notes, make necessary revisions. Eliminate notes that seem unnecessary or off the topic. Add notes to further clarify a point. If you use the Cornell Method of note taking, this is the time to add questions in the margin next to your notes and summaries in the bottom section.

19. Review your notes periodically. Studies of learning suggest that we lose up to 80 percent of what we learned within twenty-four hours of a class. Strengthen your memory pathways by frequently reviewing your notes during the semester. Try quickly reading over your notes every day for a week, then once a week thereafter. When the exam date approaches, you'll be amazed at how much you recall without painful cramming sessions.

20. Rehearse your notes aloud. By reading your notes aloud, you engage multiple senses and, especially for auditory learners, increase the amount of information you remember.

Note-Taking Exercise

In an upcoming class, take notes in a new way. Compare your notes with those of a classmate, seeing which of you has recorded more comprehensive information for later studying.

6 Gaining Self-Awareness

Despite all of my efforts to create success in college and in life, I may still find myself off course. Now is the perfect time to identify and revise the inner obstacles to my success.

I am choosing habit patterns and core beliefs that support my success.

SUCCESSFUL STUDENTS . . .	STRUGGLING STUDENTS . . .
recognize when they are off course.	unconsciously wander through life unaware of being off course.
identify their self-defeating patterns of thought, emotion, and behavior.	remain unaware of their self-defeating patterns of thought, emotion, and behavior.
rewrite their outdated Scripts, revising limited core beliefs and self-defeating patterns.	unconsciously persist in making choices based on outdated Scripts, finding themselves further and further off course with each passing year.

Recognizing When You Are Off Course

Consider this: If at first you don't succeed, something is blocking your way.

Michael Ray and
Rochelle Myers

Take a deep breath, relax, and consider your journey so far.

You began by accepting personal responsibility for creating your life as you want it. Then you chose personally motivating goals and dreams that give purpose and direction to your life. Next, you created a self-management plan and began taking effective actions. Most recently, you developed mutually supportive relationships to help you on your journey. Throughout, you have examined how to believe in yourself.

Despite all these efforts, you may still be off course—in college, in a relationship, in your job, or somewhere else in your life. Once again, you have an important choice to make. You can listen to the blaming, complaining, and excusing of your Inner Critic and Inner Defender. Or you can ask your Inner Guide to find answers to important questions such as . . .

- *What choices do I make that sabotage my success?*
- *What keeps me from cooperating with my own best interests?*
- *How can I consistently make the wise choices that create a rich, personally fulfilling life?*

The mystery of self-sabotage

Self-sabotage has probably happened to everyone who's set off on a journey to a better life. Consider Jerome. Fresh from high school, Jerome said his dream was to start his own accounting firm, earning at least $60,000 a year by his thirtieth birthday. He set long-term goals of getting his college degree and passing the CPA (certified public accountant) exam. He set short-term goals of earning A's in every class he took during his first semester. He developed a written self-management system and demonstrated interdependence by starting a study group. But at semester's end, the unthinkable happened: Jerome failed Accounting 101!

Wait a minute, though. Jerome's Inner Guide has more information. You see, Jerome skipped his accounting class three times to work at a part-time job. On another day, he didn't attend class because he was angry with his girlfriend. Then he missed two more classes when he got the flu. He was late five times because parking was difficult to find. Jerome regularly put off doing homework until the last minute because he was so

---

HARLEM (A DREAM DEFERRED)

What happens to a dream deferred?
Does it dry up
like a raisin in the sun?
Or fester like a sore—
And then run?
Does it stink like rotten meat?
Or crust and sugar over
like a syrupy sweet?

Maybe it just sags
like a heavy load

Or does it explode?

—*Langston Hughes*

busy. He didn't hand in one important assignment because he found it confusing. And he stopped going to his study group after the first meeting because . . . well, he wasn't quite sure why. As the semester progressed, Jerome's anxiety about the final exam grew. The night before, he stayed up late cramming, then went to the exam exhausted. During the test, his mind went blank.

Haven't you, too, made choices that worked against your goals and dreams . . . against your very image of who you are and who you want to become? Haven't we all! We take our eyes off the path for just a moment, and some invisible force comes along and bumps us off course. By the time we realize what's happened—if, in fact, we ever do—we can be miles off course and feeling miserable.

What's going on around here, anyway?

Unconscious forces

One of the great psychological discoveries of this century is the existence and power of unconscious forces in our lives. We now know that experiences from our past—perhaps all the way back to our birth—linger in our unconscious minds long after our conscious minds have forgotten them. As a result, we're being influenced in our daily choices by old experiences we don't even recall.

Experiments by Dr. Wilder Penfield of the Montreal Neurological Institute offer evidence that our brains may record nearly every experience we have ever had. Dr. Penfield performed brain surgery on patients who had had local anesthesia but were otherwise fully awake. During the operation, he stimulated brain cells using a weak electric current. At that moment his patients reported reexperiencing long-forgotten events in vivid detail.

Further research by Joseph LeDoux, a neuroscientist at the Center for Neural Science at New York University, suggests that the part of our brain called the amygdala stores emotionally charged but now unconscious memories. The amygdala, like a nervous watchman, examines our every experience and compares it to what happened to us in the past. When a key feature of a present event is similar to one from the past, it declares a match. Then, *without our conscious knowledge,* the alarmed amygdala hijacks our rational thought processes and demands that we respond to the present event as we learned to respond to the similar past event. The problem is, the outdated response is often totally inappropriate in our present situation. By the time the amygdala loosens its grip on our decision-making power, we may have made some very bad choices.

If many of the forces that get us off course are unconscious, how can we spot them doing their devious work in our lives? By analogy, the answer appears in a fascinating discovery in astronomy. Years ago, astronomers developed a mathematical formula to predict the orbit of any planet around the sun. Yet one planet, Uranus, failed to follow its predicted orbit. Astronomers were baffled as to why Uranus was "off course" until the French astronomer Leverrier proposed an ingenious explanation: The gravitational pull of an invisible planet was get-

We know from surgical experiences that electrical stimulation delivered to the temporal area of the brain elicits images of events that occurred in the patient's past. This is confirmation that such memories are "stored," but in most instances they cannot be voluntarily recollected. Thus, all of us "know" more than we are aware that we know.

Richard Restak, M.D.

In the entire history of science, it is hard to find a discovery of comparable consequence to the discovery of the power of unconscious belief as a gateway—or an obstacle—to the hidden mind, and its untapped potentialities.

Willis Harman

ting Uranus off course. Sure enough, when stronger telescopes were invented, the planet Neptune was discovered, and Leverrier was proven correct.

Like planets, we all have invisible Neptunes tugging at us every day. For us, these invisible forces are not in outer space; they exist in inner space, in our unconscious minds. As with Uranus, the first clue to spotting the existence of these unconscious forces is recognizing that we are off course. So, be candid. Where are you off course in your life? What goals and dreams are you moving away from instead of toward? Once you recognize where you are off course today, you can begin making the necessary course corrections that will get you where you want to be tomorrow.

I learned that I could not look to my exterior self to do anything for me. If I was going to accomplish anything in life I had to start from within.

Oprah Winfrey

Journal Entry 19

In this activity, you will recall times in your life when you were off course and you took constructive actions to get back on course. Remember, everyone gets off course at times, but only those who realize it can make positive course corrections.

1. **Write about a time when you made a positive course correction in your life.** A positive course correction changes for the better the direction in which you're headed. Examples include ending an unhealthy relationship, entering college, changing careers, stopping an addiction, choosing to be more assertive, or changing a negative belief you held about yourself, other people, or the world.

   Develop your journal entry by asking and answering questions such as the following:

   • What was I doing that was off course?

   • How did I become aware that I was off course?

   • What course corrections did I consider and which did I choose?

   • What challenges did I face in trying to make this change?

   • What benefits did I experience as a result of my change?

   • If I hadn't made this change, how would my life be different today?

2. **Write about a second time when you made a positive course correction in your life.** Develop your response using the questions you used in Step 1.

See if recalling these two positive events not only heightens your awareness of making course corrections but also raises your self-confidence in your ability to change your life's direction when necessary.

Relax, think, write.

©1990 BY SAM GROSS

Identifying Your Scripts

FOCUS QUESTIONS What habit patterns in your life get you off course? How did these habit patterns develop?

O nce you realize you're off course, you need to figure out how to get back on course. Unfortunately, the forces pulling us off course are often just as invisible to us as the planet Neptune was to Leverrier and his fellow observers of outer space.

What lies behind us and what lies before us are tiny matters compared to what lies within us.

Oliver Wendel Holmes

As observers of inner space, psychologists seek to identify what they can't actually see: the internal forces that divert human potential into human misery. In various psychological theories, these unconscious inner forces have been called names such as ego defenses, conditioned responses, programs, mental tapes, blind spots, schemas, and lifetraps.

The term we'll use to describe our internal forces was coined by psychologist Eric Berne: **Scripts.** In the world of theater, a script tells an actor what words, actions, and emotions to perform on stage. When the actor gets a cue from others in the play, he doesn't make a choice about his response. He simply responds as his script directs. Performance after performance, he reacts the same way to the same cues.

Responding automatically from a dramatic script is one sure way to succeed as an actor. However, responding automatically from a *life* Script is one sure way to struggle as a human being.

Anatomy of a Script

A psychological script is a person's ongoing program for his life drama which dictates where he is going with his life and how he is to get there. It is a drama he compulsively acts out, though his awareness of it may be vague.

Muriel James and
Dorothy Jongeward

Scripts are composed of two parts. Closest to the surface of our consciousness reside the directions for how we are to think, feel, and behave. **Thought patterns** include habitual self-talk such as *I'm too busy, I'm good at math, I always screw up, I can't write.* **Emotional patterns** include habitual feelings such as anger, excitement, anxiety, sadness, or joy. **Behavior patterns** include habitual actions such as smoking cigarettes, always arriving on time, never asking for help, exercising regularly. When people know us well, they can often predict what we will say, feel, or do in a given situation. This ability reveals their recognition of our patterns.

Deeper in our unconscious lies the second part of our Scripts, our **core beliefs.** Early in life, we form core beliefs about the world (e.g., *The world is safe* or *The world is dangerous*), about other people (e.g., *People can be trusted* or *People can't be trusted*), and about ourselves (e.g., *I'm worthy* or *I'm unworthy*). Though we're seldom aware of our core beliefs, these unconscious judgments dictate what we consistently think, feel, and do.

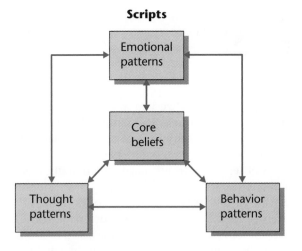

Scripts

How we wrote our Scripts

The grooves of mindlessness run deep. We know our scripts by heart.

Ellen J. Langer

Though no one knows exactly how we wrote our life Scripts as children, reasonable explanations exist. One factor seems to be **how others responded to us.** Imagine this scene: You're two years old. You're feeling lonely and hungry, and you begin crying. Your mother hurries in to pick you up. "There, there," she croons. "It's all right." She hugs you, feeds you, sings to you. You fall asleep full and content. If this happens often enough, what do you suppose you'd decide about the world, about other people, about yourself? You'd likely invent core beliefs such as *The world is kind, People will help me, I am lovable.* In turn, these beliefs would dictate your thoughts, emotions, and behaviors. With positive beliefs such as these at the core of your Scripts, very likely you'd develop optimistic thought patterns (e.g., *If I ask, I'll get help.*), positive emotional patterns (e.g., joy and harmony), and empowering behavior patterns (e.g., asking for what you want).

Now imagine the same childhood scene with a different response. You cry but no one comes. You scream louder, but still no one comes. Finally you abandon hope that anyone will respond. Imagine also that your being ignored happens often. You'd probably develop core beliefs such as *The world doesn't care about me, People won't help me, I'm not important.* You could very well develop pessimistic thought patterns (e.g., *I'm totally alone.*), negative emotional patterns (e.g., anxiety and anger), and passive behavior patterns (e.g., not asking for what you want).

Now, imagine this same scene one more time. As you're crying for attention and food, an adult storms into your room, screams "Shut up!" and slaps your face. A few experiences like this may cause core beliefs such as *The world is a dangerous and painful place, People will hurt me, I'm unlovable!* And so you may develop defensive thought patterns (e.g., *People are out to get me.*), defensive emotional patterns (e.g., fear and rage), and defensive behavior patterns (e.g., immediately fighting or fleeing at the first sign of danger).

A second factor in shaping our Scripts is **what significant adults said to us.** What did they say about the world: Is it safe or dangerous? What did they say about other people: Can they be trusted or not? And, perhaps most important, what did important adults say about us? Psychologists have a term for qualities that tell us how we "are" or "should be": **attributions.** Common attributions include *be good, be quiet, be rebellious, be devoted, be helpful, be athletic, be sexy, be tough, be independent, be dependent, be invisible, be dominant, be competitive, be smart, be confident.*

Psychologists also have a term for the qualities that tell us what we "are not" or "should not be": **injunctions.** Common injunctions include *don't be yourself, don't talk back, don't feel, don't think, don't be intimate, don't say no, don't say yes, don't get angry, don't trust, don't love yourself, don't be happy, don't be weak, don't believe in yourself, don't exist.*

A third way we write our Scripts is by **observing the behavior of significant adults.** Children notice, *What did my role models do? If it's right for them, it's right for me.* When children play, we see them trying on adult behaviors, conversations, and emotions. It doesn't take a detective to figure out where they learned them.

One more potential contributor to Scripts is **physical, mental, and emotional wounds.** In fact, such wounds may write the most self-defeating

Parents, deliberately or unaware, teach their children from birth how to behave, think, feel, and perceive. Liberation from these influences is no easy matter.
Eric Berne

The hearts of small children are delicate organs. A cruel beginning in this world can twist them into curious shapes. The heart of a hurt child can shrink so that forever afterward it is hard and pitted as the seed of a peach.

Carson McCullers

Scripts of all. A child who is mocked when she offers her opinion may avoid forever the shame of speaking her mind. A child told to shut up when he's crying may later totally shut down his emotions. A child abused or beaten when she reaches out for love may decide that all love hurts.

In these ways we develop our unique Scripts comprised of core beliefs and resulting patterns. At critical choice points we unconsciously refer to our Scripts for guidance: *What similar experience have I had in the past? What actions, thoughts, or emotions did I choose back then? Did that choice increase or decrease my pain or pleasure? Oh, look, here's a response that seemed to work back then. I'll use it again now.*

The good news about our unconscious Scripts is that their intention is always positive—always to minimize our pain, always to maximize our pleasure. Many of us made it through the mental, emotional, and physical pain of growing up with the guidance of our childhood Scripts. Some of us would not have survived without them.

But, as you might guess, there is bad news as well: When we make unconscious, Script-guided choices as adults, we often get off course. That's because the Scripts we developed in childhood seldom apply to the situations of our present lives. Imagine an actor in a Broadway show who can't stop playing a role from his grade school play! Many of us do the equivalent of this in our daily lives.

Self-defeating patterns

We first make our habits, and then our habits make us.

John Dryden

Though our unconscious Scripts are invisible, we can often see their influence in the patterns of our lives. Put a check next to any of the following patterns of thought, emotion, and behavior that are often true of you. These habits may reveal the presence of outdated Scripts that get you off course.

- ☐ 1. I act "nice" even when I don't feel like it.
- ☐ 2. I wonder if I'm "college material."
- ☐ 3. I am often angry.
- ☐ 4. I watch a lot of television.
- ☐ 5. I believe that most people don't like me.
- ☐ 6. I often turn in college assignments late.
- ☐ 7. I abuse others physically or emotionally when things don't go my way.
- ☐ 8. I worry excessively about doing things perfectly.
- ☐ 9. I think most of my classmates are smarter than I am.
- ☐ 10. I quit on goals or dreams that are important to me.
- ☐ 11. I allow a person in my life to treat me badly.
- ☐ 12. I think I don't deserve success as much as other people do.

□ 13. I miss more college classes than I should.

□ 14. I criticize myself constantly.

□ 15. I wait until the last minute to do important college assignments.

□ 16. I don't participate in class discussions.

Habit seldom loves problems, and almost never seizes opportunities.

Walter McQuade
and Ann Aikman

□ 17. I often break commitments.

□ 18. I am addicted to something (e.g., caffeine, alcohol, cigarettes, soft drinks, drugs).

□ 19. I experience severe test anxiety.

□ 20. I feel uncomfortable about asking for help.

□ 21. I hide my emotions.

□ 22. I often side-talk or daydream in my college classes.

□ 23. I seldom do my best work on college assignments.

□ 24. I am often sad or depressed.

□ 25. I get very nervous when I speak to a group.

□ 26. I keep promising to study more in college, but I don't.

□ 27. I get my feelings hurt easily.

It is not true that life is one damn thing after another— it's one damn thing over and over.

Edna St. Vincent Millay,
American Poet

□ 28. I am a loner.

□ 29. I often feel guilty about mistakes I have made.

□ 30. I am very critical of other people.

□ 31. I . . . _____

□ 32. I . . . _____

Are you aware of any other patterns—mental, emotional, or behavioral—that belong to you? If so, add them to the list above.

Journal Entry 20

In this activity, you will explore self-defeating patterns in your life that may reveal unconscious Scripts. You're about to embark on an exciting journey into your inner world! There you can discover—and later revise—the invisible forces that have gotten you off course from your goals and dreams.

1. **Write about one of your self-defeating *thought* patterns.** Choose a thought you checked on the list in the journal article or identify a thought that isn't on the list but which you have often. Remember to develop your journal paragraphs by anticipating questions that someone reading it might have about this thought pattern. (Even you might have questions when you read your journal ten years from now.) For example,

- What exactly do you think when caught in this self-defeating pattern?
- When did this pattern start?
- What may have caused it?
- What negative impact has it had on your life?

One student began by writing . . .

One of my self-defeating thought patterns is that I often wonder if I am smart enough to be successful in college. I especially think this before and after exams. For example, last Thursday I . . .

2. **Repeat Step 1 for one of your self-defeating *emotional* patterns.** Once again, choose an emotional pattern from the list in the journal article, or identify one that isn't on the list but which you often feel. *One of my self-defeating emotional patterns is that I often feel . . .*

3. **Repeat Step 1 for one of your self-defeating *behavior* patterns.** Choose one from the list in the journal article, or identify a habitual behavior that is not on the list. *One of my self-defeating behavior patterns is that I often . . .*

Relaxation is essential for getting in touch with the storehouse of experiences, thoughts, and feelings hidden away in your unconscious mind. You may therefore wish to recommit now to relaxing fully before writing each journal entry.

Relax, think, write.

The battles that count aren't the ones for gold medals. The struggles within yourself—the invisible battles inside all of us—that's where it's at.
Jessie Owens, Winner of four gold medals at the 1936 Olympics

Rewriting Your Outdated Scripts

FOCUS QUESTION How can you discover and revise the self-defeating patterns that keep you from achieving your full potential?

Once in a writing class, I was explaining how to organize an essay when a student named Diana told me she didn't understand. She asked if I'd write an explanation on the blackboard.

Earlier in the class, we'd been talking about the differences between left-brain and right-brain thinking. We'd discussed how the left side of our brain deals with logical, organized information, while the right side deals with more creative, intuitive concepts. "Sure," I said to Diana, "I hear your left brain crying out for some order. Let's see if I can help."

We don't see things as they are, we see them as we are.
Anais Nin

As I turned to write on the blackboard, she screamed, "You have no right to talk to me that way!"

I was stunned. I took a deep breath to compose myself. "Maybe we could talk about this after class," I said.

The impact of outdated beliefs

Diana and I did talk, and I learned that she was in her late thirties, a single mother of an eight-year-old daughter. Our conversation wandered for a while; then Diana mentioned that she had always disliked school. In grade school, she had consistently gotten low grades. One day, when Diana was about twelve, she overheard her father and mother talking. "I don't know what we're going to do with Diana," her father said. "She's the *half-brain* of the family."

Diana accepted as a fact other people's belief that she couldn't think or learn. She developed patterns of thoughts, emotions, and behaviors that supported this belief. She decided that school was a waste of time (thought), she exploded when anyone questioned her about schoolwork (emotion), and she was often absent (behavior). Diana barely graduated from high school, then got a menial job that bored her.

For nearly twenty years, Diana heard her Inner Critic (sounding much like her father) telling her something was wrong with her brain. Finally, another inner voice began to whisper, *Maybe—just maybe* . . . One day she took a big risk and enrolled in college.

"So what happens?" she said to me. "I get a teacher who calls me a *half-brain*! I ought to just quit college."

I used my best active listening skills: I listened to understand, not to respond. I reflected both her thoughts and her anger. I asked her to clarify and expand. I allowed long periods of silence.

Finally, her emotional storm subsided. She took a deep breath and sat back.

I waited a few moments. "Diana, I know you think I called you a 'half-brain.' But what I actually said was *left* brain. Remember we had been talking in class about the difference between left-brain and right-brain thinking? I was talking about that."

"But I *heard* you!"

We are what we think. All that we are arises With our thoughts. With our thought, We make the world.
The Buddha

"I know that's what you *heard*. But that isn't what I *said*. I've read two of your essays, and I know your brain works just fine. What really matters, though, is what *you* think! You need to believe in your own intelligence. Otherwise, you'll always be ready to hear people accuse you of being a 'half-brain' no matter what they really said."

Diana had come within an inch of dropping out of college, of abandoning her dreams of a college degree. And all because of her childhood Script.

Doing the rewrite

Until we revise our limiting Scripts, we're less likely to achieve some of our most cherished goals and dreams. That's why realizing we're off course can be a blessing in disguise. By identifying the self-defeating patterns of thought, emotion, and behavior that got us off course, we may be able to discover and revise the underlying core beliefs that are sabotaging our success.

Diana stuck it out and passed English 101. She persevered and graduated with an Associate of Arts degree in early childhood education. Today she teaches nursery school and is talking about going back to finish her bachelor's degree. Like most of us, she'll probably be in a tug of war with her Scripts for the rest of her life. But now, at least, she knows that she, and not her Scripts, can be in charge of making her choices.

One of the great discoveries about the human condition is this: We are not stuck with our Scripts. We can re-create ourselves. By revising our outdated Scripts, we can get back on course and dramatically change the outcomes of our lives for the better.

Journal Entry 21

In this activity, you will practice revising your Scripts. By doing so, you'll begin taking greater control of your life.

1. **Write a dialogue with your Inner Guide that will help you revise your Scripts.**

In this dialogue, have your Inner Guide ask you the ten questions below. After answering each question, let your Inner Guide use the active listening skills that will help you dive deep:

1. **Silence**
2. **Reflection** (of your thoughts and feelings)
3. **Expansion** (by asking for examples, evidence, and experience)
4. **Clarification** (by asking for an explanation)

Ten questions from your Inner Guide:

1. In what life role are you off course?
2. What self-defeating **thought patterns** may have contributed to this situation?
3. What different thoughts could you choose to get back on course to your goal?
4. What self-defeating **emotional patterns** may have contributed to this situation?

5. What different emotions could you choose to get back on course to your goal?

6. What self-defeating **behavior patterns** (your own) may have contributed to this situation?

7. What different behaviors could you choose to get back on course to your goal?

8. What limiting **core beliefs** (about the world, other people, or yourself) may have led you to adopt the self-defeating patterns that we've been discussing?

9. What different beliefs could you choose to get back on course to your goal?

10. As a result of what you've learned here, what new behaviors, thoughts, emotions, or core beliefs will you adopt?

A sample of a possible dialogue appears below.

Relax, think, write.

Sample dialogue with your Inner Guide

IG: In what role are you off course? [Question 1]

Me: I'm not too happy with what's going on in my role as a friend.

IG: Would you say more about that? [Expansion]

Me: My goal is to create a better relationship with Barry. But that's not happening. In fact, I haven't talked to him in weeks.

IG: What self-defeating **thought patterns** may have contributed to this situation? [Question 2]

Me: When I think about calling him, I tell myself, "Hey, I almost always call him. He hardly ever calls me. When I call, he often says he was just about to call me, but I don't believe him anymore. It would be nice if he'd call me for a change. Also, when he tells me he's going to call me back, he seldom does."

IG: And when he doesn't call, what do you tell yourself? [Expansion]

Me: That he's not a very good friend if I have to do all of the calling.

IG: What different thoughts could you choose to get back on course to your goal of having a better relationship with Barry? [Question 3]

Me: I could remind myself that he has a lot of problems with his bad back. And he has a full-time job now. I could also remind myself that whenever we do get together we have a good time, and I know that he considers me one of his best friends. I guess he's just going through a difficult time right now.

IG: So you can see many reasons why Barry might not be calling you as often as you'd like. Is that what you're saying? [Reflection]

Me: Exactly.

IG: What self-defeating **emotional pattern** may have contributed to this situation? [Question 4]

Me: When I don't hear from him for a while, I start wondering if he's a real friend. Then I get angry.

IG: So you feel angry with Barry for not keeping in closer touch. Is there anything else that you're feeling? [Reflection and Expansion]

Me: Sadness. Barry and I have been friends for more than ten years. I miss hanging out with him the way we used to.

IG: Sounds like you're feeling hurt about that loss. [Reflection]

Me: Yes.

IG: That's certainly understandable. What different emotion could you choose to get back on course to your goal? [Question 5]

Me: I guess I could just be happy about the time we do spend together. I know he's not really avoiding me on purpose. He's just got a lot to deal with in his life right now.

IG: What self-defeating **behavior patterns** (your own) may have contributed to this situation? [Question 6]

Me: Well, I have to admit that I haven't called him for quite a while.

IG: Are there any other behaviors you can think of? [Expansion]

Me: I haven't tried to set up time to spend with him, either.

IG: What different behaviors could you choose to get back on course to your goal? [Question 7]

Me: I could call him and suggest that we get together. I could also ask him how his back is doing. I know he's been having a lot of pain since his accident.

IG: What limiting **core beliefs** (about the world, other people, or yourself) may have led you to adopt the self-defeating patterns that we've been discussing? [Question 8]

Me: I believe that friends are going to abandon me. I think they're not going to really be there for me when I need them. Sometimes I wait for other people to call me just so I can get proof they're still my friends.

IG: What different core belief could you choose to get back on course to your goal? [Question 9]

Me: I guess it would help to believe that my good friends are going to be there for me. If they're not, then they weren't my friends, anyway.

IG: That sounds like a wise choice. As a result of what you've learned here, what new behaviors, thoughts, emotions or core beliefs will you commit to? [Question 10]

Me: I'll commit to calling Barry this week to see how he is. I'll also watch my emotional patterns, and if I start to get angry at him, I'll just remind myself about all the problems he has right now. I also want to look at this belief that my friends are going to abandon me. It feels real, but the friends I have now are very loyal. Oh, I just realized that I've never told Barry any of this. I think I'll also tell him how much I value him as a friend and how I feel when he doesn't call.

Strange Choices

"Do your students make really strange choices?" **Professor Assante** asked.

The other teachers looked up from their lunches. "What do you mean?" one asked.

"At the beginning of each class, I give short quizzes that count 50 percent of the final grade," **Professor Assante** replied. "One of my students comes late to every class, even though I keep telling her there's no way she can pass the course if she keeps missing the quizzes. But she keeps coming late! What is she thinking?"

"That's nothing," **Professor Buckley** said. "I've got this really bright student who comes to every class and offers perceptive comments during discussions. But the semester is almost over, and he still hasn't turned in any assignments. At this point, he's way too far behind to pass. Now that's what I call a strange choice."

"You think that's strange," **Professor Chen** said, "I'm teaching composition in the computer lab. Last week I sat down next to a woman who's working on her essay, and I suggested a way she could improve her introduction. What did she do? She stormed out of the room and slammed the door."

Professor Donnely chimed in. "Well, I can top all of you. In the third week of the semester, a student came to my office. 'Where have you been?' he asked. I said, 'Do I know you?' 'I'm in your math class,' he said. 'I've never seen you before in my life,' I told him. 'Well,' he responded, "I've been to every class, but no one ever shows up.' Then I remembered—after the first class we changed rooms. This poor soul has been sitting in an empty classroom for three weeks without asking anyone why no one else is there!"

"How about this!" **Professor Egret** said. "I had a student last semester with a 'B' average going into the final two weeks. Then he disappeared. This semester, I ran into him in the hall, and I asked him what happened. 'Oh,' he said, 'I got burned out and stopped going to all of my classes.' 'But you only had two more weeks to go. You threw away thirteen weeks' effort,' I said. You know what he did? He shrugged his shoulders and walked away. I wanted to shake him and say, 'What is wrong with you?'"

Professor Fanning said, "Talk about strange choices. I had a panel of four guest speakers in class last week when a student asked them if they'd ever had problems with procrastination. While the panelists were deciding who was going to answer the question, I said, 'Maybe they'd rather answer you later.' Okay, it was weak humor, but most of the class chuckled, and then one panelist answered the question. The next day I got a call from the dean. Seems my student told him I'd mocked her in front of the whole class, and now she's going to drop out of college. I happened to videotape the class, so

I asked her if she'd be willing to watch the tape. Later she admitted I hadn't said what she thought I had, but she still dropped out of school."

Listed below are each of the professors' students. Rank them in order of who you think *demonstrated the most self-sabotaging Scripts*. Give a different score to each student. Be prepared to explain your answer.

Most self-sabotaging ← 1 2 3 4 5 6 → Least self-sabotaging

_____ **Professor Assante's student**   _____ **Professor Donnely's student**

_____ **Professor Buckley's student**   _____ **Professor Egret's student**

_____ **Professor Chen's student**   _____ **Professor Fanning's student**

DIVING DEEPER: **For the student you ranked number 1 (most self-sabotaging), what limiting belief do you think this student may hold about him/herself, other people, or the world? How do you think this student's Script may have come into being?**

Self-Awareness at Work

Looking inward is the first place we need to look to find our own direction, not the last.

Clarke G. Carney and Cinda Field Wells in *Career Planning*

Many people spend more time choosing a video than choosing their careers. As a result, the unlucky ones later dread going to work, year after year after year. Creators, by contrast, devote time and effort to one of life's most important Quadrant II activities: conscious career planning. As a result, many of them actually like going to work.

Conscious career planning requires self-awareness. How else can you find a match between you and the thousands of career possibilities open to you? A place to start your planning is taking an inventory of your hard skills. Hard skills are the special-knowledge skills that you've learned to do throughout your life. They include such abilities as swimming, writing, programming computers, playing racquetball, solving mathematics problems, building a house, creating a budget, giving a speech, drawing blood, writing a business plan, designing a park, cooking lasagna, backpacking, playing chess, and reading. You probably learned many of your hard skills from a teacher, coach, or mentor. These skills can typically be videotaped, and they tend to be applicable only in limited and specific situations; for example, writing a business plan isn't a skill of much value when you're playing racquetball. To begin your inventory of hard skills, ask yourself, "What talents have gotten me compliments, recognition, or awards? In which school courses have I received good grades? When did I feel fully alive, extremely capable, or very smart, and what skills was I using at the time?" Finding a match between your hard skills and the demands of a career greatly improves the chances of a good fit.

Continue your self-assessment with an inventory of your soft skills. Soft skills are the ones you have developed to cope with life. They include the ones you're exploring in this book: seeing yourself as a Creator, motivating yourself, being industrious, developing relationships, being flexible, seeing lessons from every experience, managing your emotions, and feeling confident. Many of these soft skills you learned unconsciously as you faced life's challenges. Usually, they are attitudes and beliefs, so they can't be videotaped. They are as invisible as oxygen but just as important to the quality of your life. Unlike hard skills, they tend to be transferable to many situations; for example, feeling confident is valuable in a job interview, when asking for a raise, and in thousands of other situations in which you might find yourself. To create an inventory of your skills, ask yourself, "What personal qualities have earned me compliments? What accomplishments am I proud of and what inner qualities helped me achieve them?" Finding a match between your soft skills and the demands of a career further increases your chances of a good match.

To create a third component of your self-assessment, identify your personal preferences. To do so, go to your college's career center and take one of the well-known interest inventories: the *Strong Interest Inventories* (SII), the *Self-Directed Search* (SDS) or the *Myers-Briggs Type Indicator*® (MBTI®) instrument. These tools help you discover personal preferences and suggest possible college majors and career choices that will match your interests. An additional tool, the *Holland Code*, places you in one of six personality types and suggests possible careers for each. Which of the following personality types sounds most like you?

1. **Realistic** personalities prefer activities involving objects, tools, and machines. Possible Careers: mechanic, electrician, computer repair, civil engineer, forester, industrial arts teacher, dental technician, farmer, carpenter

2. **Investigative** personalities prefer activities involving abstract problem solving and the exploration of physical, biological, and cultural phenomena for the purpose of understanding and controlling them. Possible Careers: chemist, economist, detective, computer analyst, doctor, astronomer, mathematician

3. **Artistic** personalities prefer activities involving self-expression, using words, ideas, or materials to create art forms or new concepts.

Possible Careers: writer, advertising manager, public relations specialist, artist, musician, graphic designer, interior decorator, inventor

4. **Social** personalities prefer activities involving interaction with other people to inform, train, develop, help, or enlighten them. Possible Careers: nurse, massage therapist, teacher, counselor, social worker, day-care provider, physical therapist

5. **Enterprising** personalities prefer activities involving the persuasion and management of others to attain organizational goals or economic gain. Possible Careers: salesperson, television newscaster, bank manager, lawyer, travel agent, personnel manager, entrepreneur

6. **Conventional** personalities prefer activities involving the application of data to bring order out of confusion and develop a prescribed plan. Possible Careers: accountant, computer operator, secretary, credit manager, financial planner

The research of Dr. John Holland, creator of the Holland Code, shows that people tend to be satisfied in careers that are compatible with their personality type, and people are less satisfied when the match isn't there. Becoming aware of your interest preferences and personality type improves your chances of finding a satisfying career match.

Another important area of self-knowledge is your self-sabotaging Scripts. What beliefs do you hold that might keep you from pursuing or succeeding in your chosen career? For example, if one of your Scripts is to distrust other people, then it will be difficult for you to develop the support systems that will enhance your success. This awareness allows you to make a conscious choice about whether or not to revise the Script.

Self-awareness in the workplace will also help you notice when your habits get you off course. For example, you'll stop arriving at meetings late; instead, you'll arrive a few minutes early. You'll stop interrupting when others are talking; instead, you'll listen actively. You'll stop acting as if you know all the answers; instead, you'll ask others for their opinions. In short, you'll become conscious of converting your destructive behavior into constructive behavior. If you've ever had bosses or co-workers who demonstrate any of these negative behaviors, you'll know how you wished they would become conscious of what they were doing and change.

To summarize, cultivating your self-awareness will help you choose a career that you will enjoy and bring out the behaviors, beliefs, and attitudes that will help you to excel in the workplace.

Believing in Yourself: **Write Your Own Rules**

FOCUS QUESTIONS   What personal rules do you have that dictate the choices you make daily? Which of these rules will help you create high self-esteem?

Few things affect self-esteem more than our sense of personal power. When we feel like mere passengers, with no apparent choice in where we're going in life, self-esteem shrivels. When we feel like the pilots of our lives, with the power to choose wisely and reach our destinations, self-esteem grows.

I think you're going to be very surprised to discover that you may be living by rules of which you're not even aware.
Virginia Satir

Outdated Scripts can steal our sense of personal power and drag down our self-esteem. When these unconscious programs take over, we essentially turn over the controls of our lives to the scared and confused child of our past. Then we make those strange choices that push us far off course and leave us wondering, "How the heck did I get way over here?" If we want to reclaim our personal power and increase self-esteem, we need to choose wise rules to live by.

In his autobiography, *My American Journey*, Colin Powell, former chairman of the Joint Chiefs of Staff under President George Bush, shared some of the rules he has chosen to guide his life. They include *Have a vision. Share credit. Be kind.* Former first lady Eleanor Roosevelt chose these life rules: *Do whatever comes your way as well as you can. Think as little as possible about yourself; think as much as possible about other people. Since you get more joy out of giving joy to others, you should put a good deal of thought in the happiness that you are able to give.*

According to psychologist Virginia Satir, author of *The New Peoplemaking*, we are all living by rules; the important question is *Are we aware of our rules*? You'll want to become conscious of and revise any self-defeating rules that are holding you back. You'll want to identify and preserve any empowering rules that are keeping you on course. Finally, you'll want to write new rules that will support you in achieving even greater victories.

Three success rules

The most important thing is to have a code of life, to know how to live.
Hans Selye, M.D.

I have polled many college instructors, and they consistently identify three behaviors that their most successful students demonstrate. As you'll see, these rules apply just as well to creating great outcomes in other life roles such as your career and relationships. Consider, then, these three rules as the foundation of your personal code of conduct.

RULE 1: I SHOW UP.   Commit to attending every class from beginning to end. Someone once said that 90 percent of success is simply showing up. Makes sense, doesn't it? How can you be successful at something if you're not there? Studies show a direct correlation between attendance and grades (as one measure of success). At Baltimore City Community College, a study found that, on average, the more classes students missed, the lower their grades were, especially in introductory courses. If you can't get motivated to show up, maybe you need a new dream.

RULE 2: I DO MY BEST WORK.   Commit to doing your best work on all assignments, including turning them in on time. You'd be amazed at how many sloppy assignments instructors see. But it isn't just students who are guilty. A friend in business has shown me hundreds of job applications so sloppily prepared that they begged to be tossed in the trash. Doing your best work on assignments is a rule that will propel you to success in all that you do.

RULE 3: I PARTICIPATE ACTIVELY.   College, like life, isn't a spectator sport. Commit to getting involved. Come to class prepared. Listen attentively. Take notes. Think deeply about what's being said. Ask yourself how you can apply your course work to achieve your goals and dreams. Read ahead. Start a study group. Ask questions. Answer questions. If you participate at this high level of involvement, you couldn't keep yourself from learning even if you wanted to.

Some students resist adopting these three basic rules of success. They say, "But what if I get sick? What if my car breaks down on the way to class? What if . . . ?" I trust that by now you recognize the voice of the Inner Defender, the internal excuse maker.

Of course, something may happen to keep you from following your rules. You must then realize that each rule is simply your conscious *intention*. You *intend* to be at every class from beginning to end. You *intend* to do your very best work and turn assignments in on time. You *intend* to participate actively. However, you may need to break your own rules if something of a higher value (like your health) demands it. If you do miss a class for important reasons, you needn't let your Inner Critic judge you. Simply ignore its harsh judgments and attend your next class with a renewed commitment to live up to your personal rules.

Changing your habits

Exceptional students follow not only these three basic rules of success; they also add their own for college and life. By choosing personal rules, they commit to replacing their scripts with consciously chosen habits. Here are a few of my own life rules:

- I keep promises to myself and others.
- I seek feedback and make course corrections when appropriate.

> *People who lead a satisfying life, who are in tune with their past and with their future—in short, people whom we would call "happy"—are generally individuals who have lived their lives according to rules they themselves created.*
> Mihaly Csikszentmihalyi

> *I'll give you the Four Rules of Success:*
> *1. Decide what you want.*
> *2. Decide what you want to give up in order to get what you want.*
> *3. Associate with successful people.*
> *4. Plan your work and work your plan.*
> Blair Underwood, Actor

- I arrive on time.
- I do my very best work on all projects important to me.
- I play and create joy.
- I care for my body with exercise, healthy food, and good medical care.

What is hateful to you do not to your fellowman. That is the entire Law; all the rest is commentary.

The Talmud

Do I follow these rules every day of my life? Unfortunately, no. And when I don't, I soon see myself getting off course. Then I can re-elect to follow my self-chosen rules and avoid sabotaging the life I want to create.

Once we follow our own rules long enough, they're no longer simply rules. They become habits. And once our positive actions, thoughts, and feelings become habits, few obstacles can block the path to our success.

Journal Entry 22

I n this activity, you will write your own rules for success in college and in life. By following your own code of conduct, you will more likely stay on course toward your greatest dreams.

To focus your mind, ask yourself, "What do successful people do? What are their thoughts, attitudes, behaviors, and beliefs?"

Sow a thought, reap an act;
Sow an act, reap a habit;
Sow a habit, reap a character;
Sow a character, reap
a destiny.

Anonymous

1. **Title a clean journal page "MY PERSONAL RULES FOR SUCCESS IN COLLEGE AND IN LIFE." Below that, write a list of your own rules for achieving your goals in college.** List only those actions to which you're willing to commit. You might want to draw a frame around your rules to make it look like an official document.

Consider adopting the following as your first three rules:

1. I show up.
2. I do my very best work.
3. I participate actively.

2. **Write your thoughts and feelings about your personal rules.** As you write your response, consider answering questions such as the following:

- Which of my rules is the most important? Why?
- What experiences have I had that suggest the value of these rules?
- With which rules will I most easily cooperate? Why?
- Which rules will challenge me the most to keep? Why?

What if one of your rules was: I dive deep! How much would that rule improve your results in college and in life? Use the 4 E's—Examples, Experiences, Explanation, and Evidence—to dive deep in your writing.

Relax, think, write.

Especially in introductory college classes, you will be asked to memorize definitions, names, facts, and formulas. Some people have a knack for remembering such things. Fortunately for others, memory can be improved by employing a process. Before memorizing, we encode the information; during memorizing, we store it for later use; after memorizing, we attempt to retrieve what we have stored. By using the following strategies, you will find that recalling information will become easier.

Before Memorizing

1. Create a positive affirmation about memorizing. Many students hold negative beliefs about their ability to memorize. Create an affirming statement about your memory, such as, "I easily recall everything I memorize." Along with your personal affirmation, repeat this memory affirmation in order to reprogram your beliefs about your ability to memorize.

2. Choose to remember. You've used this strategy when you put your keys down and said to yourself, "Be sure to remember the keys are on the kitchen table." Likewise, tell yourself to remember what you're memorizing in college. Intention is powerful.

3. Post memory cards. Create cards with words, diagrams, formulas, or concepts you want to memorize. Post these cards where you'll see them often (mirror, refrigerator, and so on). Then go about your daily life. Over the next week or two, you will unconsciously absorb some or all of the information.

4. Plan more than one session. Research shows that memorizing over several short sessions rather than one long session aids recall. In other words, you'll probably remember more after six half-hour sessions than you will after one three-hour session.

5. Relax. Research also shows that *alpha* states, induced by relaxation, enhance memory. Before memorizing, do the progressive relaxation technique from Chapter 1, page 7, or one like it.

During Memorizing

6. Organize the information in a meaningful way. Which is easier to remember: Four random numbers (8, 9, 1, 2) or a date (1982)? Organizing the four unrelated numbers into a date allows your memory to store and recall them more easily. If the date is particularly meaningful (e.g., 1982 is the year your brother was born), it will be even easier to recall. Many of the strategies that follow are techniques for organizing information in a meaningful way.

7. Create associations. When you associate something new with something you already know, the new information is easier to recall. Suppose you want to remember the name of your new mathematics teacher, Professor Getty; you could associate his name with the Battle of Gettysburg that you studied in American history. You might even visualize him wearing a uniform and carrying a musket. Now you'll remember his name.

8. Use the loci technique. The loci technique is a variation of association. *Loci* is Latin for "place," so with this strategy, you associate a new item you want to memorize with a familiar place. Suppose you're studying parts of the brain and you need to remember the *amygdala*. Think of a familiar place, like your living room. Picture your television turned to your favorite talk show and the host introducing a woman wearing a bright red dress. The host is saying, "Please welcome Amy G. Dala." Review this mental image several times a day for two or three days. When you need to recall the *amygdala*, mentally visit your living room, turn on the television, and there's Amy G.

Dala waiting to be introduced. You can now associate other parts of the brain with additional items in your living room. Say, isn't that a neo-cortex sitting on your couch?

9. Invent word acronyms. A word acronym uses the first letter of a group of words to create a new word. If you want to memorize the names of the Great Lakes, you can use the acronym HOMES: Huron, Ontario, Michigan, Erie, Superior. In this book, you encountered the DAPPS Rule, an acronym that helps you remember the important features of a goal: Dated, Achievable, Personal, Positive, Specific. To create an acronym, simply take the first letters of the words you want to recall and rearrange them to spell a real (HOMES) or made-up (DAPPS) word.

10. Invent sentence acronyms. A sentence acronym uses the first letters of a group of words and creates a sentence. For example, music students recall the notes on the lines of a musical staff (E-G-B-D-F) by the sentence "Every Good Boy Does Fine." If you wanted to memorize the four qualities of effective visualizing (Relax, use Present tense verbs, use all five Senses, include your Feelings), you could invent the acronym sentence "Real People Seek Freedom."

11. Assign a number. When memorizing a specific number of items, identify how many there are. This number will help you know when you have forgotten one or more. For example, in your journal entry directions, you learned about the 4 E's (Examples, Experiences, Explanations, and Evidence) as ways to dive deeper as you write. Remembering that there are *four* E's (not three or five) helps you realize if you've forgotten any of them.

12. Visualize. Suppose you're trying to memorize the bones in a human hand. Look at a picture of a hand in your textbook; then close your eyes and visualize the same picture in your mind,

including the name of each bone. Go back and forth between the picture in the book and the picture in your mind until they are identical.

13. Create a concept map. A concept map shows the connections between key elements in a complex idea. It combines key advantages of visualizing and associating. Creating concept maps helps memorizing by combining the left brain's verbal and analytical skills with the right brain's spatial and creative abilities. (See example on page 69.)

14. Recite. Do you ever have trouble recalling someone's name two minutes after being introduced? Try saying the person's name immediately after being introduced. "It's nice to meet you, *Bob.*" Say his name again a few moments later. "Where do you live, *Bob*?" Reciting the name aloud firmly implants it in your memory. Try the same recitation strategy when memorizing course material.

15. Create and listen to audiotapes. Tape-record questions, leave a 10- to 15-second silence, then record the answer. The pause gives you time to fill in the answer as you listen to the tape. ("Three tools for improved self-management are . . . 15-second pause . . . a monthly planner, daily actions list, and tracking form.") You can listen to the tapes while commuting or waiting, helping you make the most of your time each day. Self-made study tapes are especially helpful for auditory learners, people who remember best what they hear.

16. Use several senses. Studies reveal that we recall information better when several senses are engaged during the learning process. Look at the item to be remembered (visual). Recite it aloud (auditory). Write it (kinesthetic).

After Memorizing

17. Repeat, Repeat, Repeat. When trying to remember a new phone number, you probably say it over and over until it sticks in your memory. So you already know the importance of *repetition* in creating a strong memory. Whatever you want to memorize, repeat it over and over to yourself.

18. Revisit visualizations. Throughout your day, recall the image (such as the bones of a human hand) that you committed to memory. Return to the original picture to fill in missing information.

19. Have others quiz you. Give friends or study group members the information you have memorized and have them test your recall. Have them ask the questions in random order so you don't become dependent on the sequence of questions for remembering the answers.

20. Go to sleep. Review what you want to memorize right before going to bed. Your brain will continue to process the information while you sleep, helping you remember it better. A quick review in the morning will solidify what you memorized the night before.

Memorizing Exercise

Suppose you were asked to memorize all of the memory strategies you just read about. How would you go about it? Fully describe your methods.

7 Adopting Lifelong Learning

As a Creator, I take personal responsibility for learning all of the information, skills, and beliefs necessary to achieve my goals and dreams.

I learn valuable lessons from every experience I have.

SUCCESSFUL STUDENTS . . .	STRUGGLING STUDENTS . . .
discover their preferred learning style, applying the effective and joyful process they used as young children to learn valuable new information and skills.	often experience frustration, boredom, or resistance when given the opportunity to learn new information or skills.
learn to make course corrections, giving them the flexibility to revise outdated behaviors or beliefs that limit their effectiveness.	hang on to ineffective behaviors or beliefs even when these get them off course.
develop wisdom from the University of Life, using problems, obstacles, mistakes, failures, and even catastrophes as valuable learning experiences.	grapple with one adversity after another without discovering the valuable life lessons they have to teach.

Discovering Your Preferred Learning Style

FOCUS QUESTIONS What is your preferred way of learning? What can you do to compensate when your instructor doesn't teach to your preferred learning style?

Learning . . . should be a joy and full of excitement. It is life's greatest adventure; it is an illustrated excursion into the mind of noble and learned men, not a conducted tour through a jail.

Taylor Caldwell

Staying on course to our goals and dreams requires us to learn so much: facts, theories, skills, and, hopefully, a generous serving of wisdom. But that shouldn't be a problem. After all, as infants we were like little learning machines. Every day was shaped by curiosity and inquiry, by gathering and sorting, by discovery and insight. Each evening found us transformed by our day's learning. Each new morning found us eager to renew our quest.

However, somewhere on life's journey, the joy of learning flickered and, for too many, went out. Take a look at a college class through your instructors' eyes: Students slouch in back rows, postures challenging: "Go ahead . . . try to teach me." Other students sit up front, pens poised, body language brightly chirping: "Go ahead . . . tell me everything I have to know for the test." But neither defiance nor compliance gets these students a meaningful education. Both approaches are merely adaptations made by learners whose spirits of personal inquiry have been wounded.

The natural learning process

The important thing is not to stop questioning. . . . Never lose a holy curiosity.

Albert Einstein

Today we can maximize our learning by returning to the natural learning process, three steps of discovery we employed so well as children.

Step 1. Ask Motivating Questions. Exceptional learners retain the curiosity of a child. They are continually asking questions. They ask questions in nearly every class. They schedule conferences with teachers and ask additional questions. Before reading a textbook, they turn chapter headings into questions, then seek answers as they read. They write effective essays and papers by asking and answering important questions about the subject. They form study groups where they ask and answer more questions. In preparation for exams, they predict test questions and answer them.

Not only is asking motivating questions valuable for excelling in college, it's also a key to learning how to live a rich, full life. By no accident, the root word of *question* is "quest." What important questions will you need to answer to succeed in the quest for your goals and dreams?

Asking just any question won't help. The quality of your questions determines the quality of your answers. And the quality of your answers determines the quality of your life. Victims ask questions such as *Why is it so hard to get what I want?* This question is merely a complaint in disguise. It diverts energy away from action. By contrast, Creators ask questions such as *What can I do differently to get what I want?* This question accepts responsibility for improving results and begins the search for effective actions.

Step 2. Gather Relevant Information.   To answer motivating questions, we need relevant information, lots of it. Everyone is constantly absorbing information, but struggling students seldom consider the quality of the data they pour into their brains. What, for example, is the value of information gained while mindlessly watching thirty hours of television each week or while listening to classmates complain endlessly about a teacher?

Successful students gather relevant information in many ways. They attend classes regularly. They initiate meaningful conversations with instructors and classmates. They read textbooks, two or three times if necessary. They find and read additional related materials on their own. They visit support labs. They do homework problems. They learn the unique vocabulary of the subject. They take notes on lectures and readings. They write journal entries. In short, they put in the necessary time on task, immersing themselves in the concepts and facts of unfamiliar subjects. College reinforces an essential truth of learning: To answer complex questions requires first a consistent effort to gather mountains of relevant information.

It's well documented that the best way to have ideas is first of all to immerse yourself in a subject for longish periods— like months or more—in which you study intensely, and then step away and do something else—go for a holiday, go out dancing, or something like that. Very often ideas come in this sort of incubation period.

Francis Crick, Winner of the Nobel Prize for medicine

Step 3. Discover Meaningful Answers.   Once you've gathered enough relevant information, relax. Review your questions, then ponder your information. Take frequent breaks. Work on something else for a while. Come back and review your questions and gathered information again and again. Sleep on it. Relax and review again. All the while, your unconscious mind will be automatically sorting and organizing random bits of information into meaningful answers. If you trust the learning process, your mind will invent answers that will astound you.

Self-Assessment: How I prefer to learn

Before reading on, take a self-assessment that will give you some insight into how your brain prefers to gather and process experiences and information.

In each group below, rank all four answers (A, B, C, D) from the *least* true of you to the *most* true of you. Give each possible answer a different score. Obviously there are no right or wrong answers; your opinion is all that matters. Remember, items that are MOST TRUE OF YOU get a 4.

Least true of you ← 1 2 3 4 → Most true of you

1. I would prefer to take a college course in

_____ A. science.

_____ B. business management.

_____ C. group dynamics.

_____ D. an independent study that I design.

2. I solve problems by

_____ A. standing back, thinking, and analyzing what is wrong.

_____ B. doing something practical and seeing how it works.

_____ C. leaping in and doing what feels right at the time.

_____ D. trusting my intuition.

3. Career groups that appeal to me are

_____ A. engineer, researcher, financial planner.

_____ B. administrator, city manager, military officer.

_____ C. teacher, social worker, physical therapist.

_____ D. entrepreneur, artist, inventor.

4. Before I make a decision, I need to be sure that

_____ A. I understand all of the relevant ideas and facts.

_____ B. I'm confident my solution will work.

_____ C. I know how my decision will affect others.

_____ D. I haven't overlooked a more creative solution.

5. I believe that

_____ A. life today needs more logical thinking and less emotion.

_____ B. life rewards the practical, hard-working, down-to-earth person.

_____ C. life must be lived with enthusiasm and passion.

_____ D. life, like music, is best composed by creative inspiration, not by rules.

6. I would enjoy reading a book titled

_____ A. *Great Theories and Ideas of the 20th Century*

_____ B. *How to Organize Your Life and Accomplish More*

_____ C. *The Keys to Developing Better Relationships*

_____ D. *Tapping into Your Creative Genius*

7. I believe the most valuable information for making decisions comes from

_____ A. logical analysis of facts.

_____ B. what has worked in the past.

_____ C. gut feelings.

_____ D. my imagination.

8. I am persuaded by an argument that

_____ A. offers statistical or factual proof.

_____ B. presents the findings of recognized experts.

_____ C. is passionately presented by someone I admire.

_____ D. explores innovative possibilities for future change.

9. I prefer a teacher who

_____ A. lectures knowledgeably about the important facts and theories of the subject.

_____ B. provides practical, step-by-step, hands-on activities with clear learning objectives.

_____ C. stimulates exciting class discussions and group projects.

_____ D. challenges me to think for myself and explore the subject in my own way.

10. People who know me would describe me as

_____ A. logical.

_____ B. practical.

_____ C. emotional.

_____ D. creative.

Total your scores for each letter and record them below:
_____ A. THINKING _____ B. DOING
_____ C. FEELING _____ D. INNOVATING

Your scores suggest the following:

30–40 = You have a strong preference to learn this way.
20–29 = You are capable of learning this way when necessary.
10–19 = You avoid this way of learning.

Whether applied to relationships at home or at work, knowledge of our brain dominance empowers us as individuals and groups to achieve more of our full potential.

Ned Herrmann

Recent discoveries about learning styles can help us maximize what we learn. These discoveries suggest that each person develops a preferred way of learning, a style that requires less effort from our brain and that produces more learning than a less preferred style of learning.

For a quick understanding of the significance of learning preferences, try signing your name twice, once with each hand. Notice that your preferred hand allows you to write quickly, easily, effectively, much as your preferred learning style allows you to learn. Your nonpreferred hand usually writes more slowly, painstakingly, ineffectively, much the way you learn with your less preferred style(s) of learning.

The evolution of learning styles theory owes a great debt to psychologist Carl Jung, whose ideas were later embraced by Katharine Briggs and her daughter Isabel Briggs Myers. They created the Myers-Briggs Type Inventory (MBTI), an assessment tool that measures sixteen psychological types. More recently, David Keirsey and Marilyn Bates created an inventory that measures four temperaments. Others, including David Kolb, Bernice McCarthy, and Ned Herrmann, have further refined assessment methods that illuminate how each individual prefers to learn. If you want an in-depth understanding of your learning style, you may wish to take one or more of the learning styles inventories listed in the bibliography.

Although there is no best way for everyone to learn, there is a best way for *you* to learn, and the self-assessment you just took begins your understanding of what that way is. Your scores indicate your order of preferences for four different learning styles: THINKING, DOING, FEELING, and INNOVATING. More specifically, your scores suggest what types of questions motivate you, how you prefer to gather relevant information, and how you prefer to discover meaningful answers.

It is very natural to teach in the same way we learn. It may be difficult for us to believe that others could learn in a way that is foreign and difficult for us.

Carolyn Mamchur

Traditional college teaching—characterized by lectures and textbook assignments—typically favors the learning styles of THINKERS, and, to a somewhat lesser degree, DOERS. As more instructors discover the importance of individual learning styles, however, they are adapting their teaching styles to help all learners maximize their academic potential. Regardless of your learning style or your instructor's teaching style, many strategies exist to help you achieve academic success.

If you encounter an instructor who doesn't teach the way you prefer to learn, take responsibility for your learning and experiment with some of the suggestions below. Perhaps most important of all is developing flexibility in how you learn. The more choices you have, the richer will be your learning experience.

In the following paragraphs, you'll discover the kinds of inquiry that motivate each learning style, the methods each style prefers for gathering relevant information, and each style's favored way for discovering meaningful answers. You may want to read about your preferred learning style first. There you'll find many options to use when your instructor doesn't teach as you prefer to learn. By looking at the other learning styles as well, you'll see additional ways to expand your menu of learning strategies.

The way a question is asked limits and disposes the ways in which any answer to it— right or wrong—may be given.

Suzanne K. Langer

A. Thinking learners

Motivating questions: Thinking learners are energized by questions that begin with "What?" *What theory supports that claim? What does a statistical analysis show? What is the logic here? What facts do you have? What experts have written about this?*

Preferred ways of gathering information: Thinkers enjoy pondering facts and theories. They learn well from instructors who present information with lectures, visual aids, problem solving by the instructor, textbook readings, independent library research, and activities that call upon logical skills, such as debates. Thinkers benefit from time to reflect on what they are learning.

Preferred ways of discovering meaningful answers: Thinkers respect logical argument and facts. They are uncomfortable with answers that depend on tradition, emotion, personal considerations, or intuition. They excel at analyzing, dissecting, figuring out, and using logic to arrive at linear, reasoned answers. Thinkers are left-brained learners.

When your instructor doesn't teach to your preferred style:
What you can do:

- Construct important "What?" questions and search for their answers.
- Construct and answer other types of questions your instructor might ask: How? Who? Why? What if?
- Read all of your textbook assignments carefully.
- Organize your lecture and reading notes in a logical fashion, using outlines and study charts wherever appropriate.
- Study with classmates who have different preferred ways of learning from your own.

Ask your instructor to do the following:

- Answer your important "What?" questions in class or in a conference.
- List important points on the blackboard or on handouts.
- Suggest additional readings in the subject.

B. Doing learners

The answers you get depend on the questions you ask. Play with your wording to get different answers.
Roger vonOech

Motivating questions: Doing learners are energized by questions that begin with "How?" *How does this work? How can I apply this? How did this work in the past? How can I do this more efficiently? How do experts do this?*

Preferred ways of gathering information: Doers enjoy taking action. They learn well from instructors who present factual information and practical skills in a step-by-step, logical manner; who then present models or examples from experts in the field; and who finally allow students to do hands-on work in guided labs or practice applications. Doers benefit from the opportunity to dive right in and do the work.

Preferred ways of discovering empowering answers: Doers honor objective testing of an idea, whether their own or an expert's. They are uncomfortable with answers based on abstract theories, emotion, personal considerations, or intuition. They excel at being unbiased, taking action and observing outcomes, following procedures, and using confirmed facts to arrive at linear, reasoned answers. Doers, like thinkers, are left-brained learners.

When your instructor doesn't teach to your preferred style:
What you can do:

- Construct important "How?" questions and search for their answers.
- Construct and answer other types of questions your instructor might ask: What? Who? Why? What if?
- Practice using the course information or skill outside of class.
- Organize your lecture and reading notes in a step-by-step fashion, using outlines and study charts wherever appropriate.
- Study with classmates who have different preferred ways of learning from your own.

Ask your instructor to do the following:

- Answer your important "How?" questions in class or in a conference.
- Explain practical applications for theories taught in the course.
- List important steps on the blackboard or on handouts.
- Demonstrate the information or skill in a step-by-step manner.
- Observe and give corrective feedback as you demonstrate your hands-on understanding of the subject.

C. Feeling learners

The meaning of my existence is that life has addressed a question to me.
          Carl Jung

Motivating questions: Feeling learners are energized by questions that begin with "Why?" or "Who?" *Why do I want or need to know this subject? Who is going to teach me? Who is going to learn this with me? Why do they want to know this information? Who here cares about me? Who here do I care about?*

Preferred ways of gathering information: Feeling learners enjoy personal connections and an emotionally supportive environment. They learn well from instructors who are warm and caring; who value feelings as well as thoughts; and who create a safe, accepting classroom atmosphere with activities like group work, role playing, and sharing of individual experiences. Feeling learners benefit from an opportunity to relate personally with both their instructors and classmates.

Preferred ways of discovering meaningful answers: Feeling learners honor their emotions and seek answers that are personally meaningful. They are uncomfortable with answers based on abstract theories or dispassionate facts. They excel at responding to emotional currents in groups, empathizing with others, considering others' feelings in making decisions, and using empathy and gut feelings to arrive at nonlinear, subjective answers. Feeling learners are right-brained learners.

When your instructor doesn't teach to your preferred style:
What you can do:

- Construct important "Who?" and "Why?" questions and search for their answers.
- Construct and answer other types of questions your instructor might ask: What? How? What if?
- Discover the value of this subject for you personally.
- Organize your notes and study materials using concept maps.
- Practice using the course information or skill with people in your life.
- Make friends with classmates and discuss the subject with them outside of class.
- Tape-record classes and listen to them during free time.
- Study with classmates who have different preferred ways of learning from your own.

Ask your instructor to do the following:

- Answer your important "Who?" and "Why?" questions in class or in a conference.
- Explain how you might make a personal application of the course information.
- Meet with you outside of class so you can get to know one another better and feel more comfortable in his or her class.
- Let you do some of the course work with a partner or in a group.

D. Innovating learners

Motivating questions: Innovating learners are energized by questions that begin with "What if?" or What else?" *What if I tried doing this another way? What else could I do with this? What if the situation were different?*

Preferred ways of gathering information: Innovators enjoy seeking new possibilities, imagining unseen futures. They learn well from instructors who encourage students to discover new and innovative applications; who allow students to use their intuition to create something new; and who use approaches such as independent projects, flexible rules and deadlines, a menu of optional assignments, metaphors, art projects, and visual aids. Innovators benefit from the freedom to work independently and let their imaginations run free.

Preferred ways of discovering empowering answers: Innovators honor personal imagination and intuition. They are uncomfortable with answers based on abstract theories, cold facts, emotion, or personal considerations. They excel at trusting their inner vision, their intuitive sense of exciting future possibilities, and their imaginations. Innovators are right-brained learners.

When your instructor doesn't teach to your preferred style:
What you can do:

- Construct important "What if?" and "What else?" questions and search for their answers.
- Construct and answer other types of questions your instructor might ask: What? How? Who? Why?
- Organize your notes and study materials using concept maps and personally meaningful symbols or pictures.
- Study with classmates who have different preferred ways of learning from your own.

Ask your instructor to do the following:

- Answer your important "What if?" and "What else?" questions in class or in a conference.
- Let you design some of your own assignments for the course.
- Use visual aids to explain concepts in class.
- Recommend a book for you to read by the most innovative or rebellious thinker in the field.
- Evaluate you with essays and independent projects rather than with objective tests.

Successful students take responsibility for not only *what* they learn in every class but also *how* they learn it. They discover how to maximize their learning regardless of the subject or the way the instructor teaches.

Journal Entry 23

I n this activity, you'll apply what you have learned about your preferred ways of learning to improve your results in a challenging course.

1. **Write about the most challenging course you are taking this semester.** Using what you just learned about how you prefer to learn, explain why the course may be difficult for you: Consider the subject matter, the teaching methods of the instructor, the textbook, and any other factors that may contribute to making this course difficult for someone with your preferred way(s) of learning. (If you are not taking a challenging course this semester, you can write about the most challenging course you have taken any time in your education.)

2. **Using what you now know about the way you prefer to learn, write about changes you can make that will help you learn this challenging subject more easily.** Refer to pages 152-156 for suggested changes.

By choosing different ways of learning in a challenging course, you can avoid the excuse-making of a Victim and apply the solution-orientation of a Creator.

Relax, think, write.

Learning to Make Course Corrections

FOCUS QUESTIONS   How can you recognize when you are off course? What three steps will help you stop doing what you've been doing and begin doing something different and more effective?

One evening at a restaurant, I went to the restroom. I pulled on the door handle, but it didn't budge. *Someone must be in there,* I thought. After a few minutes, I tried again. This time I pushed on the door. Still, it wouldn't open, so I waited a few more minutes, my irritation growing. *What inconsiderate jerk would take so long in a public restroom!* Aggravated, I yanked on the door handle again, rattling it loudly. Still no response. I was standing there fuming when a waiter walked up, took hold of the door handle, slid the door to the left, and, with a dramatic wave of his arm, beckoned me to enter the empty bathroom.

Whoops.

How many times in our lives are we this ineffective? In the face of a challenge, we repeatedly think thoughts that fail to solve our problem. We stir emotions that serve only to create a negative experience. We repeat ineffective behaviors that merely reinforce our limiting thoughts and distressing emotions. And underneath these self-defeating patterns lies a limiting core belief (like my unquestioned assumption that doors open only by swinging in or out). Had I changed my self-defeating patterns or my limiting belief, I could have solved my problem in an instant. Who knows how long I might have remained off course had not a teacher (the waiter) arrived to show me how to make a course correction?

Here's a problem for you: Draw *one straight line* that touches all three of the stars below:

Notice how your Scripts and preferred learning style dictate the way you go about solving this problem:

- **What are you thinking?** Do you think, *This is great, I love challenges like this,* or *I hate puzzles like this,* or *This is impossible,* or *Oh, I already know the answer,* or *Who cares?*

- **What are you feeling?** Do you feel excited by the challenge, or frustrated by the difficulty, or irritated by the request, or depressed by your inability to solve it immediately?

AUTOBIOGRAPHY IN FIVE SHORT CHAPTERS

CHAPTER ONE

I walk down the street.
   There is a deep hole in the sidewalk.
   I fall in.
   I am lost . . . I am helpless.
     It isn't my fault.
It takes forever to find a way out.

CHAPTER TWO

I walk down the same street.
   There is a deep hole in the sidewalk.
   I pretend I don't see it.
   I fall in again.
I can't believe I am in this same place.
     But it is my fault.
It still takes a long time to get out.

CHAPTER THREE

I walk down the same street.
   There is a deep hole in the sidewalk.
   I *see* it is there.
   I still fall in . . . it's a habit . . . but,
     my eyes are open.
     I know where I am.
It is *my* fault.
I get out immediately.

CHAPTER FOUR

I walk down the same street.
   There is a deep hole in the sidewalk.
   I walk around it.

CHAPTER FIVE

I walk down another street.

—Portia Nelson

- **What are you doing?** Do you immediately begin drawing lines to seek a solution, or sit back trying to think of a solution, or turn the page to look for the answer, or keep reading without attempting to solve the puzzle?
- **What are your unconscious core beliefs?** This puzzle is easy to solve, but most people have unconscious beliefs that keep them from seeing the answer. What belief is keeping you from solving this simple problem?

The capacity to correct course is the capacity to reduce the differences between the path you are on now and the optimal path to your objective. . . .
Charles Garfield

If your present habit patterns and beliefs aren't working to solve the puzzle, you'll have to make a course correction to solve it. The same is true in life. When you face a problem and your present answers aren't working, you need to learn to do, think, feel, or believe something different. In other words, you need to make a course correction.

The enemies of course correction are existing self-defeating patterns and an insistence that our beliefs are right. The allies of course correction are the courage to change, open-mindedness, and flexibility. Three essential steps assist you in making course corrections: test your present answers, heed feedback, and consciously revise any answers that get you off course.

Test your present answers

Teachers give tests to discover how students are doing. Whereas Victims do battle with tests, Creators cooperate. They know that test results reveal whether or not they're on course and suggest what their next best step ought to be.

Life is change. Growth is optional. Choose wisely.
Karen Kaiser Clark

So, as mentioned earlier, successful students constantly test themselves by thinking up and answering their own examination questions. They treat each opportunity to answer questions as a dress rehearsal for final exams and a way to be sure they are on course.

Whereas college instructors test us occasionally, the University of Life tests us constantly. If you have a problem, simply realize that you've enrolled in a course called Relationship 101, Money 110, Employment 202, or Health 125. Expect that the good old U. of L. will keep testing you in this subject until you master it. When you get it, Life will promote you to another course and begin testing you in that subject. The point is, nowhere on earth can you escape being tested, so you might as well cooperate and learn as much as you can from your tests.

Heed feedback

Feedback is any information from inside or outside us that reveals whether we're on course or off course. The world bombards us with feedback every day, but, sadly, many ignore it. At first, feedback taps politely on our shoulder. If we pay no heed, feedback shakes us vigorously. If we continue to ignore it, feedback may knock us to our knees, creating havoc in our lives. This havoc might look like failing out of school or having a heart attack. There's usually plenty of feedback long before the failure or the heart attack if we will only heed its message.

In college, begin thinking of yourself as an airplane pilot and each of your teachers as your personal air traffic controller. Listen as they advise, *You're on course, on course . . . whoops, now you're off course, off course . . . okay, that's right, now you're back on course.* A pilot appreciates such information. Likewise, successful students heed their instructors' feedback and use it to stay on course. They read every suggestion instructors offer on assignments; they understand the message in test scores; they request clarification of any comment they don't understand; they ask for additional feedback from classmates, other teachers, or mentors.

In life, heeding feedback looks much the same. Creators look for feedback in the results they've created in their lives. A failed relationship, a job promotion, ill health, or a serious depression all provide invaluable feedback if we will heed it. Additionally, Creators listen objectively to what others (bosses, friends, lovers, spouses, parents, even strangers) have to say. College exposes us to people of great diversity, people who can offer feedback different from what we're used to. In college, we meet people older or younger than we are, from other states and countries, of other races and cultures, and with other religious and political beliefs. If we're open to their feedback, we may hear exactly what we need to get back on course.

Revise your answers

After testing your answers and heeding feedback, the last step of course correction is revising your old answers where necessary. Whereas Victims are rigid, Creators are flexible and willing to revise self-defeating patterns and limiting beliefs.

For example, one question every college student has to answer is, "How do I write effectively in higher education?" The answer that many students bring with them from high school or work is "Get right to the point." In practice, this approach often results in writing that is closer in depth to a telegram than an essay. College instructors, however, expect effective writers to dive deep into complex issues, offering sufficient, well-organized support for their ideas. Typically, instructors' feedback—grades and comments—urges students to add more explanation, evidence, examples, and experiences.

Now, the question is: Will students revise their old answers and dive deep when writing? Or will they stay prisoners of their old answers? History is littered with the remains of individuals and nations that would not change course when their old habits and customs no longer got them the results they wanted.

A feedback mechanism registers the actual state of a system, compares it to the desired state, then uses the comparison to correct the state of the system.
Horace Freeland Judson

What is important is to keep learning, to enjoy challenge and to tolerate ambiguity. In the end there are no certain answers.
Martina Horner, president, Radcliffe College

The real voyage of discovery consists not in seeking new landscapes, but in having new eyes.

Marcel Proust

Successful students know that if they keep doing what they've been doing, they'll keep getting what they've been getting. So if they're not getting the results they want, they need to change. That's why they don't keep pulling and pushing on a door that slides from right to left, even if pulling and pushing has worked in the past. Instead, they master the skill of revising their outdated, ineffective habits and beliefs, allowing them to make essential course corrections whenever necessary.

We seldom walk to success in a straight line. With constant course corrections, however, we will get there eventually.

Journal Entry 24

I n this activity, you will practice making course corrections. Successful people are good at revising their old, ineffective ways of thinking, feeling, doing, and believing. Creators have the courage and flexibility to change.

Did you figure out how to connect the three stars with one straight line? If you were stumped, what limiting belief kept you from solving this problem? Did you assume that you were restricted to a pen or pencil with a narrow point? You weren't. In fact, the solution is to use a writing implement (such as a large crayon) with a point wide enough to cover all three stars in one straight line. Once you change your limiting belief, solving the problem is easy! How many other problems could you solve in your life if you mastered the creative art of course correction?

1. **Write about where you are presently off course in your role as a student and offer a plan for making a course correction in that same area.** Do that by using the three steps for making course corrections:

   1. *Test your answers:* Look at each of your college classes to see in which one you are most off course. Write about what your goal is for the course and where you are in the pursuit of that goal.

   2. *Heed feedback:* Write about any feedback (from inside or outside of you) informing you that you're off course. What does this feedback tell you is causing your problem? Is it your present ways of thinking, feeling, doing, or believing? If you need more feedback, ask your instructor or your Inner Guide.

   3. *Revise answers when necessary:* Write about new ways of thinking, feeling, doing, and believing that will replace your old ways and move you back on course. What will you do differently? Make a concrete plan to change.

2. **Write about where you are presently off course in another of your life roles and offer a plan for making a course correction in that same area.** Again, use the three steps for making course corrections as in Step 1. If you need more feedback, design a way to get it.

Relax, think, write.

SUCCESSES

LEARNING EXPERIENCES

GOFF

©1995 TED GOFF

Developing Wisdom

To me, earth is a school. I view life as my classroom. My approach to the experiences I have every day is that I am a student, and that all my experiences have something they can teach me. I am always asking myself, "What learning is available for me now?"

Mary Hulnick, vice-president, University of Santa Monica

As you have discovered, colleges require you to take general education courses designed to give you the essential foundation for academic success. These courses include subjects like mathematics, composition, speech, history, and science.

The curriculum of life

The University of Life also requires you to take general education courses. Its courses are a little different, however. These courses are offered by the Department of Adversities and include subjects like Problems 101, Obstacles 203, Mistakes 305, Failures 410, and, for some, a graduate course called Catastrophes 599. Tests are given often. There are no answers in the back of the book. In fact, there is no textbook in these courses, only your experiences from which to learn.

Creators believe that each course in the curriculum of life is especially designed to teach them exactly what they need to know at that moment. So they look carefully at their response to adversities: What do I **think**? How do I **feel**? What do I **do**? As always, our responses are guided by our deepest **core beliefs** about ourselves, about other people, and about the world. Adversities can destroy us or they can teach us the greatest lessons life has to offer. The choice is ours. The prize is wisdom. Wisdom, I suggest, is the deep and profound understanding that allows us to consistently make wise choices, choices that move us steadily and contentedly toward the creation of a life worth living.

Avoiding learned helplessness

Learned helplessness is the giving-up reaction, the quitting response that follows from the belief that whatever you do doesn't matter.
Martin Seligman

Psychologist Martin Seligman, author of *Learned Optimism,* has spent years studying how people respond to adversity. He compares experiencing adversity to being punched in the stomach. The punch will hurt and maybe even knock the person down. Some people get back up. Others stay down for the count. Folks who stay on the floor typically believe that nothing they try will make any difference. They feel helpless and quit.

These people are not necessarily any less capable than others, but they *believe* they're helpless in the face of adversity. So they are. Their belief becomes their reality. They have learned to be Victims.

Seligman says people quit when they believe the causes of their difficulties are **permanent, pervasive,** and/or **personal.** A student who fails an exam may explain her defeat by saying, *I'll never pass these exams* (permanent), *I mess up everything I do* (pervasive), and *I'm so stupid* (personal). These, of course, are the harsh self-judgments of her Inner Critic. The Inner Critic's self-blame brings a Victim to her knees, and she quits.

There are no mistakes, no coincidences, all events are blessings given to us to learn from.
Elizabeth Kübler-Ross

The student who responds to her failure more positively is listening to very different inner voices. According to Seligman, the inner conversation of an optimistic student attributes her failure to causes that are **temporary, specific,** and **impersonal.** She thinks, *Okay, I failed, but I know I can do better next semester* (temporary—she can improve the situation in the future), *I'm doing fine in my other courses* (specific—the problem is limited to this one area of her life), and *I'll be able to do better when I make more time to study* (impersonal—the problem is not a flaw in her, rather something she can fix by changing her behavior). Her Inner Guide likely believes, *I'll do better next time because I'll learn from my failure and do something different.* This hopeful version of reality allows her to stand up, brush herself off, and get back on course wiser than before.

Lessons from adversity

The research of Seligman and others shows that adversity teaches many people to doubt their ability to go on. By contrast, other people learn to have hope even in the face of life's inevitable challenges. This lesson allows them to focus on solutions rather than problems, to keep going instead of quitting. People who overcome adversity learn the great wisdom that each challenge has to teach.

Earlier, you read the story of Luanne, the student who passed English 101 on her seventh try. Luanne could very well have quit after any of her previous six "failures," but somehow she had learned to persevere. Luanne's experience demonstrates that *you have not truly failed until you quit.* Once you quit, all possibilities for success die. Some people need only one try to succeed; others need many. Wise people know that perseverance is a critical ingredient of success. But Luanne didn't succeed just because she persevered. She succeeded because she was also willing to learn a new way to overcome her obstacles and to change what she had been doing for six previous semesters. And that is a sign of wisdom also.

The roll call of the world's successful people is full of "students" of life's adversities. R.H. Macy stumbled seven times before his department store became immensely profitable. Henry Ford didn't taste success in the automobile industry until he had experienced going broke five times. Winston Churchill failed the sixth grade on his way to becoming prime minister of England. Albert Einstein didn't learn to read until he was seven. Walt Disney went bankrupt before building Disneyland. Abraham Lincoln lost six elections for various political offices before being elected the sixteenth president of the United States.

Don't settle in college for being stuffed full of facts and information while starving for wisdom. Courses in the University of Life offer you deeper insights into yourself, other people, and the world. Adversities can not only show you how to stay on course to a particular goal; they can also teach you how to make the choices that create a rich, personally fulfilling life. And that is the greatest wisdom of all.

> *I have learned that success is to be measured not so much by the position that one has reached in life as by the obstacles which he has overcome while trying to succeed.*
>
> Booker T. Washington

Journal Entry 25

In this activity, you will explore an adversity in your life. By doing so, see if you can discover the wisdom it has to teach you.

1. **Have your Inner Guide interview one of your biggest adversities, seeking the lesson it has to offer. Write out their dialogue.** Interview a present problem, obstacle, mistake, or failure. Have your Inner Guide ask each of the eleven questions below and let your adversity answer. Have your Inner Guide demonstrate effective listening skills, including asking your adversity to expand or clarify its answers where appropriate. Ask for examples, experiences, evidence, and explanation. Label each comment with IG (Inner Guide) or ADV (Adversity)

1. Adversity, what is your name?
2. Why are you such a challenge for me?
3. How have I attempted to deal with you in the past? What did I think, feel, and do?
4. What have been my results?
5. How have you defeated my attempts to overcome you until now?
6. What personal qualities will I need to get beyond you?
7. What different thoughts will I need to get beyond you?
8. What different emotions will I need to get beyond you?
9. What different actions will I need to get beyond you?
10. What different beliefs (about the world, other people, or myself) will I need to get beyond you?
11. What wisdom have you come to teach me?

2. **Title a clean page in your journal "MY WISDOM." Look back over past journals and find places where you expressed your growing wisdom about life. Then write ten or more of these wisdom statements.** See the next page for some examples of wisdom from students.

Relax, think, write.

CASE STUDY IN CRITICAL THINKING

A Fish Story

One September morning, on their first day of college, two dozen first-year students made their way into the biology laboratory. They sat down six at a lab table and glanced about for the professor. Because this was their first college class, most of the students were a bit nervous. A few introduced themselves. Others kept checking their watches.

At exactly nine o'clock, the professor, wearing a crisply pressed white lab coat, entered the room. "Good morning," he said. He set a white plate in the middle of each table. On each plate lay a small fish.

"Please observe the fish," the professor said. "Then write down your observations." He turned and left the room.

The students looked at each other, puzzled. This was *strange!* Oh, well. They took out scrap paper and wrote notes such as, *I see a small fish.* One student added, *It's on a white plate.*

Satisfied, they set their pens down and waited. And waited. For the entire class period, they waited. A couple of students whispered that it was a trick. They said the professor was probably testing them to see if they'd do some-

Student Wisdom

- The better choices I make, the better my life will be—life is all about choices.
- I am not a passenger in my life. I am the driver, and every turn I make creates my future.
- When I set goals that mean something to me, I feel my energy go up.
- I always thought life had to be hard. Now I see that, for the most part, my life is only as hard as I choose it to be.
- When I break a huge task into chunks and do a little bit every day, I can accomplish great things.
- Just because I believe something doesn't make it true. I need to keep an open mind for better ways of thinking, feeling, doing, and believing.
- I can't be anyone else but me, though, in the past, I sure have tried.
- Spending all of my time hating someone leaves me little time to love myself.
- In the past I have spent more energy on getting people to feel sorry for me than I have on accomplishing something worthwhile.
- I am always looking for ways to cut corners, to get out of doing what's necessary. It doesn't work. I have to do my best in order to be successful.
- The person I lie to the most is me. It's time I tell myself the truth.

thing wrong. Time crawled by. Still they waited, trying to do nothing that would get them in trouble. Finally, one student mumbled that she was going to be late for her next class. She picked up her books and stood. She paused. Others rose as well and began filing out of the room. Some looked cautiously over their shoulders as they left.

When the students entered the biology lab for their second class, they found the same white plates with the same small fish already waiting on their laboratory tables. At exactly nine o'clock, the professor entered the room. "Good morning. Please take out your observations of the fish," he said.

Students dug into their notebooks or book bags. Many could not find their notes. Those few who could held them up for the professor to see as he walked from table to table.

After visiting each student, the professor said, "Please observe the fish. Write down all of your observations." Then he left, closing the door behind him.

The students looked at one another, more puzzled. They peered at the fish. Those few who had found their notes glanced from the fish to their notes and back again. Was the professor crazy? What else were they supposed to notice? It was only a stupid fish.

About then, one student spied a book on the professor's desk. It was a book for identifying fish, and she snatched it up. Using the book, she quickly discovered what kind of fish was lying on her plate. She read eagerly, recording in her notes all the facts she found about her fish. Others saw her and asked to use the book, too. She passed the book to other tables, and her classmates soon found descriptions of their fish. After about fifteen minutes the students sat back, very pleased with themselves. Chatter died down. They waited. But the professor didn't return. As the period ended, all the students carefully put their notes away.

The same fish on the same white plate greeted each student in the third class. The professor entered at nine o'clock. "Good morning," he said. "Please hold up your observations." All of the students held up their notes immediately. They looked at each other, smiling, as the professor walked from table to table, looking at their work. Once again, he walked toward the door. "Please . . . *observe* the fish. Write down all of your observations," he said. And then he left.

The students couldn't believe it. They grumbled and complained. This guy is nuts. When is he going to teach us something? What are we paying tuition for, anyway? Students at one table, however, began observing their fish more closely. Other tables followed their example.

The first thing all of the students noticed was the biting odor of aging fish. A few students recorded details about the fish's color that they had failed to observe in the previous two classes. They wondered if the colors had been there originally or if the colors had appeared as the fish aged. Each group measured its fish. They poked it and described its texture. One student looked in its mouth and found that he could see light through its gills. Another student found a small balance beam, and each group weighed its fish. They passed around someone's pocket knife. With it, they sliced open the fish and examined its insides. In the stomach of one fish they found a smaller fish. They wrote quickly, and their notes soon overflowed onto three and four sheets of paper. Finally someone shouted, "Hey, class was over ten minutes ago." They carefully placed their notes in three-ring binders. They said good-bye to their fish, wondering if their finny friends would be there on Monday.

They were, and a vile smell filled the laboratory. The professor strode into the room at exactly nine o'clock. The students immediately thrust their notes in the air. "Good morning," the professor said cheerfully, making his way from student to student. He took longer than ever to examine their notes. The students shifted anxiously in their chairs as the professor edged ever closer to the door. How could they endure the smell for another class period? At the door, the professor turned to the students.

"All right," he said. "Perhaps now we can begin."

—Inspired by Samuel J. Scudder, "Take This Fish and Look at It" (1874).

- **If you had been in this biology lab class, what lessons about college and life would you have learned from the experience?**

DIVING DEEPER: **When you think you have discovered one life lesson, dive deeper and find another even more powerful wisdom. And then another and another.**

Lifelong Learning at Work

The intellectual equipment needed for the job of the future is an ability to define problems, quickly assimilate relevant data, conceptualize and reorganize the information, make deductive and inductive leaps with it, ask hard questions about it, discuss findings with colleagues, work collaboratively to find solutions and then convince others.

Robert B. Reich, former Secretary of Labor

Some students believe that once they graduate from college they'll finally be finished with studying and learning. In fact, a college diploma is merely a ticket into the huge University of Work. In 1995 alone, U.S. employers spent more than 55 billion dollars for employee training, according to the American Society for Training and Development.

Continuing education in the workplace includes instruction in hard skills, such as mastering a new product line, a computer system, or government regulations. Companies also offer their employees instruction in many of the same soft skills that you're learning in this book, skills such as listening, setting goals, and managing your time and work projects. In fact, soft skills are in such demand in the workplace today that top training consultants charge thousands of dollars *per day* to teach these skills to employees of American businesses.

Smart workers take full advantage of the formal classes provided by their employers. They also take full advantage of the informal classes provided by the University of Life. In this university, you have the opportunity to learn from every experience you have, especially those on the job. Lifelong learners aren't devastated by a setback, such as having a project crumble or even losing their job. They learn from their experiences and come back stronger and wiser than ever. A report by the Center for Creative Leadership compared executives whose careers got off course with those who did well. Although both groups had weaknesses, the critical difference was this: Executives who did *not* learn from their mistakes and shortcomings tended to fail at work. By contrast, those executives who *did* learn the hard lessons taught by their mistakes and failures tended to rebound and resume successful careers.

Your work-world learning begins as soon as you get serious about finding your ideal job. Unless you're sure about your career path, you'll have much research to do. Even if you do feel sure about your career choice, further research might lead to something even better. More than 20,000 occupations and 40,000 job titles exist today, and you'll want to identify careers that match the personal talents and interests you identified in your self-assessment.

Your college's library or career center probably has a number of great resources to learn about careers. For example, computerized programs such as DISCOVER, SIGI PLUS, CHOICES, and CIS may be available to explore thousands of career possibilities. Helpful books include the *Dictionary of Occupational Titles* (DOT), which offers brief descriptions of several thousand occupations; *The Guide for Occupational Exploration* (GOE), another source of occupational options; and the latest edition of the *Occupational Outlook Handbook* (OOH), which provides information about the demand for various occupations. With these resources, you can learn important facts about careers you may never even have heard of, including the nature of the work, places of employment, training and qualifications required, earnings, working conditions, and employment outlook. Keep in mind that in today's fast-paced world, occupations will be available when you graduate that don't even exist today.

Ned Herrmann, creator of the Brain Dominance Inventory, wrote, "Experience has shown that alignment of a person's mental preferences with his or her work is predictive of success and satisfaction while nonalignment usually results in poor performance and dissatisfaction." So use your discoveries in this chapter about your preferred thinking styles to help you choose a compatible career. See Figure 1 for some examples.

When you have narrowed your career choices, you may want to learn even more before committing yourself. To get the inside scoop on how a career may fit you, get some hands-on experience. Find part-time or temporary work in the field, apply for an internship, or even do volunteer work. At one time I thought I wanted to be a veterinarian, but one summer of working in a veterinary hospital quickly taught me that it was a poor career match for me. I'm sure glad I found out *before* I went through veterinary school!

Now it's time for your job interviews. Keep in mind that most employers are looking for someone who can learn the new position and keep learning new skills for years to come. In fact, a 1989 U.S. Department of Labor study found that employers of entry-level workers considered specific technical skills less important than the ability to learn on the job. So, how can you present yourself in the interview as a life-long learner? First, of course, have a transcript with good grades to demonstrate your ability to learn in college.

Figure 1: Learning Preferences and Compatible Careers

A. Thinking Learner: biologist, stock broker, engineer, city manager, science teacher, computer designer/programmer, computer technician, detective, educational administrator, radiologist, electrical engineer, financial planner, lawyer, chemist, mathematician, medical researcher, physician, statistician, veterinarian

B. Doing Learner: reporter, accountant, librarian, bookkeeper, clinical psychologist, credit advisor, historian, environmental scientist, farmer, hotel/motel manager, marketing, military, police, realtor, school principal, technical writer

C. Feeling Learner: actor, social worker, clergy, sociologist, counseling psychologist, humanities teacher, human resource development, public relations, journalist, musician, teacher, nurse, occupational therapist, organizational development consultant, recreational therapist, sales, writer

D. Innovating Learner: dancer, poet, advertising design, florist, psychiatrist, artist, creative writer, entrepreneur, fashion artist, playwright, film maker, graphics designer, humorist, inventor, landscape architect, nutritionist, photographer, editor, program developer

Be ready for questions like, "How do you keep up with advancements in your field? What workshops or seminars have you attended? What kind of reading do you do?" Go to the interview prepared to ask good questions of your own. And demonstrate that one of the things you're looking for in a particular job is its ability to help you keep learning your profession.

Today's work world is marked by downsizing and rightsizing. Companies are operating with leaner staffs, and this means that every employee is critical to the success of the business. It also means that someone who can't keep up with inevitable changes is expendable. One powerful way to give yourself a competitive advantage is to continually learn new skills and knowledge, even before you need them on your job. When your supervisor says, "Does anyone here know how to use a desk-top publishing program?" you'll be able to say, "Sure, I can do that." Another way to keep learning on the job is to seek out feedback. Superior performers want to hear what others think of their work, realizing that this is a great way to learn to do it even better.

According to Anthony J. D'Angelo, author of the *College Blue Book*, world knowledge doubles every 14 months. Suppose he's way off, and knowledge actually doubles every 5 years as others claim. That still means we'll have to keep learning a little every day just to keep pace and a lot every day to get ahead. Educator Marshall McLuhan once said, "The future of work consists of *learning* a living (rather than *earning* a living)." His observation becomes truer with each passing day. Future success at work belongs to the life-long learners.

Believing in Yourself: **Develop Self-Respect**

FOCUS QUESTIONS What is your present level of self-respect? How can you raise your self-respect, and therefore your self-esteem, even higher?

Self-respect is the core belief that I AM AN ADMIRABLE PERSON. If self-confidence is the result of **what** I do, then self-respect is the result of **how** I do it.

Two crucial choices that build or tear down my self-respect are whether or not I live with integrity and whether or not I keep my commitments.

Live with integrity

Always aim at complete harmony of thought and word and deed.
Mohandas K. Gandhi

The foundation of integrity is my personal value system. What is important to me? What experiences do I want to have? What experiences do I want others to have? Do I prize outer rewards such as cars, clothes, compliments, travel, fame, or money? Do I cherish inner experiences such as love, respect, excellence, security, honesty, wisdom, or compassion?

Integrity derives from the root word *integer,* meaning "one" or "whole." Thus we create integrity by choosing words and deeds that are one with our values. Many students say they value their education, but their actions indicate otherwise. They leave assignments undone; they do less than their best work; they miss classes; they come late. In short, their choices contradict what they say they value. Choices that lack integrity tear at a conscious person's self-respect.

One of my great integrity tests occurred years ago when I left teaching to find a more lucrative career. I was excited when hired as a management trainee at a high-powered sales company. Graduates of this company's five-year training program were earning more than thirty times what I had earned as a teacher. I couldn't wait!

My first assignment was to hire new members of the company's sales force. I gave applicants an aptitude test that revealed whether they had what it took to succeed in sales. When the scores came back, the sales manager would tell me whether or not the applicants had qualified. If so, I'd offer them a sales position. Lured by dreams of wealth, many of them left the security of a steady salary for the uncertainty of a commission check. Unfortunately, few of them lasted more than a few months. They sold to their friends. They struggled. They disappeared.

Before long, I noticed an unsettling fact: No applicant ever failed the aptitude test. Right after this realization, I interviewed a very shy man who was a lineman for the local telephone company. He was only a year from early retirement, but he was willing to give up his retirement benefits for the promise of big commissions. If ever someone was wrong for sales, I thought, this was the person. I knew he'd be making a terrible mistake to abandon his security for the seductive promise of wealth. Surely here was one person who wouldn't pass the aptitude test. But he did.

"In fact," the sales manager told him in person, "you received one of the highest scores ever. How soon can you start?"

"Errr . . . well, let's see. It's Friday. I guess next week? If that's okay."

That night, after the sales manager had left, I went into his office and located the lineman's folder. I opened it and found the test results. His score was zero. The man had not even scored!

All weekend, my stomach felt as though I had swallowed acid. My self-respect sank lower and lower. My Inner Defender kept telling me it was the lineman's choice, not mine. It was his life. Maybe he'd prove the aptitude test wrong. Maybe he would make a fortune in sales. My Inner Guide just shook his head in disgust.

On Monday, I phoned the lineman and told him his actual score.

He was furious. "Do you realize what I almost did?"

I thought, *Do you realize what I almost did?* Two weeks later I quit. Soon after, my stomach felt fine.

Each time you contradict your own values, you make a withdrawal from your self-respect account. Each time you live true to your values, you make a deposit. Here's a quick way to discover what you value and whether you are living with integrity: Ask yourself, *What qualities and behaviors do I admire in others? Do I ever allow myself to be less than what I admire?*

When you find that your choices are out of alignment with your values, you need to revise your dreams, goals, thoughts, feelings, actions, or beliefs. You can't abandon what you hold sacred and still retain your self-respect.

Keep commitments

Now let's consider another choice that influences your self-respect. Imagine that someone has made a promise to you but doesn't keep it. Then he makes and breaks a second promise. And then another and another. Wouldn't you lose respect for this person? What do you suppose happens when the person making and breaking all of these promises is YOU?

True, your Inner Defender would quickly send out a smoke screen of excuses. But the truth would not be lost on your Inner Guide. The fact remains: You made commitments and broke them. This violation of your word makes a major withdrawal from your self-respect account.

This above all; to thine own self be true
And it must follow, as the night the day,
Thou canst not then be false to any man.
Polonius,
in Shakespeare's *Hamlet*

You will always be in fashion if you are true to yourself, and only if you are true to yourself.
Maya Angelou

To make a deposit in your self-respect account, keep commitments, especially to yourself. Here's how:

- **Make your agreements consciously.** Understand exactly what you're committing to. Say "no" to requests that will get you off course; don't commit to more than you can handle just to placate others.
- **Use Creator language.** Don't say, *I'll try to do it.* Say, I **will** *do it.*
- **Make your agreements important.** Write them down. Tell others about them.
- **Create a plan; then do everything in your power to carry it out.**
- **If a problem arises or you change your mind, renegotiate** (don't just abandon your promise).

The person we break commitments with the most is, ironically, ourselves. How are you doing in this regard? Here's some evidence: How are you doing with the commitment you made to your dream in Journal Entry 8? How are you doing with your thirty-two-day commitment from Journal Entry 13?

If you haven't kept these commitments (or others), ask your Inner Guide, *What did I make more important than keeping my commitment to myself?* A part of you wanted to keep your agreement. But another, stronger part of you obviously resisted. Pursue your exploration of this inner conflict with total honesty and you may uncover a self-defeating pattern or limiting core belief that is crying out for a change. Our choices reveal what we truly value.

Keeping commitments often requires overcoming enormous obstacles. Rosalie had postponed her dream of becoming a nurse for eighteen years while raising her two children alone. Shortly after enrolling in college, her new husband asked her to drop out to take care of his two sons from a former marriage. Rosalie agreed, postponing her dream once more. Now back in college ten years later, she made what she called a "sacred vow" to attend every class on time, to do her very best on all work, and to participate actively. This time she was committed to getting top grades all the way to her nursing degree. Finally her time had come.

Then, one night she got a call from one of her sons who was now married and had a two-year-old baby girl. He had a serious problem: His wife was on drugs. Worse, that day she had bought two hundred dollars worth of drugs on credit, and the drug dealers were holding Rosalie's granddaughter until they got paid. Rosalie spent the early evening gathering cash from every source she could. All night she lay awake, waiting to hear if her grandchild would be returned safely.

At six in the morning, Rosalie got good news when her son brought the baby to her house. He asked Rosalie to watch the child while he and his wife had a serious talk. Hours passed, and still Rosalie cared for the baby. Closer and closer crept the hour when her college classes would begin. She started to get angrier and angrier as she realized that once again she was allowing others to pull her off course. And then she remembered that she had a choice. She could stay home and feel sorry for herself, or she could do something to get back on course.

At about nine o'clock, Rosalie called her sister who lived on the other side of town. She asked her sister to take a cab to Rosalie's house, promised to pay the cab fare, and even offered to pay her sister a bonus to watch the baby.

"I didn't get to class on time," Rosalie said. "But I got there. And when I did, I just wanted to walk into the middle of the room and yell, 'YEEAAH!! I MADE IT!!'"

If you could have seen her face when she told the class about her ordeal and her victory, you would have seen a woman who had just learned one of life's great lessons: When we break a commitment to ourselves, something inside of us dies. When we keep a commitment to ourselves, something inside of us thrives. That something is self-respect.

Character, simply stated, is doing what you say you're going to do. A more formal definition is: Character is the ability to carry out a worthy decision after the emotion of making that decision has passed.

Hyrum W. Smith

Journal Entry 26

In this activity, you will explore strengthening your self-respect. People with self-respect honor and admire themselves not just for *what* they do but for *how* they do it.

1. **Write about a time when you passed an integrity test.** Tell about an experience when you were greatly tempted to abandon one of your personal values. Describe how you decided to "do the right thing" instead of giving in to the temptation.

2. **Write about a time when you kept a commitment that was difficult to keep.** Fully explain the commitment you made to yourself or to someone else, and discuss the challenges—both inner and outer—that made it difficult for you to keep this promise. Explain how you were able to keep the commitment despite these challenges.

Remember, asking motivating questions leads to meaningful answers. Anticipate questions a curious reader might ask you about your stories . . . and answer them.

Relax, think, write.

Developing effective study skills is obviously a key to success in college. But studying doesn't end with graduation. Employees in today's fast-changing world must know both how to earn a living and how to "learn" a living. To excel in a challenging career after college, you'll need to learn even more than you ever learned in college. This section offers some effective strategies for learning well in college and beyond. Experiment and see which ones appeal to your preferred learning style.

Before Studying

1. Create a positive affirmation about studying. You may hold negative beliefs about studying that will sabotage your success. If so, create an affirming statement about studying, like, *"I love learning new things."* Along with your personal affirmation, repeat this study affirmation in order to reprogram your beliefs about studying.

2. Relax. Remember, you learn best when your brain is experiencing *alpha* waves. Therefore, before studying, use the progressive relaxation technique on page 7 or your own way of relaxing.

3. Create an ideal study space. Having one comfortable place where you always study has many advantages. You have the study materials you need close at hand. You aren't distracted by unfamiliar sights or sounds. And your mind becomes accustomed to shifting into study gear whenever you enter your study area. Design your study area so you always enjoy being there. Minimum requirements include a comfortable chair, plenty of light, room to spread out your materials, and space to store your books and supplies. Personalize your study area to make it even more inviting. For example, display pictures of loved ones or add plants. Do whatever it takes to create a space you look forward to entering.

4. Make a list of important assignments. The daily actions list on page 81 is ideal for this purpose.

Put the most urgent assignments on the top of your daily actions list. As you study, check off each completed item; then go to the next one. This method allows you to use your valuable study time efficiently.

5. Plan to study your challenging subjects first. Tackle difficult subjects when your mind is alert and more receptive to new information. Save your easier subjects for dessert.

6. Arrange to be undisturbed. Do whatever is necessary to minimize interruptions. Tell friends and relatives not to contact you during your regular study hours. Put a Do-Not-Disturb sign on your door. Let your answering machine take telephone calls. If necessary, study where no one can easily disturb you, such as at your college library. Protect the sanctity of your study time.

7. Tell yourself "I will remember what I'm about to study." Simply telling yourself to remember what you are studying increases your ability to recall the information later.

8. Do a data dump. Write down everything you already know about the subject you're preparing to study. This activity starts your brain thinking about the subject at hand. It's the mental equivalent of stretching your muscles and warming up before playing a sport.

9. Form a study group. Studying with other Creators is a great way to improve your study efficiency. Follow the suggestions on pages 105–106 to ensure that your study group functions at top form.

During Studying

10. Play soft, instrumental music in the background. Studies show that listening to instrumental music with about 60 beats per second induces *alpha* brain waves and therefore enhances learning. Classical music of the baroque period is ideally suited for this purpose.

11. Change subjects after forty-five to sixty minutes. Studies of learning reveal that we recall the most

© Lynn Johnston Productions, Inc./Dist. by United Feature Syndicate, Inc.

from the beginning and ending of a study session. Changing tasks periodically provides more beginnings and endings. You'll typically learn more from three one-hour sessions, each on a different subject, than you will with one three-hour session on the same subject.

12. Take a short break every thirty minutes or so. Get up and stretch. Walk around. Get a drink of water. Stretch and walk around a little more. Now return to your studying refreshed.

13. Study during your peak learning times. Some people are most alert in the morning, whereas others are most alert in the evening. And some come alive in the middle of the day. Investing one hour of studying in your prime time is probably worth two (or more) hours of studying in your off times. Schedule your day to use your peak learning times for studying.

14. Create Q&A cards. On one side of a 3″ × 5″ card, write a question (Q) that your instructor might ask on a test. Create questions from both class discussions and readings. Remember, you can create questions by simply turning textbook headings and key terms into questions. On the back of the Q&A cards, write the answers (A). Show these questions to your instructor, con-

firming that they'll lead you to important answers in the course. Carry Q&A cards with you everywhere. Pull them out for a quick review whenever you have a few extra minutes. If you study them only twenty minutes per day, that's over two hours of extra studying each week during time you might otherwise have wasted. You can also use Q&A cards to great benefit in study group sessions.

15. Create comparison charts. College courses often expose you to the similarities among and differences between a number of people, events, or theories. When this is the case, create a comparison chart that places the various items you're studying next to one another so you can see the similarities and differences. For an example, look at the charts at the beginning of each chapter in this book. Notice how each chart clearly compares the beliefs, behaviors, and attitudes of Successful Students with those of Struggling Students. You can do the same sort of a comparison with many subjects you will take.

16. Create study sheets containing key math and science formulas. Use the study sheets to solve practice problems, being sure you understand each step.

17. Review briefly every day. Repetition strengthens memory, so set aside a minimum of ten to fifteen minutes daily for reviewing your courses. Review your Q&A cards, comparison charts, study sheets, or class notes regularly, and you'll be pleased to see how easily you recall the information later. Ideal times to review are right before going to sleep or directly upon waking in the morning.

18. Use the postage stamp method. Here's my favorite way to study in the week before a test. Seven days before the test, summarize all the information you need to know for the test, writing everything on one side of a full sheet of paper (8.5 inches by 11 inches). Every couple of hours, read and study the summarized information for thirty minutes. Six days before the test, copy these same study notes onto a sheet of paper half as large as the first one—condensing ideas as necessary—and study the information for several thirty-minute sessions that day. Five days before the test, copy all of your study notes onto a sheet of paper half again as large (4.25 inches by 5.5

inches), once more studying the information for several thirty-minute sessions that day. Each day thereafter, transfer the information onto a study sheet half as large as the previous one and study from it. By now you are creating abbreviations, acronyms, and symbols to get all the information on your shrinking study sheet. When your notes are on a piece of paper about the size of a postage stamp, study them right up to the exam. On the way into the exam, roll your tiny piece of paper into a tiny ball and toss it in the trash. You are ready for the test.

After Studying

19. Review, Review, Review. The key to retaining information is moving it from short-term memory to long-term memory. Repetition is the key. Shortly after your study period, spend ten minutes reviewing the key concepts or terms you learned. Two hours later review again for ten minutes. Review once more before going to sleep. For

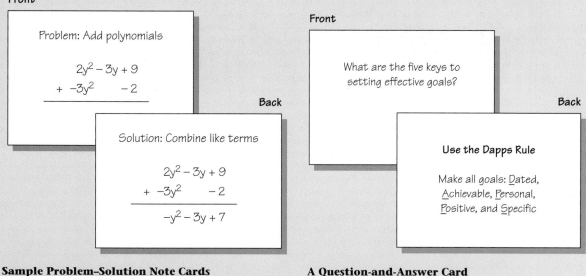

Front

Problem: Add polynomials

$$2y^2 - 3y + 9$$
$$+ \ -3y^2 \qquad - 2$$
_____

Back

Solution: Combine like terms

$$2y^2 - 3y + 9$$
$$+ \ -3y^2 \qquad - 2$$
_____
$$-y^2 - 3y + 7$$

Front

What are the five keys to setting effective goals?

Back

Use the Dapps Rule

Make all goals: <u>D</u>ated,
<u>A</u>chievable, <u>P</u>ersonal,
<u>P</u>ositive, and <u>S</u>pecific

Sample Problem–Solution Note Cards   **A Question-and-Answer Card**

the next three days, review these same concepts or terms daily for about five minutes. Next, review them weekly for about five minutes each time. This repeated review takes little effort but creates much learning.

20. Create an instant replay of your study session. Run a movie in your mind of your entire study session. For example, mentally reconstruct conversations with your study partner(s), picture your Q&A cards, visualize your comparison charts. Best of all, do this mental review at times that would otherwise be wasted, like when commuting or standing in a line.

21. Discuss concepts often. Conversation solidifies learning. Whenever possible, talk about new concepts with study partners and your instructors.

22. Teach what you learn. Find people who will assume the role of your students. Tell them, "I learned something new in class today, and I'd like to see if I can explain it clearly enough for you to understand." One student I knew put her children to bed each night in a most creative way; she donned hand puppets and delivered animated lectures to her children about what she had learned that day.

23. Seek tutoring. If you don't understand something you're studying or need more one-on-one explanations, go to the tutoring center on your campus to get help. If the first tutor you see isn't much help, ask for a different tutor the next time.

Studying Exercise

Interview successful students and ask for their favorite study strategies. See if you can discover additional strategies not on the list above.

8 Developing Emotional Intelligence

Creating worldly success is meaningless if I am unhappy. That means I must take responsibility for creating the quality of not only my outcomes but also my inner experiences.

I create my own happiness.

SUCCESSFUL STUDENTS . . .	STRUGGLING STUDENTS . . .
understand emotional intelligence, using feelings as a compass for staying on course to their goals and dreams.	allow themselves to be overwhelmed by emotions, making unwise choices that push them off course.
effectively reduce distress, managing and soothing emotions of upset such as anger, fear, and sadness.	take no responsibility for managing their emotions, instead acting irrationally on impulses of the moment.
create flow, feeling joyful and contentedly absorbed in their choices of work and play.	frequently experience boredom or anxiety in their lives.

Understanding Emotional Intelligence

FOCUS QUESTIONS	What is emotional intelligence? How can you use your emotions as a compass to stay on course to a rich, fulfilling life?

During final exam period one semester, I heard a painful shriek from the nursing education office. Seconds later, a student charged out of the office, screaming, scattering papers in the air, and stumbling down the hall. A cluster of concerned classmates caught up to her and desperately tried to comfort her. "It's all right. You can take the exam again next semester. It's okay. Really." She leaned against the wall, eyes closed. She slid down the wall until she sat in a limp heap, surrounded by sympathetic voices. Later, I heard that she dropped out of school.

At the end of another semester, I had the unpleasant task of telling one of my hardest-working students that she had failed the proficiency exams. Her mother had died during the semester, so I was particularly worried about how she would handle more bad news. We had a conference, and upon telling her the news, I began consoling her. For about a minute, she listened quietly and then said, "You're taking my failure pretty hard. Do you need a hug?" Before I could respond, she plucked me out of my chair and gave me a hug. "Don't worry," she said, patting my back. "I'll pass next semester," and sure enough, she did.

For most of us, life presents bumpy roads now and then. We fail a college course. The job we want goes to someone else. The person we love doesn't feel the same. Our health gives way to sickness. How we handle the resulting emotional distress is critical to the outcomes of our lives.

Success depends on much more than high IQs and academic success. Karen Arnold and Terry Denny at the University of Illinois studied eighty-one valedictorians and salutatorians from the 1981 graduating classes from Illinois high schools. They found that ten years after graduation, only 25 percent were at the highest level of those of similar age and chosen professions. Actually, many were doing significantly less well. What seems to be missing for these academic stars is **emotional intelligence.**

An experiment during the 1960s shows just how important emotional control is to success. Four-year-old children at a preschool were told that they could have one marshmallow immediately, or if they could wait for about twenty minutes, they could have two. Over a dozen years later, experimenters examined the differences in the lives of the one-marshmallow (emotionally impulsive) children and the two-marshmallow (emotionally intelligent) children. The adolescents who as children were able to delay gratification were found to be superior to their counterparts as high school students and to score an average of 210 points higher on SAT tests. Additionally, the two-marshmallow teenagers had borne fewer children out of wedlock and had experienced fewer

I know it is hard to accept, but an upset in your life is beneficial, in that it tells you that you are off course in some way and you need to find your way back to your particular path of clarity once again.

Susan Jeffers

In the realm of emotions, many people are functioning at a kindergarten level. There is no need for self-blame. After all, in your formal education, how many courses did you take in dealing with feelings?

Gay and Kathlyn Hendricks

problems with the law. Clearly the ability to endure some emotional discomfort in the present in exchange for greater rewards in the future is a key to success.

Components of emotional intelligence

In his book *Emotional Intelligence,* psychologist Daniel Goleman suggests that mastery of our emotions requires the ability to do the following:

1. **Recognize our emotions as they occur.** This ability might seem easy; surprisingly, for many, it is difficult. As children, many of us learned to minimize, maximize, or substitute our emotions. These three emotional patterns will be explained below.

2. **Manage our distressing emotions in a positive way.** This ability allows us to shake off or soothe our emotional upsets so that we can bring reason and purpose to our decisions.

3. **Control impulses and motivate ourselves.** This ability gives us the self-control and willpower necessary to delay gratification, as the two-marshmallow kids did. We learn to sacrifice immediate pleasure for future achievement.

4. **Recognize others' emotions (empathy).** This ability is one that we explored in Chapter 5, Employing Interdependence. Empathy is demonstrated by such responses as listening actively, respecting differences, and having compassion for others.

5. **Handle feelings that come up in a relationship.** This ability (along with empathy) allows us to develop the relationships that are essential to achieving our greatest success. We demonstrate this ability by positively resolving disagreements, avoiding defensiveness, negotiating compromises, cooperating with others, and avoiding self-righteous judgments.

Every great, successful person I know shares the capacity to remain centered, clear and powerful in the midst of emotional "storms."
Anthony Robbins

Knowing your own emotions

The foundation of emotional intelligence is a keen awareness of our emotions as they rise and fall. None of the other abilities can exist without this one. However, three self-defeating patterns learned in childhood too often thwart this ability.

Minimizing emotions causes people to become numb to their current emotions; minimizers typically say they aren't feeling anything or they state what they are thinking and, inappropriately, label it a feeling. *Maximizing* emotions causes people to exaggerate their feelings; maximizers become overwhelmed by the flood of their strong emotions. *Substituting* emotions causes people to replace an "unacceptable" emotion with an "acceptable" emotion; substitutors, for example, may express inappropriate anger instead of sadness upon the loss of someone or something important to them.

Here are some steps toward becoming more attuned to your emotions:

Build a vocabulary of feelings. Learn the names of emotions you might experience. There are dozens. How many can you name beyond anger, fear, sadness, and happiness?

Be mindful of emotions as they are happening. Learn to identify and express emotions in the moment. Be aware of the subtleties of emotion, learning to make fine distinctions between similar feelings such as sadness and depression.

Understand what is causing your emotion. Look behind the emotion. See when anger is caused by hurt feelings. Notice when anxiety is caused by irrational thoughts. Realize when sadness is caused by disappointments.

Recognize the difference between a feeling and resulting actions. Feeling an emotion is one thing; acting on the emotion is quite another. Emotions and behaviors are separate experiences, one internal, one external. Note when you tend to confuse the two, as a student did who said, "My teacher made me so upset I had to drop the class." One can be upset with a teacher and remain enrolled in the class.

You will never reach your full potential without emotional intelligence. No matter how academically bright you may be, emotional illiteracy will limit how much you achieve. Emotions that run wild can destroy you; emotions that fuel motivation and guide your wise choices can propel you successfully to your goals and dreams.

> *Academic intelligence has little to do with emotional life. The brightest among us can founder on the shoals of unbridled passions and unruly impulses; people with high IQ's can be stunningly poor pilots of their private lives.*
>
> Daniel Goleman

Journal Entry 27

> *It made me feel better sometimes to get something down on paper just like I felt it. It brought a kind of relief to be able to describe my pain. It was like, if I could describe it, it lost some of its power over me. I jotted down innermost thoughts I couldn't verbalize to anyone else, recorded what I saw around me, and expressed feelings inspired by things I read.*
>
> Nathan McCall

In this activity, you will explore your ability to understand your own emotions and recognize them as they are occurring. This ability is the foundation for all other abilities constituting emotional intelligence.

1. **Write about an experience when you felt ANGER or RAGE.** Describe fully what happened and your emotional reaction. Because emotions are difficult to describe, you may want to try a comparison like this: *Anger spread through me like a fire in a pile of dry hay.* Of course, you will compose your own comparison.

2. **Write about an experience when you felt FEAR or ANXIETY.** Again, describe fully what happened and your emotional reaction. Consider another comparison, such as *I trembled as though I was the next person to stand before a firing squad.*

3. **Write about an experience when you felt SADNESS or DEPRESSION.** Try another comparison, such as *For weeks, depression wrapped me in a profound darkness.*

4. **Write about an experience when you felt HAPPINESS or JOY.** Did you consciously choose to create this emotion, or did it happen spontaneously? A possible comparison: *Joy bubbled like champagne in my soul, and I laughed uncontrollably.*

5. **Describe any emotional changes you experienced *as you described* each of these four experiences. What insight might your experience here suggest about emotions?** If you weren't aware of any changes in your present emotions as you described past emotions, write as best you can about why that might be so.

Relax, think, write.

Reducing Distress

FOCUS QUESTION   What can you do to calm distressing feelings that make life unpleasant and threaten to get you off course?

B ecause life's adversities are inevitable, so is their accompanying distress. Although no one is exempt from distress, Victims and Creators react quite differently.

A deal with the devil

Of all the drugs and the compulsive behaviors that I have seen in the past twenty-five years, be it cocaine, heroine, alcohol, nicotine, gambling, sexual addiction, food addiction, all have one common thread. That is the covering up, or the masking, or the unwillingness on the part of the human being to confront and be with his or her human feelings.

Richard Miller, M.D.

To manage their moods, Victims make unwise choices that reduce distress in the moment while putting their future in jeopardy. This is a deal with the devil.

A Victim's greatest concern when feeling distress is to minimize discomfort. When upset, Victims blame, complain, and make excuses. They insult others, break promises, drink alcohol to excess, flee challenges, threaten, fight, take numbing drugs, watch television for hours, or spend money foolishly. Like the impulsive children of the marshmallow experiment, they seek instant release from discomfort and an immediate experience of pleasure, giving little thought to the impact on their futures. While every strong emotion is a call to action, Victims respond with one impulsive, immature choice after another. Little wonder Victims move further and further off course.

THE FAR SIDE® By GARY LARSON

"You know, we're just not reaching that guy."

The Far Side® by Gary Larson © 1982 FarWorks, Inc. All Rights Reserved. Used with permission.

Take responsibility for your inner experience

When you take full responsibility here and now for all of your feelings and for everything that happens to you, you never again blame the people and situations in the world outside of you for any unhappy feelings that you have.

Ken Keyes

Creators, on the other hand, learn to recognize, accept, and fully experience distressing feelings. They know that healthy emotions deliver powerful messages and, when heeded, eventually pass out of consciousness. Like everyone, Creators want to experience positive emotions, but they know that managing emotions intelligently means making wise choices even in the grip of distress. They know they are responsible not only for the results they create in their outer world but also for the emotions they generate in their inner world.

Because Creators are skilled at identifying their emotions early, they take positive actions before their rational processes are hijacked by emotional upset. Here's a menu of proven strategies for managing the three most common distressing emotions: Anger, Fear, and Sadness.

ANGER Healthy anger declares a threat or injustice against us or someone we care about. Perceiving this violation, our brain signals our body to release catecholamines (hormones) that fuel our strength and will to fight. Creators become conscious of oncoming anger through changes like flushed skin, tensed muscles, and increased pulse rates.

With this awareness, Creators can pause and wisely choose what to do next rather than strike out impulsively. Emotions don't ask rational questions, so we must. For example, Creators ask, *Will I benefit from releasing my anger, or will it cost me dearly?*

When you perceive a true injustice, use the energy produced by your anger to right the wrong. To avoid being overwhelmed by anger and doing something you will regret later, however, here are some effective strategies:

Change your physiology: Allow the chemical bath of anger-producing hormones about twenty minutes to recede. Here's how:

- *Separate.* Go off and be alone, allowing time to regain your ability to make rational, positive choices.

- *Exercise.* Moving vigorously assists in reducing anger-fueling hormones in your body.

- *Relax.* Slowing down also aids in calming your body, returning control of your decisions to you (as long as you don't spend this time obsessively thinking about the event that angered you).

Change your thoughts: As we know, thoughts stir emotional responses, so revising anger-producing thoughts calms us. Here's how:

- *Reframe.* Look at the problem from another angle. Search for a benign explanation for the anger-causing event. If you realize you were wronged unknowingly, unintentionally, or even necessarily, you can often see the other person's behavior in a less hostile way.

- *Elevate.* Rise above the moment and see the angering event in the larger picture of your life and notice how little importance it really has. Consider, "Will this really matter one year from now?"

- *Distract yourself.* Consciously shift your attention to something pleasant, stopping the runaway train of angry thoughts. Involve yourself with uplifting conversations, movies, books, music, video games, puzzles, or similar diversions.

- *Identify the hurt.* Anger is often built upon hurt: Someone doesn't meet me when she said she would. Below my anger I'm hurt that she seems to care about me so little. Shift attention from anger to the deeper hurt.

- *Forgive.* Take offending people off the hook for whatever they did, no matter how offensive. Don't concern yourself with whether *they* deserve forgiveness; the question is whether *you* deserve the emotional relief of forgiveness. The reason for forgiveness is primarily to improve *your* life, not theirs. We close the case to free ourselves of the daily self-infliction of poisonous judgments. Of course, forgiveness doesn't mean we forget and allow them to misuse us again.

FEAR   Healthy fear delivers a message that we are in danger. Our brain then releases hormones that fuel our energy to flee. Many Victims, though,

The sign of intelligent people is their ability to control emotions by the application of reason.

Marya Mannes

Living life as an art requires a readiness to forgive.

Maya Angelou

exaggerate dangers, and their healthy fear is replaced by paralyzing anxiety or terror about what could go wrong.

Creators become conscious of oncoming fear, terror, or anxiety through their body's clear signals, especially shallow breathing, increased pulse rate, and "butterflies" in the stomach. With this awareness, Creators can pause and wisely choose what to do next rather then fleeing impulsively from or constantly worrying about a nonthreatening person or situation.

One area where fear hinders academic performance is test anxiety; unless you minimize your distress you will be unable to demonstrate effectively what you know. Here are some wise choices to avoid being hijacked by fear:

Change your physiology: As with anger, allow the fear-producing chemicals to recede. Here's how:

- *Relax.* Slowing down helps you reclaim mastery of your thoughts and resulting emotions (but don't spend this time thinking about the original cause of your fear).
- *Breathe deeply.* Fear constricts. Keep oxygen flowing through your body to reverse the physiological impact of fear.

Change your thoughts: Changing your thoughts soothes irrational fears. Here's how:

- *Detach.* Once you have prepared fully, there is no more you can do. Worrying won't help. So do everything you can to ready yourself for a challenge, and then let the outcome take care of itself.
- *Reframe.* Ask yourself, "If the worst happens, can I live with it?" If you fail a test, for example, you won't like it, but could you live with it? (If not, consider seeking help to regain a healthy perspective.)
- *Visualize success with safety.* Create a mental movie of yourself achieving your ideal outcomes. Play the movie over and over until it becomes stronger than your fear.
- *Assume the best.* Victims often create fear through negative assumptions. Suppose your professor says, "I want to talk to you in my office." Resist assuming that the conversation is about something bad. In fact, if you're going to assume, why not assume it's something wonderful?
- *Distract yourself.* As with anger, consciously replacing fearful thoughts with pleasant ones will help stop the anxiety. So involve yourself with engaging activities that will take your thoughts on a pleasant diversion.
- *Face the fear.* Do what you fear, in spite of the fear. Most often you will learn that your fear was just a False Expectation Appearing Real.

SADNESS Healthy sadness overtakes us upon the loss of someone or something dear. Fully grieving our loss is essential, for only in this way do we both honor and resolve our loss. Unhealthy sadness, however, becomes a lingering depression, a dark, helpless feeling that anesthetizes us, keeping us from moving on to create a positive experience of life despite our loss.

Anxiety . . . sabotages academic performance of all kinds: 126 different studies of more than 36,000 people found that the more prone to worries a person is, the poorer their academic performance, no matter how measured— grades on tests, grade-point average, or achievement tests.
Daniel Goleman

If your images are positive, they will support you and cheer you on when you get discouraged. Negative pictures rattle around inside of you, affecting you without your knowing it.
Virginia Satir

Creators become conscious of oncoming or lingering depression through their body's clear signals of low energy, constant fatigue, and lack of a positive will to perform meaningful tasks. With this awareness, Creators wisely take steps to climb out of the dark pit of depression into the light of a full, rich life. Here are some wise choices to avoid being hijacked by depression:

Change your physiology: You want to help your body produce natural hormones that will elevate your mood. Here's how:

- *Exercise.* Moving vigorously helps your body create a natural chemical high that combats depression.
- *Laugh.* Like exercise, laughter is physiologically incompatible with depression. So rent a funny movie, go to a comedy club, read joke books or cartoons, visit your funniest friend.
- *Breathe deeply.* Like fear, depression constricts. Keep breathing deeply to offset the physiological impact of depression.
- *Do something (anything!) toward your goals.* Get moving. Get a result, no matter how small. Accomplishment combats depression.

Change your thoughts: As with other distressing emotions, changing our thoughts soothes depression. Here's how:

- *Challenge pessimistic beliefs.* Depression thrives on pessimism. Dispute beliefs that make the loss seem permanent, pervasive, or personal. Think, instead, how life will improve over time, how the loss is limited to only part of your life, and how the cause is not a personal flaw, but something you can remedy with an action.
- *Socialize with friends and loved ones.* Isolation usually intensifies depression. Socializing reengages you with people who matter and helps you gain a healthier perspective on your loss.
- *Help others in need.* Assisting people less fortunate not only distracts you from the source of your sadness, but it also reminds you that, despite your loss, you still have much to be grateful for.
- *Focus on the positive.* Identify your blessings and victories. Appreciate what you have instead of regretting what you don't. See positive alternatives.
- *Find the opportunity in the problem.* At least, learn the lesson life has brought you and move on. At best, turn your loss into a gain.

Choose your attitude

When dealing with distress, the critical issue is, *Do you manage your emotions or do they manage you?* If you have made an honest effort to manage your emotions and they have defied you still, you may wish to seek the help of a counselor or therapist. But if it's inspiration you seek, look to Viktor E.

The greater part of our happiness or misery depends on our dispositions and not our circumstances.
Martha Washington

The greatest discovery of my generation is that human beings, by changing the inner attitudes of their minds, can change the outer aspects of their lives.
William James

Frankl, a psychiatrist imprisoned in the Nazi concentration camps during World War II. In his book *Man's Search for Meaning,* Frankl relates how he and other prisoners rose above their unspeakable suffering to create a more positive inner experience.

In one example, Frankl tells of a particularly bleak day when he was falling into deep despair. With terrible sores on his feet, he was forced to march many miles in bitter cold weather to a work site, and there, freezing and weak from starvation, he endured constant brutality from the guards. Frankl describes how he "forced" his thoughts to turn to another subject. In his mind he imagined himself "standing on the platform of a well-lit, warm and pleasant lecture room." Before him sat an audience pleased to hear him give a lecture on the psychology of the concentration camp. "By this method," Frankl says, "I succeeded somehow in rising above the situation, above the sufferings of the moment, and I observed them as if they were already of the past."

I discovered I always have choices and sometimes it's only a choice of attitude.
Judith M. Knowlton

From his experiences and his observations, Frankl concluded that everything can be taken from a person but one thing: "the last of the human freedoms—to choose one's attitude in any given set of circumstances, to choose one's own way."

Creators claim the power to choose their outcomes whenever possible and to choose their attitudes always.

Journal Entry 28

In this activity you will practice changing your emotional response to a distressing situation in your life.

1. **Write a conversation between you and your Inner Guide about a distressing situation that now exists in your life.** Begin by fully describing the situation to your Inner Guide. Then continue the conversation, having your Inner Guide ask questions that help you *discover and apply three or more strategies for managing your distressing emotions.* Label your own comments with ME and your Inner Guide's comments with IG. Let your Inner Guide use all of the skills of a great listener as it helps you to take responsibility for your inner experience of life.

2. **Write about what you have just learned or relearned about managing your emotions.** Mention any changes you will make in your life as a result of what you have learned. Remember the power of the 4 E's—Examples, Experiences, Explanation, and Evidence—to improve the quality of your writing.

Relax, think, write.

Creating Flow

FOCUS QUESTIONS What are you doing when you feel most happy to be alive—when you become so absorbed that time seems to disappear? How can you create more of these peak experiences in your life?

Happiness has been called the goal of all goals, the true destination of all journeys. After all, why do we pursue any goal or dream? Isn't it for the positive experience our quest will create?

For centuries, explorers of human nature have wondered how we can consciously and naturally create happiness. Psychologist Mihaly Csikszentmihalyi has called highly enjoyable periods of time **flow states.** Flow is characterized by total absorption in what one is doing, an altered sense of time (usually seeming to pass more quickly than usual, though sometimes more slowly), and a loss of self-consciousness (concern about yourself). His studies offer insights into how we can purposely create such inner experiences.

Csikszentmihalyi believes that the key to creating flow lies in the interaction of two factors: the challenge a person *perceives* himself to be facing and the related skills he *perceives* himself to possess. Note the word "perceive." Once again, we're reminded that the quality of our inner experience is dependent upon what we *believe* to be true.

Let's consider examples of three possible relationships of skill level and challenge. First, when a person's perceived skill level is higher than the perceived challenge, the result is *boredom:* Think how bored you'd feel if you took an introductory course in a subject in which you were already an expert.

Second, when a person's perceived skill level is lower than that needed to meet the perceived challenge, the result is *anxiety:* Think how anxious you'd feel if you took an advanced mathematics course before you could even add and subtract.

Third, when the individual's perceived skill level is equal to or even slightly below the challenge level, the result is often *flow:* Recall one of those extraordinary moments when you lost yourself in the flow—

TO BE OF USE

The people I love the best
jump into work head first
without dallying in the shallows
and swim off with sure strokes almost out of sight.
They seem to become natives of that element,
the black sleek heads of seals
bouncing like half-submerged balls.

I love people who harness themselves, an ox to a heavy cart,
who pull like water buffalo, with massive patience,
who strain in the mud and the muck to move things forward,
who do what has to be done, again and again.

I want to be with people who submerge
in the task, who go into the fields to harvest
and work in a row and pass the bags along,
who stand in the line and haul in their places,
who are not parlor generals and field deserters
but move in a common rhythm
when the food must come in or the fire be put out.

The work of the world is common as mud.
Botched, it smears the hands, crumbles to dust.
But the thing worth doing well done
has a shape that satisfies, clean and evident.
Greek amphoras for wine or oil,
Hopi vases that held corn, are put in museums
but you know they were made to be used.
The pitcher cries for water to carry
and a person for work that is real.

—*Marge Piercy*

maybe while conversing with a challenging thinker or playing a sport you love with a well-matched opponent. In flow, participation in the activity is its own reward; the outcome doesn't matter.

CREATING FLOW

Skill level HIGH and challenge level LOW = Boredom

Skill level LOW and challenge level HIGH = Anxiety

Skill level EQUAL TO or SLIGHTLY BELOW challenge level = Flow

---

Being able to enter flow is emotional intelligence at its best; flow represents perhaps the ultimate in harnessing the emotions in the service of performance and learning.
Daniel Goleman

According to Csikszentmihalyi, activities that are likely to create a flow experience offer us

- specific goals and clear rules about how to achieve the goals.
- challenges that can be adjusted up or down to match our skill level.
- clear feedback about how we're doing.
- the capacity to screen out distractions.

Nadja Salerno-Sonneberg, one of the world's great concert violinists, has found her source of flow in creating music. "Playing in the zone is a phrase that I use to describe a certain feeling on stage, a heightened feeling where everything is right," she says. "By that I mean everything comes together. Everything is one . . . you, yourself, are not battling yourself. All the technical work and what you want to say with the piece comes together. It's very, very rare but it's what I have worked for all my life. It's just right. It just makes everything right. Nothing can go wrong with this wonderful feeling."

Work and flow

When do you suppose a typical working American experiences the most flow? After work? On the weekends? On vacations? If these are your guesses, you'll be surprised by what Csikszentmihalyi found: Typical working adults report experiencing flow on their jobs three times more often than during free time.

The best career advice to give the young is "Find out what you like doing best and get someone to pay you for doing it."
Katherine Whitehorn

The lesson is clear: If you want to create a positive experience of life, engage in work that appeals to your natural inclination, your inborn desires. When will you have time for boredom if you wake up every morning excited about your day's work?

Carolyn, a twenty-year-old student, was studying to be a nurse, but that was the career her mother wanted for her. Carolyn's dream was to dance, but part of us—perhaps our Inner Critic—will do anything to keep the peace, to stay safe, to make things a little more pleasant in the moment. "If I even mention dancing, my mother goes nuts," Carolyn confided. "It's not worth the hassle to fight her."

Another more spirited part of us—probably our Inner Guide—hangs on to our dreams. That spirit urges us to pursue work we truly love.

Which part will you heed? Your career is a critical choice that will profoundly affect the quality of your life. Carolyn had responsible options besides giving up her dream. She could have dropped out of college and gotten a job to pay her bills while pursuing her dancing career. She could have completed her nursing degree and then worked as a nurse while pursuing her dancing career.

The last time I saw Carolyn (about a year after our first conversation), I asked her what she was doing.

"I'm still in the nursing program," she said.

"Any dancing in your life?"

"I've sort of stopped thinking about that."

As best I could tell, Carolyn had abandoned her dreams.

When you study people who are successful as I have over the years, it is abundantly clear that their achievements are directly related to the enjoyment they derived from their work.

Marsha Sinetar

Have you? Let's revisit your written goals and dreams. Is this the work you would choose if you had absolutely no restrictions? Are you headed for a career that represents your passion? Or are you like one of my students, who said, "My goal is to be an accountant. I hate math, but I hear accountants make a lot of money."

For the next couple of decades at least, you'll probably spend many of your waking hours at work. You don't have to settle for just a paycheck. Some people do what they love. Why shouldn't you?

I spent more than a year of my life doing work I disliked, and I know how quickly my inner experience turned sour. I woke up many mornings with a stomachache. I lived for weekends, but by Sunday afternoon I began to dread Monday morning. Finally, I heeded the feedback from my emotional distress and sought work where I was happy. I urge you to follow your bliss. This choice may require self-discipline to get you through the education or training necessary to qualify for your desired career, but it's worth all the discomfort in the present for all the rewards in the future.

Play and flow

The supreme accomplishment is to blur the line between work and play.

Arnold Toynbee

What do you do when you're not working? People who successfully create a positive experience of life have a knack for having fun. Staying connected to the little kid inside of them, they make time to play. The luckiest (wisest?) among us even get paid to play.

Effective self-management includes scheduling time for recreation. True *recreation* is a Quadrant II activity and deserves time in your weekly written plan. Make time to play basketball, learn a new computer game, play an instrument, dance, watch a movie, ride a horse, go shopping, collect coins, plant a garden, put together a puzzle—something you love to do.

Be open to spontaneous play as well. Tell a joke. Skip along the sidewalk between classes. Crawl around the floor with a baby. Go to a matinee. Call a friend you haven't seen in years and talk like Donald Duck.

Don't put off having fun because money is tight; play for free. Go to a park. Write a poem. Throw a Frisbee. Play chess. Climb a mountain.

Notice the activity that's missing in these lists: television. If you watch a lot of television, you should know what Csikszentmihalyi found in his study of flow. Students reported experiencing flow five times more often while doing homework than they did while watching TV. Television, he discovered, relaxes your mind, but it also lowers your alertness, mental focus, satisfaction, and creativity.

I finally figured out the only reason to be alive is to enjoy it.

Rita Mae Brown

One more point remains to be made about the benefits of creating flow in work and play. Not only does flow improve your inner experience, but it also promotes your professional and personal growth. Each time you create flow by testing your present skills against a new challenge, your skills improve. To create flow the next time, you have to increase the difficulty of the challenge, which, in turn, offers an opportunity to improve your skills once again. Over time, by creating flow again and again, your skills improve greatly, and this growth adds even more to the happiness in your life.

Journal Entry 29

In this activity, you will explore ways to create flow in your life. The more flow you create day to day, the more positive will be your inner experience of life.

1. **Write about a specific past experience when you experienced flow in any part of your life.** Remember, flow is characterized by total absorption in what you're doing, an altered awareness of time, and a sense of performing at your very best.

2. **Write about your perfect work of the future, the kind that you believe will create the most flow in your life.** Think about past or present work experiences. Explore the feelings these jobs generated in you (particularly boredom, anxiety, flow). Then let your imagination run free. Design your perfect job, its challenges, rewards, fellow workers, hours, location, environment. Consider everything that will make this work something you would love to do *even if you didn't get paid.*

Try as much as possible to be wholly alive, with all your might, and when you laugh, laugh like hell and when you get angry, get good and angry. Try to be alive. You will be dead soon enough.

William Saroyan

3. **Write about how you could bring more flow into your life through play.** Use past experiences as feedback, but let your imagination design fun that you would like to create in the future. Which recreational activities have you tried that you would like to do more of? Which have you never tried but might give you a flow experience?

Consider illustrating this journal entry with drawings, stickers, or pictures cut from magazines.

Relax, think, write.

After Math

When **Professor Bishop** returned mid-term exams that Monday morning, he said, "In 20 years of teaching math, I've never seen such low scores. Can anyone tell me what the problem is?" He ran a hand through his graying hair and waited. No one spoke. "Don't you people even care how you do?" Students fiddled with their test papers. They looked out of the window. No one spoke. Finally, Professor Bishop said, "Okay, Scott, we'll start with you. What's going on? You got a 35 on the test. Did you even *study*?"

Scott, 18, mumbled, "Yeah, I studied. But I just don't understand math." Other students in the class nodded their heads. One student muttered "Amen, brother."

Professor Bishop looked around the classroom. "What about the rest of you?" he said. Silence reigned for a full minute. Suddenly, **Michael**, 23, stood up and snarled, "You're a damn joke, man. You can't teach, and you want to blame the problem on us. Well, I've had it. I'm dropping this stupid class. Then I'm filing a grievance. You better start looking for a new job!" He stormed out of the room, slamming the door behind him.

"Okay, I can see this isn't going anywhere productive," Professor Bishop said. "Class is canceled. I want you all to go home and think about why you're doing so poorly. And don't come back until you're prepared to answer that question honestly." He picked up his books and left the room.

An hour later, Michael was sitting alone in the cafeteria when his classmates Scott and **Kia**, 20, joined him. Scott said, "Geez, Michael, you really went off on Bishop! You're not really going to drop his class, are you?"

"Already did!" Michael snapped as his classmates sat down. "I went right from class to the registrar's office. I'm outta there!"

I might as well drop the class myself, Kia thought. Ever since her fiancé had called off their engagement ten months before, she had been too depressed to do her homework. Familiar tears blurred her vision.

Scott said, "I don't know what it is about math. I can study for hours, but come test time, I get so freaked it's like I never studied at all. My mind just goes blank." Thinking about math, Scott started craving something to eat.

"Where do you file a grievance against a professor around here, anyway?" Michael asked.

"I have no idea," Scott said.

"What?" Kia answered.

Michael stood and stomped off to file a grievance. Scott went to buy some French fries. Kia put her head down on the cafeteria table and tried to swallow the burning sensation in her throat.

Listed below are the characters in this story. Rank them in order of their *emotional intelligence*. Give a different score to each character. Be prepared to explain your choices.

Most emotionally intelligent←1 2 3 4→Least emotionally intelligent

_____ **Professor Bishop**   _____ **Scott**
_____ **Michael**   _____ **Kia**

DIVING DEEPER: **Imagine that you have been asked to mentor the person whom you ranked number 4 (least emotionally intelligent). Other than seeing a counselor, how would you suggest that this person handle his or her upset in a more emotionally intelligent manner?**

Emotional Intelligence at Work

During nearly twenty years working as a consulting psychologist to dozens of companies and public agencies, I have seen how the lack of emotional intelligence undermines both an individual's and a company's growth and success, and conversely how the use of emotional intelligence leads to productive outcomes at both the individual and the organizational levels.

Hendrie Weisnger, *Emotional Intelligence at Work*

Imagine this: The local store manager of a large retail chain sends a one-line e-mail to her department heads: "Quarterly sales figures on my desk by 9:00 A.M. tomorrow!" The head of the men's wear department reads the e-mail, feels insulted by the demanding tone, and fires back an angry e-mail response: "I've been working here a hell of a lot longer than you have, and I don't need your nasty reminders about when sales reports are due. You might try treating people more like colleagues and less like servants awaiting your every command." On an impulse, he copies his response to the company president and the five vice-presidents at the store's national headquarters.

How much lost time and productivity do you think will result from this brief exchange of two e-mails? How much damage will be done to their professional relationship and their ability to work well together in the future? How might their reputations and careers suffer when others hear rumors of this incident?

Or, how different might this event have evolved if the head of the men's wear department had made a different, more emotionally intelligent choice? Suppose he'd read the store manager's e-mail, taken a deep breath, and read it again? Feeling angry at what appeared to be the manager's dictatorial tone, what if he had waited about 30 minutes before responding? During that time, maybe he would have done a relaxation process. Maybe he would have recalled that the store manager has always been very respectful of him since she took over the store six months before. Having calmed his initial emotional upset, suppose he now went to the store manager's office and asked for a brief meeting? "You know," he says to her in this revised scene, "I just read you're e-mail about turning in the third-quarter sales figures, and I got that you're angry or upset. Is there something we need to talk about?" "What? Oh no," she responds, "there's no problem. I meant to send you a reminder last week, but I'm so far behind in my paper work that I forgot. Then, when I remembered this morning, I wrote the e-mail while I was doing five other things. Sorry if it sounded like I was upset with you. On the contrary, I think you're doing a terrific job!"

Another name for emotional intelligence in the workplace is "professionalism." Professionals are aware of their own feelings. They've developed methods for managing distressing feelings, not allowing themselves to respond impulsively while in their grip. Professionals know how to motivate themselves to do their work with excellence and they consistently meet project deadlines, even when this means delaying gratification in other areas. They're good at perceiving emotions in others, and they know how to communicate effectively, building alliances rather than destroying them. Notice that in the revised scene above, the department head doesn't reply to his manager with another e-mail. He communicates with the store manager in person. Little decisions like this one make all the difference when it comes to building a reputation as a business professional. And that reputation can be destroyed with one careless tantrum.

Your emotional intelligence begins to impact your work life as soon as you consider a career path. If you choose work for which you have no passion, no emotional commitment, you're starting your career with a huge handicap. Unmotivated by the outcomes or experiences of your work, you'll likely cut corners, doing less than is necessary to propel your career to success. By contrast, when you match your interests and talents to your career choice, you'll find work stimulating and success more likely. As Shoshana Zuboff, a psychiatrist and professor at Harvard Business School put it, "We only will know what to do by realizing what feels right to us."

Emotional intelligence continues to support your success during your job search. Chances are, every applicant invited for an interview has the training to do the job. So, what will distinguish you from the crowd? One answer lies in what employers are looking for beyond job skills. A 1997 survey of major corporations, done by the American Society for Training and Development, discovered that four out of five companies seek emotional intelligence as one of the qualities they look for in new employees. Realizing this, you'll know to communicate not only your academic and job-related skills, but your emotional intelligence competencies as well.

Employers have good reason to seek employees with emotional intelligence: It's critical to success. In his book *Working with Emotional Intelligence,* Daniel Goleman writes, "We now have twenty-five years' worth of empirical studies that tell us with a previously unknown precision just how much emotional intelligence matters for success." Goleman presents his analysis of what 121 companies reported as the necessary competencies for success in 181 different career positions. He found that two out of three of the abilities considered essential for effective job performance were emotional competencies. Put another way, according to employers themselves, emotional competence matters *twice* as much as IQ and technical expertise in job effectiveness.

You might think that the soft skills associated with emotional intelligence would be less important for those in highly intellectual fields like engineering, computer science, law, or medicine. Paradoxically, the exact opposite is true. Since academic success and high intelligence are required of all who enter these careers, virtually everyone in these careers is "smart." However, not everyone is emotionally intelligent. In these professions, there is more variation in the "soft" domain than there is variation in education and IQ. Therefore, if you're at the top end of the emotional intelligence scale, you have a great advantage over your emotionally illiterate colleagues. As Goleman puts it, " 'Soft' skills matter even more for success in 'hard' fields."

While emotional intelligence is important in entry-level positions, as one moves up the ladder into leadership positions, it becomes essential. According to Goleman, employers report emotional intelligence as making up 80–100 percent of the skills necessary to be an outstanding leader. As just one example of its importance, leaders are charged with motivating others to move persistently toward company goals and missions. They need to be able to spot and resolve conflicts that happen in their work force, because such upsets, if not dealt with effectively, can get an individual, group, division, or even the whole company off course.

Doug Lennick, executive vice president at American Express Financial Advisors, sums up the case for emotional intelligence in the work place: "The aptitudes you need to succeed start with intellectual horsepower—but people need emotional competence, too, to get the full potential of their talents. The reason we don't get people's full potential is emotional incompetence."

Believing in Yourself: **Develop Self-Love**

FOCUS QUESTIONS How much do you love yourself? What can you do to love yourself even more?

Ultimately, for most of us, the journey comes down to the same issue: learning to love freely. First ourselves, then other people.

Melody Beattie

S elf-love is the core belief that **I AM LOVABLE.** It's the unwavering trust that, no matter what, I will always love myself and other people will love me as well.

Self-love is vital to success. It empowers us to make wise, self-supporting choices instead of impulsive, self-destructive ones. These wise choices create a rich, full life of outer achievement and inner happiness.

Adults who have difficulty loving themselves typically felt neglected or abandoned as children. Many grew up in families in which they felt unappreciated and unloved. What meager love they did experience was often little more than a short-lived reward for adapting to their parents' expectations and demands. For children who felt unloved, each new day meant a desperate search for something they could say or do to earn approval from others.

A student in my English class once wrote an essay about the outrageous stunts she'd done to become head rabbit for her fifth grade's spring festival. As she read her story, everyone laughed loudly. Afterward, someone asked, "Why did you go to all that trouble just to be the head rabbit?"

Markeya paused. "Simple. The head rabbit got to wear the best costume." Then a serious look came over her face. "The truth is, I thought people would like me more if I was the head rabbit." She paused again. "And, I guess I hoped that *I* would like me more, too."

Like Markeya, we may believe that self-love depends upon our outer accomplishments and what others think of them. This kind of self-love is conditional: *I'll love myself **after** I earn my degree, **after** I get a great job, **after** I marry the perfect person, **after** I buy my dream house. . . .*

Self-esteem is the capacity to experience maximal self-love and joy whether or not you are successful at any point in your life.

David Burns, M.D.

If the belief that accomplishment creates self-love were accurate, then why do so many people who appear successful on the outside feel so empty on the inside? Worldly success will not fill all the empty places in our souls. But love for ourselves will.

Design a self-care plan

If we felt unloved as a child, we may need to learn how to love ourselves as adults and do so without confusing self-love with egotism, arrogance, or self-righteousness.

First, we might ask, *How do we know when other people truly love us?* Isn't it when they treat us well, when they consider our welfare along with their own, concern themselves with our success and happiness, treat us with respect even when our behavior seems least deserving, give us honest feedback, and make sacrifices for the betterment of our lives? Don't we feel loved when others nurture the very best in us with the very best in them?

Our parents' job was to love and nurture us when we were children. Some parents did a great job; some did a terrible job. Most parents probably fell somewhere in between. Now that we are adults, we are responsible for continuing (or beginning) our own nurturing. The more we care for ourselves, the more we feel lovable. And the more we feel lovable, the more overflow of compassion and love we have for others.

Nurturing yourself today begins with a conscious self-care plan. As you consider the following options for nurturing yourself, look for choices you could adopt to increase your self-love.

Nurture yourself physically. People who love themselves make wise choices to nurture their bodies for a long, healthy life. How's your diet? The next time you're about to eat or drink something, ask yourself: *Would I be proud to offer this to someone I truly loved?* This question will raise your awareness, encouraging you to make wiser choices about eating and drinking. Visit your college's health office or library for valuable information on improving your diet.

Do you exercise regularly? Even moderate exercise done routinely helps most people stay stronger and healthier. Regular exercise strengthens the immune system and produces hormones that give us a natural sense of well-being. Your physical education department can help you begin a safe, effective, and lifelong exercise program.

Do you have habits that injure your body? Do you drink too much coffee, smoke cigarettes, drink alcohol to excess, take dangerous drugs? If so, you may wish to give up the immediate pleasure of such substances for the improved health you'll gain. Substance abuse is misnamed. You're not abusing the substance—you're abusing yourself. Would you abuse someone you truly loved? Your college's health office can also provide you with information on how to stop these self-destructive habits. Additional community resources include Alcoholics Anonymous (A.A), Narcotics Anonymous (N.A.), Overeaters Anonymous (O.A.), and other twelve-step programs.

Here are additional ways to nurture your body: Get enough rest. Swing on a swing. Have regular medical checkups. Hug someone dear to you. Laugh until your sides ache. Take a bubble bath. Go dancing. Get a massage. Do nothing for an hour. Stretch like a cat. Breathe deeply. Relax.

Nurture yourself mentally. How you talk to yourself, especially when you're off course, will greatly influence your sense of self-love. Whenever you begin to condemn yourself, stop. Replace your negative judgments with positive, supportive comments.

You may find it difficult at first to choose self-loving thoughts rather than self-criticism. To help, try separating the doer from the deed. If you fail a test, your Inner Critic wants to label you a failure. But your Inner Guide knows you're not a failure; you're a person who, with many other successes in life,

The extent to which we love ourselves determines whether we eat right, get enough sleep, smoke, wear seat belts, exercise, and so on. Each of these choices is a statement of how much we care about living.

Bernie Siegel, M.D.

I believe that the black revolution certainly forced me and the majority of black people to begin taking a second look at ourselves. It wasn't that we were all that ashamed of ourselves, we merely started appreciating our natural selves . . . sort of, you know, falling in love with ourselves just as we are.

Aretha Franklin

got one F on one test. Keep your self-talk focused on facts, not judgments. When you create an undesired outcome, learn from the experience, forgive yourself for your shortcomings, and move on.

Here are some other ways to nurture yourself mentally: Say your affirmation(s) often, read uplifting books (many are listed in the bibliography), ask a motivating question and seek the answer, learn new words, visualize your success, balance your checkbook, sing or listen to a song with positive lyrics, analyze a difficult situation and make a decision, teach someone something you know how to do.

Nurture yourself emotionally. The very times you need self-love the most are often the times you feel self-love the least. You may be feeling shame instead of self-acceptance, helplessness instead of competence, self-contempt instead of self-respect, self-loathing instead of self-love.

An emotional antidote for toxic self-judgments is *compassion*. Treat yourself with the same kindness you'd offer a loved one who's struggling to make sense of this huge, confusing, and sometimes painful world. Realize that how you treat yourself as you go through difficult times—judgmentally or compassionately—is what will continue to affect your self-love long after the difficult times have passed.

The First Best-Kept Secret of Total Success is that we must feel love inside ourselves before we can give it to others.
Denis Waitley

Here are some other ways to nurture yourself emotionally: Feel your feelings, share your feelings with a friend, write about your feelings in your journal, see an uplifting and inspiring movie, spend time with loved ones, listen to inspiring music, do something special for yourself, remind yourself that strong feelings, like storms, will pass.

Deep self-love is the ongoing inner approval of who you are regardless of your current outer results. You are not your results. When you learn to love yourself even when you're off course, your belief in yourself will soar.

Journal Entry 30

In this activity, you will explore ways to develop greater self-love. Typically, people who love themselves achieve many of their goals and dreams and, regardless of the outer circumstances of their lives, often experience positive feelings.

1. **On a blank journal page, draw a circle. Within the circle, create a representation of your most LOVABLE INNER SELF.**
   If people could get a glimpse of you without your protective scripts, patterns, and habits, this is what they'd see. Such a drawing is called a "mandala." Like an affirmation, a mandala represents your ideal self, your greatest potential as a human being, the self you are in the process of creating. This drawing needs to make sense only to you. Use colors, words, or shapes as appropriate. Feel free to add personal photographs, pictures, and words cut from magazines.

One of the ways I nurture my own soul is by waking every morning around four-thirty and spending two hours by myself—for myself— doing yoga, visualization, meditation, or working on dreams. . . . Another way I nurture my soul is by keeping a daily journal. . . . This is what my two solitary hours in the morning are about— experiencing the core of my soul and discovering the truth that I have to live.

Marion Woodman

2. **Outside of the mandala circle, write different ways that you could take care of yourself PHYSICALLY, MENTALLY, and EMOTIONALLY.** In this way you are creating a self-care plan for the LOVABLE INNER SELF depicted in your mandala. Look back at the text for examples of ways to nurture yourself physically, mentally, and emotionally.

3. **On the next page in your journal, write an explanation of your mandala and the Self-Care Plan that you have created.** Think of questions an inquisitive reader would ask you, and let your Inner Guide answer them. For example, What is the significance of the drawings, shapes, words, lines, and colors that you have chosen to represent your full potential as a human being? What personal characteristics have you depicted as representing your best self? Why are these qualities important to you? In what ways have you decided to take care of yourself? And why have you chosen these particular ways to nurture yourself?

Relax, think, write.

Three factors determine how well you score on tests. The first is how well you have prepared. The second is how well you take tests. The third is how much you have learned from previous tests. The strategies below will enable you to maximize your scores on various kinds of tests.

Before a Test

1. Create a positive affirmation about taking tests. Create an affirming statement about test taking, like "I love taking tests and showing how much I've learned." Along with your personal affirmation, repeat this test-taking affirmation to reprogram your beliefs about your ability to succeed on tests.

2. Find out what information will be covered on the test. Ask your instructor questions such as the following: *Will the test cover everything from the beginning of the course or only since the mid-term? Will the test cover only material covered in lecture or from the readings as well?* You can plan your studying better when you understand what you are responsible for knowing.

3. Find out how you will be tested. How you prepare for a test depends on the kind of questions you will be asked. Is the test multiple-choice, true-false, fill-in-the-blank, matching, short answer, problem solving, essay, or some other format? To find out, ask your professor. Better yet, if your professor schedules special study sessions, be there. Such sessions provide a perfect opportunity for discovering both what will be on the test and how you will be tested.

4. Set a study schedule. To maximize your learning efficiency, spread your study sessions over time. Avoid cramming! Use your self-management tools (Chapter 4) to schedule and track your studying.

5. Predict test questions. Either by yourself or with a study group, create and take a practice test.

If you've created Q&A cards, these become your test. Besides readying yourself mentally, a practice test also prepares you emotionally. Having a dress rehearsal helps calm nerves and reduce test anxiety.

6. Visualize your success. Create a mental movie of yourself taking the exam with confidence, understanding every question, finishing on time, and receiving your test back with a high grade. Play this positive movie in your mind often.

7. Get to the exam room early and find a comfortable place. Set up your supplies (pens, pencils, paper, white-out, allowed books, calculator, and so on). Have a clock or watch so you can manage your time. You might even bring a picture that inspires you, like a photo of your family or one of you in a graduation gown. If it's a long exam, you might want to bring water and snacks, if they are allowed.

During a Test

8. Right before the exam is handed out, relax, say your affirmation(s), and visualize your success once more. If you have read your assignments, studied regularly, attended classes, and done everything that successful students do, this last-minute mental preparation will enable you to do your best work on the test.

9. Skim the test. Get an immediate overview of the whole test. Discover where the easy and difficult questions are. Understand the point value of each question or each part of the test. This information will allow you to make strategic choices about how to take the test. While skimming, you may even notice the answer to one question revealed in another question.

10. Read and follow the directions carefully. If you give a great answer to a question that wasn't asked, you won't do well. Likewise, if the directions allow you the option of marking two or more multiple-choice answers and you mark only one,

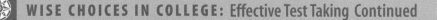

you'll probably lose points. Be sure you understand exactly what you are to do, and do it.

11. Do easy questions first. Easy points build confidence for the rest of the test. Return to the unanswered questions later, doing the ones with higher point values first. Following this plan, if you run out of time, you've earned the most points possible.

12. For multiple-choice questions: 1. Read the question and decide on an answer first; then look for that answer in the list of choices. 2. If you aren't sure, eliminate obvious incorrect answers and choose from those remaining. 3. When eliminating, cross out answers with qualifiers like *all, always, never, must,* or *every.* 4. When eliminating, also look for grammatical clues to cross out an answer (e.g., the subject in the question doesn't agree with the verb in a possible answer). 5. If two of four possible answers are similar (e.g., have similar words like *independent* and *interdependent*), choose one of them as correct. 6. Look for answers contained in other questions. 7. If the question is based on a reading passage, read the questions before reading the passage; look for answers as you read the passage.

13. For true-false questions: 1. Answer questions you know first. 2. If any part of the statement is false, the entire statement is false. 3. If the question contains a qualifier like *all, every, never,* or *always,* the answer is probably false. 4. If the question contains a qualifier like *some, a few, occasionally,* or *sometimes,* the answer is probably true.

14. For fill-in-the-blank questions: 1. Make sure your answer fits grammatically into the sentence (e.g., don't insert a noun if the space in the sentence requires a verb). 2. See if the answer is revealed in another question on the test.

15. For short-answer questions: 1. Begin your answer with the key part of the question. Suppose the question is "What are the advantages of using a tracking form?" Begin your answer, "The advan-

tages of using a tracking form include . . ." 2. Plan your answer to fit in the space provided whenever possible.

16. For matching questions: 1. First, match the pairs you know. 2. Next, match any remaining pairs. 3. Cross out pairs as you match them so you can see which choices remain.

17. For essay questions: 1. Underline key words in the question. Words like *compare and contrast, describe,* and *explain the cause* require different sorts of responses. Be sure to do what is requested. 2. Brainstorm by jotting down ideas related to the question. 3. Organize your ideas in a way compatible with your preferred learning style (an informal outline or a concept map). 4. Organize your answer so it's easy to read and understand. Creating a clear organization not only helps you write an effective essay; it also allows your professor to follow your ideas easily and give you maximum points for your ideas. 5. Reword the question and make it the first sentence of your answer. 6. Answer questions your reader may have about your ideas. For example, readers often want to know "Why?" and "How do you know?" 7. Offer specific support for your ideas. As you know, the 4 E's are ideal for adding powerful support. 8. Write a conclusion that summarizes the main points you have made. 9. Proofread carefully for grammar, spelling, and punctuation errors. 10. If your handwriting is difficult to read, recopy for neatness. Consider printing, writing on every other line, and writing on one side of the paper only.

18. For mathematics tests: 1. Jot down on the test itself any formulas necessary to solve the problem. 2. Estimate the answer. When finished, compare your answer with your estimate. If they are very different, check your computations. 3. Write out every step of your solution; even if you get the final answer wrong, the instructor may give you partial credit. 4. Revisit each question and confirm that you have done all that was asked. 5. Double-check all calculations.

19. Review your answers. If you finish with time to spare, don't leave yet. Return to the parts with the most points available and check your answers. Check other parts in descending order of points available. Bring white-out to the exam for making corrections neatly. Remain at the exam until you've thoroughly reviewed each question and every answer.

20. Offer an answer for every question. Unless there's a penalty for wrong answers, guess at any questions that remain blank. Even for an essay question, write something. You might pick up a few more points.

21. Match questions to the answer sheet. If the test has a separate answer sheet (as many standardized tests do), confirm that your answers are correctly matched to the appropriate question.

After a Test

22. Reward yourself. No matter how you did on the test, treat yourself for your efforts in preparing for and taking the test. Go out to dinner, take a bubble bath, rent a movie, tell a friend how hard you worked.

23. Get the correct answers to all questions you missed and study them. Ask the instructor for the correct answers. If you don't get the answers from the instructor, ask classmates. Creators may miss a question once, but they never miss it twice.

24. Review your exam to see what you can learn about yourself as a test taker. How many points did you miss because of poor preparation (you didn't understand the material)? How many points did you lose because of carelessness (you got the plus and minus signs reversed in a math problem)? How many points did you miss because of poor time management (you ran out of time and lost points on questions you could have answered)? How many points did you miss because of anxiety (your mind went blank)? With this information you'll be able to make a study plan that will create a better grade next time.

Test-Taking Exercise

Create a twenty-five-question test for a difficult course you are now taking; write out your answers to each question. Include five questions each of the following kinds: (1) true-false, (2) matching, (3) fill-in-the-blank, (4) multiple-choice, and (5) short-answer or essay questions. Or, for a mathematics course, prepare problems like the ones you have been studying. Design your questions so that a student who answers them well will be demonstrating the essential knowledge/skills covered in this course. Have a meeting with your instructor and ask for feedback on the quality of your questions and answers. Revise them based on what you discover in the conversation with your instructor.

9 Staying On Course to Your Success

SUCCESSFUL STUDENTS . . .	STRUGGLING STUDENTS . . .
gain self-awareness, consciously employing behaviors, beliefs, and attitudes that keep them on course.	make important choices unconsciously, being directed by self-sabotaging habits and outdated life scripts.
adopt lifelong learning, finding valuable lessons and wisdom in nearly every experience they have.	resist learning new ideas and skills, viewing learning as fearful or boring rather than as mental play.
develop emotional intelligence, effectively managing their emotions in support of their goals and dreams.	live at the mercy of strong emotions such as anger, depression, anxiety, or a need for instant gratification.
believe in themselves, seeing themselves as capable, lovable, and unconditionally worthy human beings.	doubt their competence and personal value, feeling inadequate to create their desired outcomes and experiences.

Planning Your Next Steps

FOCUS QUESTIONS	How have you changed while keeping your journal? What changes do you still want to make?

You are the only one who can ever determine whether you are successful or not. . . . When it comes right down to it, the grades you give yourself are the grades that count.

Shad Helmstetter

Congratulations on completing this part of your life's journey. Your efforts and successes are signs of great things to come! Let us recall the highlights:

First, we saw that our choices create the outcomes and experiences of our lives, and the foundation of our success is **PERSONAL RESPONSIBILITY**—the ability to make wise choices that keep us on course without interfering with the right of others to do the same. Although in reality we are *not* responsible for everything that occurs in our lives, holding this belief motivates us to find and act upon options we might otherwise overlook. Accepting personal responsibility, therefore, maximizes the control we have over the outcomes and experiences of our lives.

Next, we explored how **SELF-MOTIVATION** energizes us from within. We saw that choosing personally meaningful goals and dreams generates a powerful inner drive, and the more specifically we visualize our future life, the more likely we are to make it a reality. Although we can't expect to create our every desire, by committing to clear goals and dreams, we generate the positive energy necessary for moving ahead.

Then, we considered the power of effective **SELF-MANAGEMENT**. We saw that dreams become reality when we effectively manage our efforts to stay on course, consistently doing first what is important. We explored the illusion of time management, realizing that all we can actually manage is our own choices. To that end, we examined written self-management tools that help us take effective actions toward our goals and dreams. Finally we examined how focus and persistence together create self-discipline, a key to making our dreams come true.

Destiny is not a matter of chance; it is a matter of choice. It is not a thing to be waited for; it is a thing to be achieved.

William Jennings Bryant

Following this, we examined the value of **INTERDEPENDENCE**. In this chapter, we saw how people mature from dependence to independence and finally to interdependence. Interdependent people build networks of mutually supportive people who help one another create lives worth living. By developing effective listening and communication skills, interdependent people strengthen relationships, helping them achieve more in their lives while enjoying the journey.

At this point, we asked why we can do so many things right yet still get off course, observing how we are often unknowingly controlled by our Scripts. While exploring **SELF-AWARENESS**, we sought to uncover self-defeating patterns of behavior, thought, and emotion, as well as our limiting core beliefs. Now more conscious of some of our Scripts, we began rewriting some of the outdated inner programs that get us off course.

In Chapter 7, we looked at **LIFELONG LEARNING**. We began by discovering the steps of effective learning and our preferred learning styles so that we could maximize our efforts to learn in college and beyond. We also looked at how to use feedback to constantly monitor how we are doing and to make course corrections whenever necessary. Then we explored how to turn adversity into wisdom by acknowledging our perpetual enrollment in the University of Life.

Coming near the end of our journey, we reflected on the important part that emotions play in our lives and acknowledged that no worldly success is meaningful without a positive inner experience of life. Therefore, we considered ways for developing **EMOTIONAL INTELLIGENCE**, acknowledging that we are as responsible for what we create in our inner world as we are for what we create in our outer world. We learned the components of emotional intelligence and used this knowledge to explore how to reduce distress and create more flow and happiness in our lives.

Throughout our journey, we looked at **WISE CHOICES IN COLLEGE**, learning and practicing effective, time-tested study strategies for maximizing what we learn in college.

In each chapter we paused to explore the center of our experience—our "selves." There, we discussed the essential nature of **BELIEVING IN OURSELVES**. Unless we do, our outdated Scripts will likely sabotage all of our efforts to succeed. So we looked at various strategies for developing core beliefs such as self-acceptance, self-confidence, self-respect, and self-love. On this transformational journey, we have been slowly but surely rewriting our limiting Scripts so that we can tap our greatest potential and create rich, personally fulfilling lives.

Choices and changes

In a profound sense, each human life has the potentiality of becoming an art work. To that degree, each of us can become an artist-in-life with our finest creation being our own Self.

Ira Progoff

Your life is a work of art, you are the artist, and choices are your medium. All that you now have is the sum of the choices you have made in the past. All that you will create in the future is the sum of the choices you make from this moment on.

Whatever you realistically wish to have, do, or be, you have the possibility to create, if you believe you can, and if you are willing to do whatever it takes. Your greatest limitations are inside you, not outside you, and that means that you will probably have to make changes in order to achieve your dreams.

Change, although not easy, is required of those who would be Creators. At any moment, we can shed the invisible chains of our Scripts, walk away from our self-imposed limitations, and create a new life.

Although our travels together are coming to an end, your journey has really just begun. Look out there to your future. What do you want? What are you willing to do to get it? Make a plan and go for it!

Realize that you will probably get off course. But know that you have the strategies—both outer and inner—to get back on course. Before you head out again toward your dream, take a moment to assess your tools. Review the table of contents of this book. Look over the chapter openers, which compare the choices of successful and struggling people. Skim the pages to remind yourself of the many strategies you have learned. Know also that at any time you can come back to these pages and to your journal to remind yourself of whatever you forget. In that way, you can stay on course.

Assess yourself, again

It isn't where you came from; it's where you're going that counts.

Ella Fitzgerald

On the next page is a duplicate of the questionnaire you took in Chapter 1. Take it again. (Don't look back at your previous answers yet.) In Journal Entry 31, you will compare your first scores with your scores today, and you'll consider the changes you have made. Acknowledge yourself for your courage to grow. Look, also, at the changes that you still need to make if you are to continue evolving into your best self.

You have much of what you need to achieve your dreams. The rest you can learn on your journey. Be bold! Begin today!

Self-Assessment

You can take this self-assessment on the Internet by visiting the *On Course* web site at the College Survival discipline student page located at *http://college.hmco.com/collegesurvival/students*.
You'll receive your score immediately . . . and see how others scored as well.

Read the statements below and score each one according to how true or false you believe it is about you. To get an accurate picture of yourself, consider what **IS** true about you (not what you want to be true). Obviously there are no right or wrong answers. Assign each statement a number from zero to ten, as follows:

Totally false   0 1 2 3 4 5 6 7 8 9 10   Totally true

1. ___ I control how successful I will be.
2. ___ I'm not sure why I'm in college.
3. ___ I spend most of my time doing important things.
4. ___ When I encounter a challenging problem, I try to solve it by myself.
5. ___ When I get off course from my goals and dreams, I realize it right away.
6. ___ I'm not sure how I learn best.
7. ___ Whether I'm happy or not depends mostly on me.
8. ___ I'll truly accept myself only after I eliminate my faults and weaknesses.
9. ___ Forces out of my control (like poor teaching) are the cause of low grades I receive in school.
10. ___ If I lose my motivation in college, I know how to get it back.
11. ___ I don't need to write things down because I can remember what I need to do.
12. ___ I have a network of people in my life that I can count on for help.
13. ___ If I have habits that hinder my success, I'm not sure what they are.
14. ___ When I don't like the way an instructor teaches, I know how to learn the subject anyway.
15. ___ When I get very angry, sad, or afraid, I do or say things that create a problem for me.
16. ___ When I think about performing an upcoming challenge (like taking a test), I usually see myself doing well.
17. ___ When I have a problem, I take positive actions to find a solution.
18. ___ I don't know how to set effective short-term and long-term goals.
19. ___ I remember to do important things.
20. ___ When I have a difficult course in school, I study alone.
21. ___ I'm aware of beliefs I have that hinder my success.
22. ___ I don't know how to study effectively.
23. ___ When choosing between doing an important school assignment or something really fun, I usually do the school assignment.
24. ___ I break promises that I make to myself or to others.
25. ___ I make poor choices that keep me from getting what I really want in life.
26. ___ I have a written plan that includes both my short-term and long-term goals.
27. ___ I lack self-discipline.
28. ___ I listen carefully when other people are talking.
29. ___ I'm stuck with any habits of mine that hinder my success.
30. ___ When I face a disappointment (like failing a test), I ask myself, "What lesson can I learn here?"
31. ___ I often feel bored, anxious, or depressed.
32. ___ I feel just as worthwhile as any other person.

33. ___ Forces outside of me (like luck or other people) control how successful I will be.
34. ___ College is an important step on the way to accomplishing my goals and dreams.
35. ___ I spend most of my time doing unimportant things.
36. ___ When I encounter a challenging problem, I ask for help.
37. ___ I can be off course from my goals and dreams for quite a while without realizing it.
38. ___ I know how I learn best.
39. ___ My happiness depends mostly on what's happened to me lately.
40. ___ I accept myself just as I am, even with my faults and weaknesses.
41. ___ I am the cause of low grades I receive in school.
42. ___ If I lose my motivation in college, I don't know how I'll get it back.
43. ___ I use self-management tools (like calendars and to-do lists) that help me remember to do important things.
44. ___ I know very few people whom I can count on for help.
45. ___ I'm aware of the habits I have that hinder my success.
46. ___ If I don't like the way an instructor teaches, I'll probably do poorly in the course.
47. ___ When I'm very angry, sad, or afraid, I know how to manage my emotions so I don't do anything I'll regret later.
48. ___ When I think about performing an upcoming challenge (like taking a test), I usually see myself doing poorly.
49. ___ When I have a problem, I complain, blame others, or make excuses.
50. ___ I know how to set effective short-term and long-term goals.
51. ___ I forget to do important things.
52. ___ When I have a difficult course in school, I find a study partner or join a study group.
53. ___ I'm unaware of beliefs I have that hinder my success.
54. ___ I've learned to use specific study skills that work effectively for me.
55. ___ I often feel happy and fully alive.
56. ___ I keep promises that I make to myself or to others.
57. ___ I make wise choices that help me get what I really want in life.
58. ___ I live day to day, without much of a plan for the future.
59. ___ I am a self-disciplined person.
60. ___ I get distracted easily when other people are talking.
61. ___ I know how to change habits of mine that hinder my success.
62. ___ When I face a disappointment (like failing a test), I feel pretty helpless.
63. ___ When choosing between doing an important school assignment or something really fun, I usually do something fun.
64. ___ I feel less worthy than other people.

Transfer your scores to the scoring sheets on the next page. For each of the eight areas, total your scores in columns A and B. Then total your final scores as shown in the sample.

Self-Assessment Scoring Sheet

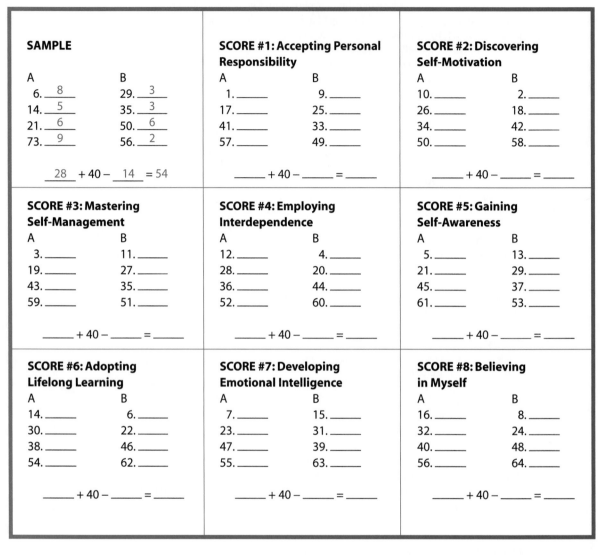

SAMPLE

A		B	
6.	8	29.	3
14.	5	35.	3
21.	6	50.	6
73.	9	56.	2

28 + 40 − 14 = 54

SCORE #1: Accepting Personal Responsibility

A		B	
1.		9.	
17.		25.	
41.		33.	
57.		49.	

_____ + 40 − _____ = _____

SCORE #2: Discovering Self-Motivation

A		B	
10.		2.	
26.		18.	
34.		42.	
50.		58.	

_____ + 40 − _____ = _____

SCORE #3: Mastering Self-Management

A		B	
3.		11.	
19.		27.	
43.		35.	
59.		51.	

_____ + 40 − _____ = _____

SCORE #4: Employing Interdependence

A		B	
12.		4.	
28.		20.	
36.		44.	
52.		60.	

_____ + 40 − _____ = _____

SCORE #5: Gaining Self-Awareness

A		B	
5.		13.	
21.		29.	
45.		37.	
61.		53.	

_____ + 40 − _____ = _____

SCORE #6: Adopting Lifelong Learning

A		B	
14.		6.	
30.		22.	
38.		46.	
54.		62.	

_____ + 40 − _____ = _____

SCORE #7: Developing Emotional Intelligence

A		B	
7.		15.	
23.		31.	
47.		39.	
55.		63.	

_____ + 40 − _____ = _____

SCORE #8: Believing in Myself

A		B	
16.		8.	
32.		24.	
40.		48.	
56.		64.	

_____ + 40 − _____ = _____

Carry these scores to the corresponding boxes in the chart on the next page, writing them in the "Your Score" column.

Choices of Successful Students

Your score	Successful students . . .	Struggling students . . .
Score _____	**accept self-responsibility,** seeing themselves as the primary cause of their outcomes and experiences.	see themselves as Victims, believing that what happens to them is determined primarily by external forces such as fate, luck, and powerful others.
Score _____	**discover self-motivation,** finding purpose in their lives by discovering personally meaningful goals and dreams.	have difficulty sustaining motivation, often feeling depressed, frustrated, and/or resentful about a lack of direction in their lives.
Score _____	**master self-management,** consistently planning and taking purposeful actions in pursuit of their goals and dreams.	seldom identify specific actions needed to accomplish a desired outcome. And when they do, they tend to procrastinate.
Score _____	**employ interdependence,** building mutually supportive relationships that help them achieve their goals and dreams (while helping others do the same).	are solitary, seldom requesting, even rejecting, offers of assistance from those who could help.
Score _____	**gain self-awareness,** consciously employing behaviors, beliefs, and attitudes that keep them on course.	make important choices unconsciously, being directed by self-sabotaging habits and outdated life scripts.
Score _____	**adopt lifelong learning,** finding valuable lessons and wisdom in nearly every experience they have.	resist learning new ideas and skills, viewing learning as fearful or boring rather than as mental play.
Score _____	**develop emotional intelligence,** effectively managing their emotions in support of their goals and dreams.	live at the mercy of strong emotions, such as anger, depression, anxiety, or a need for instant gratification.

Score _____	**believe in themselves,** seeing themselves capable, lovable, and unconditionally worthy as human beings.	doubt their competence and personal value, feeling inadequate to create their desired outcomes and experiences.

Interpreting your scores: A score of . . .

0–39	Indicates an area where your choices will **seldom** keep you on course.
40–63	Indicates an area where your choices will **sometimes** keep you on course.
64–80	Indicates an area where your choices will **usually** keep you on course.

Journal Entry 31

I n this activity, you will examine the changes you have made since the beginning of this course, and you'll plan your next steps toward success in college and in life.

1. **In your journal, write the eight areas of the self-assessment and transfer your two scores from the chart on pages 11–12 (1st test) and the chart on pages 211–212 (2nd test), as follows:**

1st Test	2nd Test	
_____	_____	1. Accepting personal responsibility
_____	_____	2. Discovering self-motivation
_____	_____	3. Mastering self-management
_____	_____	4. Employing interdependence
_____	_____	5. Gaining self-awareness
_____	_____	6. Adopting lifelong learning
_____	_____	7. Developing emotional intelligence
_____	_____	8. Believing in myself

And the end of all our exploring
Will be to arrive where we started
And know the place for the first time.
                    T.S. Eliot

2. **Comparing the results from the two self-assessment questionnaires, write about the area(s) in which you feel you**

have changed for the better. Remember to consider Creator questions that you will answer in your discussion. During your writing, remember also to use the four E's to support your opinions and ideas. Dive deep!

3. **Further comparing the results from the two self-assessment questionnaires, write in depth about the area(s) in which you most want to continue improving.** Remember the saying "If you keep doing what you've been doing, you'll keep getting what you've been getting." With this understanding in mind, identify the specific changes you'd like to make in your behaviors, thoughts, emotions, and beliefs in the months and years to come.

Whatever you can do, or dream you can, begin it. Boldness has genius, power and magic in it. Begin it now.
Johann Wolfgang vonGoethe

By the way, if one of your scores went down over the semester, consider that this result may indicate not that you became less effective but that you are now more aware of what's necessary to excel in this area.

4. **Write one last entry in which you sum up the most important discoveries that you have made about yourself while keeping your journal so far. Dive deep!**

Before writing, take a few moments to relax using the method that works best for you. As always, you will get much more value from this journal entry and from your life if you take time to relax, collect your thoughts, and dive deep.

Relax, think, write.

Bibliography

*An asterisk beside an entry indicates it as highly recommended.

*Adams, Kathleen. *Journal to the Self: Twenty-two Paths to Personal Growth.* Warner Books, 1990.

Anderson, Walter. *Courage Is a Three Letter Word.* Random House, 1986.

Angelou, Maya. *Wouldn't Take Nothing for My Journey Now.* Random House, Canada, 1993.

Bradshaw, John. *Creating Love.* Bantam Books, 1992.

*————. *Homecoming.* Bantam Books, 1990.

*Brandon, Nathaniel. *How to Raise Your Self Esteem.* Bantam Books, 1988.

Burns, David, M.D. *Feeling Good.* William Morrow, 1980.

Buzan, Tony. *Make the Most of Your Mind.* Simon and Schuster, 1977.

Capacchione, Lucia. *The Creative Journal.* Newcastle, 1989.

Carnegie, Dale. *How to Win Friends and Influence People.* Pocket Books, 1936.

Chapman, Joyce. *Live Your Dream.* Newcastle, 1990.

Chopra, Deepak, M.D. *Unconditional Life.* Bantam Books, 1991.

*Covey, Stephen R. *7 Habits of Highly Effective People.* Simon and Schuster, 1989.

*Csikszentmihalyi, Mihaly. *Flow: The Psychology of Optimal Experience.* Harper and Row, 1990.

————. *Finding Flow.* Basic Books, 1997.

deBono, Edward. *deBono's Thinking Course.* Facts on File, 1982.

Dewey, John. *Experience and Education.* Collier Books, 1938.

Dyer, Wayne. *You'll See It When You Believe It.* Morrow, 1989.

Ferrucci, Piero. *What We May Be.* J.P. Tarcher, 1982.

*Frankl, Viktor E., M.D. *Man's Search for Meaning.* Washington Square Press, 1959.

Garfield, Charles. *Peak Performers.* Avon Books, 1986.

Gawain, Shakti. *Creative Visualization.* Bantam Books, 1979.

*Glasser, William. *Reality Therapy.* Harper and Row, 1965.

*Goleman, Daniel. *Emotional Intelligence.* Bantam Books, 1995.

Gordon, Thomas, M.D. *Parent Effectiveness Training.* NAL Penguin, 1970.

Griessman, B. Eugene. *The Achievement Factors.* Dodd, Mead, 1987.

Harmon, Willis, and Howard Rheingold. *Higher Creativity.* J.P. Tarcher, 1984.

Harris, Thomas. *I'm OK, You're OK.* Harper and Row, 1967.

*Helmstetter, Shad. *Choices.* Simon and Schuster, 1989.

Hendricks, Gay, and Kathlyn Hendricks. *Conscious Loving.* Bantam Books, 1990.

*Herrmann, Ned. *The Creative Brain.* The Ned Herrmann Group. 1989.

Hill, Napoleon. *Think and Grow Rich.* Fawcett Crest, 1960.

James, Muriel, and Dorothy Jongeward. *Born to Win.* Addison-Wesley Publishing, 1978.

Jampolsky, Gerald, M.D. *Teach Only Love.* Bantam Books, 1983.

John-Roger and Peter McWilliams. *Life 101.* Prelude Press, 1991.

Keirsey, D., and M. Bates. *Please Understand Me.* Prometheus Nemesis Books. 1978.

*Keyes, Ken, Jr. *Handbook to Higher Consciousness.* Living Love Publishing, 1975.

Lao Tzu. *Tao Te Ching.* Trans. Vitor H. Mair. Bantam Books, 1990.

Lawrence, G. *People Types and Tiger Stripes.* 3rd ed. Center for Applications of Psychological Type, 1983.

Lerner, Harriet Goldhor. *The Dance of Intimacy.* Harper and Row, 1989.

Maltz, Maxwell. *Magic Power of Self-Image Psychology.* Prentice Hall, 1964.

Mamchur, Carolyn. *Cognitive Type Theory and Learning Style.* Association for Supervision and Curriculum Development, 1996.

Mandino, Og. *A Better Way to Live.* Bantam Books, 1990.

Mazlow, Abraham H. *Toward a Psychology of Being.* Van Nostrand Reinhold, 1968.

McCall, Nathan. *Makes Me Wanna Holler.* Random House, 1994.

McQuade, Walter, and Ann Aikman. *Stress.* Bantam Books, 1974.

Merrill, A. Roger. *Connections: Quadrant II Time Management.* Publishers Press, 1987.

Metcalf, C. W., and Roma Felible. *Lighten Up.* Addison-Wesley, 1992.

Meyers, David. *The Pursuit of Happiness.* Avon Books, 1992.

Moore, Thomas. *Care of the Soul.* HarperCollins, 1992.

Myers, Isabelle. *The Myers-Briggs Type Indicator.* Consulting Psychological Press, 1962.

Ornstein, Robert. *Multimind.* Houghton Mifflin, 1986.

Ostrander, Sheila, and Lynn Schroeder. *Superlearning.* Dell, 1979.

Peck, M. Scott, M.D. *A Different Drum.* Simon and Schuster, 1987.

———. *Further Along the Road Less Traveled.* Simon and Schuster, 1993.

*———. *The Road Less Traveled.* Simon and Schuster, 1978.

Postman, Neil, and Charles Weingartner. *Teaching as a Subversive Activity.* Dell, 1969.

Progroff, Ira. *At a Journal Workshop.* Dialogue House Library, 1975.

Restak, Richard, M.D. *The Mind.* Bantam Books, 1988.

Riley, Pat. *The Winner Within.* G.P. Putnam's Sons, 1993.

Ringer, Robert J. *Million Dollar Habits.* Wynwood Press, 1990.

Robbins, Anthony. *Awaken the Giant Within.* Simon and Schuster, 1991.

Rogers, Carl. *Freedom to Learn.* Charles E. Merrill, 1969.

———. *On Becoming a Person.* Houghton Mifflin, 1969.

*Satir, Virginia. *The New Peoplemaking.* Science and Behavior Books, 1988.

Schutz, Will. *Profound Simplicity.* Bantam Books, 1979.

Segal, Jeanne. *Raising Your Emotional Intelligence.* Henry Holt, 1997.

*Seligman, Martin. *Learned Optimism.* Alfred A. Knopf, 1991.

———. *What You Can Change and What You Can't.* Alfred A. Knopf, 1994.

Sher, Barbara, and Annie Gottleib. *Wishcraft: How to Get What You Really Want.* Ballantine, 1986.

Siegel, Bernie S., M.D. *How to Live Between Office Visits.* HarperCollins, 1993.

———. *Love, Medicine and Miracles.* Harper and Row, 1986.

Silva, Jose, and Philip Miele. *The Silva Mind Control Method.* Simon and Schuster, 1977.

*Smith, Hyrum W. *The 10 Natural Laws of Successful Time and Life Management.* Warner Books, 1994.

*Steiner, Claude M. *Scripts People Live.* Bantam Books, 1974.

Stone, Hal, and Sidra Stone. *Embracing Your Inner Critic.* HarperCollins, 1993.

Tannen, Deborah. *You Just Don't Understand.* Ballantine, 1990.

vonOech, Roger. *A Whack on the Side of the Head.* Warner Books, 1983.

Waitley, Denis. *Seeds of Greatness.* Pocket Books, 1983.

———. *Psychology of Winning.* Nightingale-Conant, 1988.

Young, Jeffrey, E., and Janet S. Klosko. *Reinventing Your Life.* Dutton, 1993.

Zilbergeld, Bernie, and Arnold A. Lazarus. *Mind Power.* Ballantine Books, 1987.

Appendix

---

1. What Is the Internet?

The Internet is an exceptionally large computer network that spans a large part of the world we live in, with a number of tremendously powerful capabilities for sharing and communicating information between the people (users) of this network through their computers.

Technically speaking, all computers connected to the Internet have the capability of sharing information and communicating with each other. In many ways, the Internet works similar to the telephone system we are all familiar with and use every day. People who have telephones in their homes or places of business are connected to their local telephone company's network and are able to communicate with other people who have telephones locally, nationwide, and around the world (through the use of long-distance and overseas telephone networks).

Sending a fax, for example, over the telephone line, whether to a business down the street or to an individual half a world away, is a relatively simple process. One only needs to know the telephone number of the party receiving the fax, turn on the fax machine, make the connection, insert the document to be faxed into the machine, and the job is finished.

Information transmitted over the Internet works in a very similar fashion: documents are shared on this world network by first converting them into a form that can be stored on computers (unless they're already in that form), connecting the computer to the Internet, establishing a connection with the receiving party or with an intermediate party (such as a mail server), and sending the document to its destination using one of the Internet tools designed for that purpose, such as electronic mail (e-mail) or file transfer protocol (FTP).

Speaking again from a technical point of view, information shared and communicated via the Internet pathway is always first converted from its original form into electronic form, which means it is translated into bits and bytes of electrical information the computer can understand and process. Once it has been converted into electronic form, computers have exceptionally powerful capabilities for storing, compressing, and transmitting such information to other computers on the Internet in an extremely efficient and reliable manner.

Using the Internet can be enjoyable, and students who are willing to take the time to learn the minimal skills required gain the multitude of advantages it has to offer. Unlike the many commands and skills necessary to effectively use the power of other computer applications such as word processing, spreadsheets, desktop publishing programs, and database management systems, Internet software tools tend to be designed for less technically sophisticated users and are usually quite easy for most students to learn. Basic facility with a web browser that gives access to a gigantic volume of Internet resources, for example, can be acquired in 15 minutes or less.

2. Getting Connected

How to Gain Access to the Internet

A computer connected through a local-area network (LAN), such as a PC or Macintosh in a campus computer lab, media center, or library, is needed to access the Internet. Alternatively, students may connect directly from home or residence hall through a modem that connects the computer to the Internet via the telephone line. Some schools have even started supplying students living in residence halls with direct Ethernet connections. Extra software (and sometimes hardware, such as a circuit board in the computer) may be needed to complete the connection. The student must have a user account with an Internet service provider (ISP) or with the computer system on campus. An account gives the student access privileges to connect to other computers locally and, through the Internet, worldwide.

Cost

For many student Internet users, there is no cost whatsoever to use the power and capabilities of the Internet through their campus computer networks. Since colleges and universities consider these resources and communication capabilities educationally valuable, many have acquired this technology for the benefit of their students. In addition to four-year colleges and universities, many community colleges, high schools, vocational and technical institutions, public libraries, and even elementary schools are connecting to the Internet in ever-expanding numbers. For students who access the Internet from their own personal computers, an Internet Service Provider (ISP) will usually cost between fifteen and twenty dollars per month.

3. Useful Applications of the Internet

E-mail

The advantages for the student who gains facility with e-mail communications over the Internet simply cannot be overstated. This communication tool is the primary (and most heavily used) application of the Internet, and literally millions of e-mail messages are exchanged among Internet users daily. It's a simple tool to learn, and sending an e-mail message through the Internet is even easier than mailing a letter through the post office: one only needs to address the e-mail to the recipient, type in the subject of the message, type the message itself, and send it on its way, where it will arrive in minutes (instead of the days it takes through the conventional postal system).

Students can exchange e-mail with other students in their classes at the school they are attending or with those at other educational institutions elsewhere. Further, they can use it to exchange communications with faculty and staff members at their college. (Many instructors currently use e-mail to distribute course materials, including syllabi, class and lecture notes, review and supplementary materials, student feedback, and even to conduct online quizzes and exams.)

Students writing term papers or conducting research can communicate directly via e-mail with researchers in their field of study. Many valuable professional contacts can be made in this fashion. Students pursuing internships or employment opportunities can use e-mail to contact representatives of companies or organizations in which they are interested.

It's a very simple process for a student who has Internet access with an account to subscribe to free, e-mail-based newsletters, magazine mailing lists, and user groups in their areas of interest or investigation. Politically inclined students may easily send letters to their elected representatives expressing their viewpoints on issues of concern. The applications of e-mail communications are many for the enterprising student.

A Word on E-mail Addresses

E-mail addresses at educational institutions follow the format: username@ machine.domain.edu where *username* is the log-in name of the Internet user, *machine* is the name of the computer being used, *domain* is the name of the institution, company, or facility that is "hosting" the user's account, and *.edu* is an abbreviation for "educational institution." An example of a mythical e-mail address for a user in the engineering department at the University of Michigan may be: *rjones@engin.umich.edu* where *rjones* is the user's log-in name, *engin* corresponds to a computer server used by the engineering department, followed by *umich*, which is the domain name for the University of Michigan. Commercial e-mail addresses end with the suffix *.com* (rather than *.edu*), government institutions with *.gov*, and military installations with *.mil*.

World Wide Web

The Web is an outstanding mechanism for locating and browsing resources located throughout the world's great libraries, universities, and research institutions. There is no doubt that the Web is the most exciting recent development in Internet tools for users seeking information rapidly across a very large variety of disciplines and types of information. The growth rate of organizations, educational institutions, research centers, businesses of all types, and individuals that are providing free information for distribution worldwide on the Web is simply astronomical. (For example, in 1994, the Web grew by a factor of 350,000 percent!)

As a student, you have the luxury of free access to all of this easy-to-locate and rapidly available information in an almost limitless range of subjects when you become a capable Internet user and have access to the tools required for web browsing and information retrieval. Although not all Internet connections provide access to the Web, most educational institutions are providing those services and the tools (Web browsers) needed to access them because of the Web's exceptional importance and applicability for students and faculty engaged in learning and research.

Using Search Engines

Finding information on the Internet and the Web has been greatly simplified with the development of huge database search engines developed to scan the Web for any topic you wish to explore. Powerful search engines can be reached by clicking your browser's net search button or entering the proper URL addresses in the "Location" window on your Internet page. Popular search engines include Yahoo *(http://www.yahoo.com)*, Excite *(http://www.excite.com)*, Infoseek *(http://guide.infoseek.com)*, Alta Vista *(http://altavista.digital.com)*, Google *(http://www.google.com)*, and Lycos *(http://www.lycos.com)*. Once at the search engine of your choice, type in key words for your search, using quotes around words that are a part of a phrase (for example "goal setting" or "time management"), submit your query, and review your returns. Using specific key words will reduce the number of hits—you will be amazed at the number of sources the search engine will identify as relevant to your search. In addition to web-search capabilities, some search engines (such as Yahoo) also offer free e-mail accounts.

Setting Bookmarks

Most web browsers allow you to save web page titles and URLs for future reference. If you visit a site to which you want to return later, set a bookmark to place it on a list for future reference. Experienced web surfers tend to develop very comprehensive and well-indexed bookmark files, allowing them to return to sites of interest quickly and conveniently. To bookmark a page on the Web, hold down your computer's control key and press the letter "D." That page is now stored in your bookmarks for a later return visit.

A Caution about Information on the Web

Remember, *anyone* can place his or her thoughts on the Internet with no review of the content . . . ANYONE! To assess the quality of Internet information, be a critical thinker and ask questions like these: Who is the source (person or group) of the information? How respected or reliable is this source? What does this source stand to gain if I believe the information? What sort of evidence is offered to support the ideas presented? In short, approach all information on the Web with a critical eye. Don't fall victim to web exploitation.

Citing the Web as a Source

Works appearing on the Web should be cited exactly like any other print material. Add the electronic address (URL) of the source at the end of the entry. For example:

"Documenting Sources From the World Wide Web." *Modern Language Association on the Web*. 9 July 1998 <http://www.mla.org/set_stl.htm>

Visit the MLA web site *(http://www.mla.org)* for the most up-to-date information on documenting sources.

4. Useful Web Sites

Many web sites are useful to students, and many of those sites contain links to other valuable sites on the Web. Here are some sites you may wish to visit.*

Self-Responsibility

Take one of these "locus of control" tests on line and find out how well you take responsibility for the outcomes in your life (results reported instantly).
http://www.queendom.com/lc.html (42 items)
http://www.cl.uh.edu/edu/awl/survey/locus.html (29 items)

An editorial on personal responsibility from the Georgia Tech student newspaper.
http://cyberbuzz.gatech.edu/nique/issues/fall1996/nov22/editorials2-s.html

Self-Motivation

The importance of self-motivation.
http://www.d.umn.edu/student/loon/acad/strat/motivate.html

Strategies for effective goal-setting.
http://www.mindtools.com/page6.html
http://www.topachievement.com/goalsetting.html

Affirmations for success.
http://www.ozemail.com.au/~caveman/Creative/Resources/affirmations.htm

Self-Management

An abundance of time management principles and information at these sites:

*   All of these links can be accessed online by visiting the *On Course* web site at the College Survival discipline student page located at *http://college.hmco.com*. Due to the changing nature of the Internet, please be advised that the links listed here may have changed or been removed from their main servers since the time of publication. For the most accurate and up-to-date information, bookmark the useful web sites page for easy access to updates.

http://www.mindtools.com/page5.html
http://www.keithellis.com/bootstraps2.8.html
http://www.d.umn.edu/student/loon/acad/strat/time_man_princ.html

Are you a procrastinator? Find out with this 40-question quiz.
http://www.queendom.com/tests/procrastination.html

Ten strategies for overcoming procrastination.
http://www.ucc.vt.edu/stdysk/procrast.html

Relationships

How well do you communicate? Take this 32-item test on-line and get your results immediately.
http://www.queendom.com/communic.html

Communication skills.
http://www.mindtools.com/page8.html

Are you a good roommate? This quick quiz will tell you. Have your roommate take it, too!
http://www.queendom.com/minitests/roommate.html

Self-Awareness

Are your beliefs optimistic or pessimistic? This quick on-line quiz will let you know.
http://www.queendom.com/optimist.html

Take the Keirsey Temperament Sorter on-line and get your results immediately.
http://www.keirsey.com/cgi-bin/keirsey/newkts.cgi

Are you an introvert or extrovert? Take this test on-line and find out (28-item test with results reported instantly).
http://www.queendom.com/extraver.html

Lifelong Learning

Information about the brain and learning, including lateral thinking, mind-mapping, and puzzles to test your creative problem-solving abilities.
http://www.ozemail.com.au/~caveman/Creative/

Information about multiple intelligence, a theory by Harvard psychologist Howard Gardner that human beings can be intelligent in eight different ways: verbal/linguistic, logical/mathematical, visual/spatial, bodily/kinesthetic, musical, interpersonal, intrapersonal, and naturalistic.
http://www.newhorizons.org/trm_gardner.html
http://www.cogs.susx.ac.uk/users/zahraar/mi1.htm

Discover if your preferred learning style is visual, auditory, or tactile.
http://www.hcc.hawaii.edu/intranet/committees/FacDevCom/guidebk/teachtip/lernstyl.htm

Discover even more about your preferred learning style.
http://adulted.about.com/aboutcanada/adulted/gi/dynamic/offsite.htm?site=http://www2.ncsu.edu/unity/lockers/users/f/felder/public/ILSdir/ilsweb.html

What is your IQ (Intelligence Quotient)? Take a 60-item test on-line and get the answer immediately.
http://www.queendom.com/iq.html

Stretch your mind with puzzles and brain teasers.
http://www.queendom.com/mindgames/mindgame.html

Study Skills

Study tips are abundant at the following web sites (most hosted by colleges or universities):
http://www.iss.stthomas.edu/studyguides/
http://uhs.bsd.uchicago.edu/scrs/vpc/vpc.html
http://www.utexas.edu/student/lsc/handouts/stutips.html
http://euler.slu.edu/Dept/SuccessinMath.html (math tips)
http://www.adm.uwaterloo.ca/infocs/Study/studyindex.html
http://www.dartmouth.edu/admin/acskills/#study
http://www.unc.edu/depts/unc_caps/TenTraps.html
http://www.grcc.cc.mi.us/biosci/studyski/forbstud.html
http://www.barcharts.com/keys.htm
http://www.ucc.vt.edu/stdysk/stdyhlp.html

Emotional Intelligence

Short article on Emotional Intelligence and a quiz to discover your EQ (Emotional Quotient).
http://www.utne.com/lens/bms/eq.html

What is your EQ (Emotional Intelligence Quotient)? Take an emotional intelligence test on-line and get your results immediately. (It takes about 30 minutes to complete the 70-item test, but it's worth the time.)
http://www.queendom.com/emotionaliq.html

How well do you cope with stress? This on-line test will give you an answer (45 questions).
http://www.queendom.com/coping.html

Self-Esteem

Do you believe in yourself? Take a self-esteem inventory on-line and get your results immediately (30 questions).
http://www.queendom.com/selfest.html

Do you take good care of yourself? This on-line quiz will give you feedback on whether you care enough to give yourself a healthy lifestyle.
http://www.queendom.com/lifestyl.html

Financial Aid

Information about financial aid resources for students. Here you can search some of the best scholarship and fellowship databases in the United States and Canada. The term scholarship refers to awards intended primarily for undergraduate students. The term fellowship refers to awards intended primarily for graduate and postgraduate students.
http://www.finaid.org/
http://www.ed.gov/offices/ope/express.html
http://www.fastweb.com/

Links to a variety of general scholarship and fellowship databases.
http://www.finaid.org/finaid/awards.html
http://www.studentservices.com

On-Line Sources For Doing Research

Links to established web-based scholarly journals that offer access to English language article files without requiring user registration or fees (from the University of Houston).
http://info.lib.uh.edu/wj/webjour.htm

Links to on-line reference-type resources such as dictionaries, encyclopedias, almanacs, biographies, consumer guides, calendars, college and graduate school

directories, atlases, geography books, grants and scholarships, medical information, and style manuals. Very extensive!
http://www.libraries.rutgers.edu/rul/

Library on the Web includes a tutorial on the Internet, search engines, tools for locating Internet e-mail addresses, library catalogs, reference books on-line, government-related resources, employment information, grants, and general subject indexes for business, the humanities, social sciences, and sciences.
http://www.stetson.edu/departments/library/ref.html

Links to topics such as current affairs, business, computers, economics, educational research, electronic books, personal finance, ethnic interests, humor, literature, on-line magazines and newspapers, medicine, music, politics, science, and sports. Excellent index.
http://www.gmi.edu/gmi_official/acad/mech-eng/region29.htm

Virtual library subject catalog containing a comprehensive index of an enormous number of topics accessible through the World Wide Web.
http://vlib.org/Overview2.html

Careers

Here's a thorough overview of job hunting.
http://www.jobhuntersbible.com/index.html

Take a 22-item test and discover what career may be suitable for your personality.
http://www.ventura.com/jsearch/unique/29063/jshome2e.html

Find out what careers you can pursue with various majors.
http://www.uncwil.edu/stuaff/career/majors.htm

See what occupations are in demand by searching the jobs posted on the On-line Career Center's electronic job bulletin board.
http://www.occ.com/

This site is a source of many job openings.
http://www.jobbankusa.com/

More information about careers in demand.
http://www.careercity.com/

Miscellaneous

Inspirational quotations
http://www.motivateus.com/

Calculate your Grade Point Average
http://www.twsu.edu/~ucwww/wsugpa.html

5. A Note of Caution: Beware of Viruses

It can be dangerous to open a document or start a computer program that has been received through the Internet from any unknown source. For example, in April 1997, a program with the title "AOL 4FREE" was being sent to thousands of Internet users via attachment to unsolicited e-mail messages (that is, junk mail). When unwary recipients opened this document, it caused the entire contents of their disk drives to be destroyed—causing irreparable damage to the files stored on their computer systems! Such "virus-infected" programs exist in widespread numbers on the Internet—and can be spread easily among computers using e-mail attachment and FTP.

Adhering to the following suggestions will increase your protection against damage inflicted by software viruses:

- Always keep a current backup of important files stored on diskettes.

- Remain wary of any documents or files received from individuals (especially of an unknown identity or origin) on the Internet.

- Ensure that the latest virus protection software is installed on any computer system that connects to the Internet. Consult with your computer system administrator, lab attendant, or instructor for information on this issue.

Acknowledgments

Page 30: From "The Road Not Taken" from *The Poetry of Robert Frost*, edited by Edward Connery Lathem, © 1969 by Henry Holt & Co., LLC. Reprinted by permission of Henry Holt & Co., LLC.

Page 72: "Notice" from *Mysteries of the Body*. Copyright © 1984 by Steve Kowit. Reprinted by permission of the author.

Page 120: Outline sample from Carol Kanar, *The Confident Student*, Third Edition, p. 178. Copyright © 1998 by Houghton Mifflin Company. Used by permission.

Page 121: From Walter Pauk, *How to Study in College*, Sixth Edition, p. 205. Copyright © 1997 by Houghton Mifflin Company. Used by permission.

Page 124: "Dream Deferred" ("Harlem") From *The Collected Poems of Langston Hughes* by Langston Hughes, copyright © 1994 by The Estate of Langston Hughes. Used by permission of Alfred A. Knopf, a division of Random House, Inc.

Page 158: "Autobiography in Five Short Chapters." Copyright © 1993 by Portia Nelson from the book *There's a Hole in My Sidewalk*. Reprinted by permission of Beyond Words Publishing, Hillsboro, OR.

Page 165: Inspired by "Take This Fish and Look at It" by Samuel J. Scudder, 1874.

Page 177: Notecard sample from Carol Kanar, *The Confident Student*, Third Edition, p. 353. Copyright © 1998 by Houghton Mifflin Company. Used by permission.

Page 177: From James F. Shepard, *College Study Skills*, Sixth Edition, p. 191. Copyright © 1997 by Houghton Mifflin Company. Used by permission.

Page 181: Adapted text (Components of Emotional Intelligence) from Daniel Goleman, *Emotional Intelligence*, (New York: Ballantine Books, 1995), p. 43.

Page 189: "to be of use" from *Circles on the Water* by Marge Piercy, copyright © 1982 by Marge Piercy. Used by permission of Alfred A. Knopf, a division of Random House, Inc.

Index